Multicultural Theatre and Drama

Multicultural Theatre and Drama

T. Sai Chandra Mouli

AUTHORSPRESS
Publishers of Scholarly Books

Worldwide Circulation through Authorspress Global Network

First Published 2011

by

Authorspress

Editorial

Q-2A Hauz Khas Enclave,

New Delhi-110 016

e-mail: authorspress@yahoo.com

Marketing

E-35/103, Jawahar Park

Laxmi Nagar, Delhi-110 092

e-mail: authorspress@yahoo.com

Multicultural Theatre and Drama

ISBN 978-81-7273-584-5

Printed in India at Tarun Offset, Delhi.

Preface

> I am not an employee of yours or a borrowed convict;
> I'm not an assigned servant to whom you are God.
>
> — *Hal Porter*

Man and movement are inalienable. Human civilisation evolved from nomadic stage to rooted existence. Movement leads to dislocation, which in turn results in merger of margins and new boundaries on the rise. Everyone is a migrant, some way or the other. Human development and blooming of cultures stem from migration, adaptation and absorption. No one is an island. No society can sustain itself without contact with and contribution from other societies. Migration in search of better living conditions and ambition to amass wealth always triggered fresh waves of dislocations and subsequent nostalgia and a craving to compensate through creative works offering a safety valve to release pent-up feelings and longings.

Multiculturalism may acquire significance in monolingual and monotheistic contexts. But, in a multilingual context like India, existence and fusion of numerous subcultures manifests what obtains as multiculturalism elsewhere. Past blends with the present in shaping the future of humankind. History is both subjective and objective. Perception makes all the difference. Cultural memories tend to make an immense impact on human psyche. History and culture coalesce to strengthen memories and myths merge with modernity in creative works to offer a new perspective. Breakers on a vast seashore best illustrate human mind and predicament.

In today's unipolar world hierarchies, authority, subordination and subsequent exploitation still persist. Globalisation has offered avenues for enrichment of a few sections; for the subaltern light at the end of the tunnel is yet a distant dream. Desires remain unfulfilled, aspirations evaporate and sweat on the brow still tastes the same.

Devouring disenchantment demands vehemently means of redressal of grievances.

As in all primitive societies today too enactment of human life in all its hues offers a solace, a solution, and sets one contemplating on possible twists and gyrations at play in determining one's fate. Theatre and theatrical performances across the globe still retain the pristine charm and power of the bygone eras. Muticutural drama and study of theatre in diverse environment offer unprecedented opportunities to trace the evolution of theatre, shedding ample light on the divergent dramatic techniques employed to sustain the attention of the audience across cultures.

Oral tradition as it existed in the past, offering support at crucial junctures in unfolding of the plot and liberal use of myths in projecting vexing problems of the present and pragmatic solutions suggested or offered in mitigating the suffering of the protagonist make drama in multicultural milieu most sought after avenue of entertainment and edification, in spite of the relentless onslaught on the pores unleashed by new market dynamics that dictate and determine the required measure and mode of entertainment through Television telecasts and digital delight delivered through technological up gradation.

Post-war feelings of futility, a sense of vacuum, generated proper conditions for the absurd theatre to evolve, exposing the limitations of humankind in the fast changing scenario. Experiments carried out in different locales on the themes and presentation of action, not forgetting shifting stage craft, yielded rich dividends in making multicultural drama most fascinating genre in world literature.

Multiculturalism has travelled far away alluringly from the original concept of limited application and reference to the creative work of the Afro-American writers in USA. Canada is a veritable crucible for multicultural creative output. Australia, UK and many European countries along with newly liberated Asian nations have unhesitatingly adopted multiculturalism as their governing policy to survive and emerge stronger in global market. Thus, dominant cultures and languages have meekly made way to the oppressed and suppressed subaltern to raise voice vehemently, confidently to proclaim proudly his hitherto deliberately ignored treasure-trove of cultural, literary legacy in the language of the coloniser. A sort of paying back Prospero! India is in the forefront of offering multicultural literature not only on account of her hoary past, but by the indomitable spirit of her resilience, her ability to absorb and radiate salient features of all cultures, and faiths so firmly fused and splendidly harmonised. Very rarely found anywhere in the world !

Experiences may look personal but feelings are universal. Mortification may seem to be individual; hurt, bruised souls are global in nature. Hence, all literature emerging from mutilingual and multicultural contexts echo a major song of discrimination and its ramifications resulting in resistance, revolt and regeneration of a new social order, where all cultures are received with uniform regard and evaluated with a common benchmark.

This volume offers eighteen research papers in addition to an interview with a well established writer who is known for his integrity and uncompromising administrative acumen. An honest endeavour is made to showcase salient features of drama in different countries, in addition to incorporating information on theatre in different regions in India.

I am grateful to all contributors who have extended unstinted cooperation. I am obliged to Prof S. Robert Gnanamony, Prof Saumitra Chakravarty, Prof Megha Trivedi, Dr. C.G.K.Murthy, Dr. Bhagabat Nayak, Dr. K.S.Anish Kumar, Dr. Lata Mishra, Dr. Lipi Pushpa Nayak, Dr. V.Kadambari, Dr. A.Madhavi Latha, Dr. Santhan Haridas, Dr. Shanta Naik, Dr. Asish Gupta, Dr. Ram Sharma and D.Suganya. I am beholden to Dr. Hrisikesh Panda for his superb support in executing this work through his illuminating interview.

I am deeply indebted to my motivator Sudarshan Kcherry, Managing Director of Authorspress, New Delhi, for showering Supreme SAI blessings in conceiving and completing this project. His constant encouragement and loving concern for me and my work enable me to carry on comfortably. I thank the staff at Authorspress for bestowing best attention in giving this book a pleasant shape.

It is fervently hoped that this anthology receives unreserved support of discerning lovers of literature. Constructive criticism is solicited for improving expression and content in future editions.

T. Sai Chandra Mouli

Our Contributors

A. Madhavi Latha, Lecturer in English, KVR Govt. Degree College for Women, Kurnool, Andhra Pradesh.

Ashish Gupta, Asstt. Professor English, Deptt. of Research & Postgraduate Studies, J.H.Govt.P.G.College, Betul, Madhya Pradesh.

Bhagabat Nayak, Department of English, Kandarpur College, Siddheswarpur, Cuttack-754117, Orissa.

C.G.K. Murthy, I.I.S., Former Director of Press Information Bureau, Hyderabad, Andhra Pradesh.

D. Suganya, Research Scholar, Mother Teresa Women's University, Kodaikanal, Tamil Nadu.

Hrishikesh Panda, I.A.S., Addl. Secretary, Dept. of Panchayat Raj, Govt. of India, New Delhi.

K.S. Anish Kumar, Assistant Professor of English, Bharathidasan University College, Perambalur, Tamil Nadu.

Keyur K.Parekh, Sr. Grade Lecturer in English, Arts & Commerce College, Kakanpur, At. & Po. Kakanpur-388713, Ta. Godhra, Dist. Panchmahals, Gujarat.

Lata Mishra, Asst. Professor of English, Govt. K.R.G. (Autonomous) P.G. College, Gwalior, Madhya Pradesh.

Lipipuspa Nayak, Associate Professor of English, K.B.College, near Bhubaneshwar, Orissa.

Megha Trivedi, Principal-Academics, ELITE Research Centre, Gwalior, Madhya Pradesh.

N. Shanta Naik, Asst. Professor of English, Maharaja's College, University of Mysore, Mysore, Karnataka.

Ram Sharma, Sr Lecturer in English, J.V.College, Baraut, Baghpat, Uttar Pradesh.

S. Robert Gnanamony, Professor of English, Kalasalingam University, Krishnan Koil-626190, Tamil Nadu.

Santhan Haridas, Poet, Kalavihar, Thiruvananthapuram, Kerala.

Saumitra Chakravarty, Professor & Head, Dept. of English, V.V.S.College, Bangalore, Karnataka.

T.S. Chandra Mouli, Former Professor of English, Railway College, Secunderabad, Andhra Pradesh.

V. Kadambari, Associate Professor in English, Ethiraj College For Women, Chennai, Tamil Nadu.

Contents

1

The Marginalised Bushed as Fuzzed Moths: A Reading of Wendy Lill's *The Occupation of Heather Rose*

— S. Robert Gnanamony

Introduction

In this paper an attempt is made to valorise the claim and voice of the Canadian Indians and the marginalised like the Metis in the canons of Canadian texts, thereby their 'silenced' voices could also reach the outside world. I have taken the contemporary Canadian playwright Wendy Lill's play *The Occupation of Heather Rose* and tried to see how impossible it is to ignore the muted agony of Canada's originary people in the Canadian canon. An attempt is also made to highlight how the play crosses the boundary lines of the rigidity of genres that tells us that in the postmodern times the text evolves in interaction with dynamic and cultural context, and its aim, if at all there is one, is to disturb our peace and complacency.

Taking an overview of Canada's literary canon, one could see that there are only two literatures that constitute the country's canon—the predominant Anglophone and the Francophone (Quebec) literatures. They both mostly give a unified notion of Canadian identity. Very seldom a legitimate space is provided to the literature of the marginalised and the aborigines; their identity is seldom recognised. This paper makes an impassioned plea to space in the Canadian canon the repressed and the silent voice of the Snake Island Indians who are 'a broke people' and such kindred souls living in neglected reserves elsewhere in the country. Heather Rose, the white nurse in her encounter with these people, though fired with a missionary zeal, feels bushed as a fuzzed moth very much as the Canadian marginalised people the native Indians.

The pluralising of poetics follows certain general characteristics. Contrarily, artists coming from subaltern communities, colonised collectivities, and native people produce artistic works different from mainstream majority cultures. As Vincent B. Leitch points out:

> Minority literatures exhibit distinctive images, rhythms, characters, themes, structures, genres, and styles (92).

If one looks into pluralising poetics one could understand that to some extent even the white women like Wendy Lill in a Western country like Canada constitute long-standing oppressed subcultures; as has been observed by Vincent B. Leitch:

> they are minorities and therefore, any discussion of the pluralising of poetics should take into account the literary work of these women as a distinct area of inquiry (92).

Wendy Lill's *The Occupation of Heather Rose* was produced in many theatres like Prairie Theatre Exchange, Tarragon Theatre, Globe Theatre, Vancouver Arts club, Eastern Front Theatre and Theatre Northwest across Canada in 1986 and thereabouts and was nominated along with three other plays of her for the Governor General's Literary Award for Drama. The other plays of Wendy Lill nominated for the Governor General's Award were *The Glace Bay Miner's Museum* (1996), *All Fall Down* (1994), and *Corker* (1998). Between June 1997 and June 2004, Wendy Lill was the Member of Parliament for Dartmouth and the Culture communications critic for the Federal New Democratic Party (NDP). Her broad sense of Canada, socially and politically, is reflected in her dual life as a politician and a prolific playwright. Her writings carry her sense of socio-politico concerns. A desire for social justice permeates in Lill's eight published plays. One could discern the abuse of power, especially over women and minorities, at the centre of these socially conscious works. Earlier she, with the help of a couple of her artist-friends, founded the Eastern Front Theatre in Dartmouth. In each of her plays, Lill presents protagonists oppressed by social powers that appear beyond their control and management; yet the majority of her characters never lose hope for a better world. In *The Occupation of Heather Rose*, Lill presents a well-meaning white nurse attempting, yet failing, to do good on a remote Native reserve in Canada's North. Many critics have viewed her devotion to social justice as didactic theatre, yet for others it represents provocative, social activist theatre at its best. Her plays have been highly regarded in Canada and beyond.

Reading through Wendy Lill's play one could see that she is trying to show to the outside world the conflictual relationship that the natives/first people have with the outside world, especially the White settlers. By presenting their problems she is negotiating for them a global space for greater visibility and recognition. At the same time, she has not failed to narrate the sacrifices of some other-centred people who do everything in their power for the other and thus the like Heather Rose find themselves in a precarious position of being neither here nor there, and thus either permanently out of place or unable to move away after dedicating their selves to the people in the reserves. Even though Heather Rose feels a sense of displacement in the play, she makes the reserve her place of choice for living and is trying to forge relationships with the marginalised.

In Canada in the past one hundred years an effort has been made to have a national theatre and also to establish a Canadian Theatre canon. It must reflect the national character. In the early days the notion of the Canadian character was spelt to be "rugged, Nordic, pure, and Anglo-Saxon to the bone" (Alan Filewod 16). I must hasten to add that this notion of national character is not the be-all and end-all and it gets revised from time to time. It has almost been an obsession. As Canadian culture to many Canadian authors like Arthur Beverley Baxter is mostly visualised as an extension of the

British culture, the Canadian dramatists did not fall into that trap and tried hard to wriggle out from the British and American stranglehold in order to have a distinct Canadian cultural content. They maintained that Canadian drama must necessarily be a celebration of Canadian nationhood and Canadian culture because both have attained full maturity. Canadian playwrights have produced over a couple of decades hundreds of plays in order to give the Canadian audiences a steady diet of Canadian experience rather than American and British culture and experience. The problem before the Canadian artists in the formative years had been to stop Canada from cultural absorption of the vast commercial power of the United States. They had a nagging question before them. How to preserve the Canadian identity? They should also be clear what exactly was Canadian identity. They had to contend with arch-imperialist poets like Wilfred Campbell who saw themselves as citizens of a "Vaster Britain". It is natural that "the antidote to Americanism was plainly Imperialism, a renewed emphasis on the 'British Connexion'" (Alan Filewod 17). It may be borne in mind in this connection what Alan Filewod writes about Canada's obsession with a national theatre. He tries to analyse why the Canadian artists failed to establish a Canadian national theatre. The reason that he forwards is

> [...] Canada's complex experience of colonialism, in which the theatre has been identified throughout our history as a site for a debate on the nature of nationhood. What makes this complex is that the evolution of the theatre as an expression of post-colonialism coincides with the historical transformation of the theatre as a cultural industry (15).

In the case of the marginalised in Canada, the centre has not fallen apart leaving the margins in a state of turmoil as in the postcolonial states. As Prafulla C. Kar et.al. in their Introduction to *Theory and Praxis* observe:

> Both postmodernism and postcolonialism are implicated in the game of toppling the centred subject [...] in replacing

> the centre with the margins [...] (18), in the case of the Canadian natives no such organised effort is made to topple the centre.

What exactly the reader finds in the experience of Heather Rose with the natives is the natives' subliminal archetypal essentialising common traits in human nature. Heather Rose finds in her day-to-day fragmented, and fractured experience the commonality of human experience wherever they are. The neglected side of this experience of the natives should be made part of the Canadian National History and the literature that brings out the stifled voices of the reserve-dwellers be part of the school/ university curriculum so that the world will at least wake up to their cries and do something useful to these neglected lot. That is the focus of this paper.

Heather Rose's absolute dedication to the Natives in the reserves need not be taken as an isolated event. In fact there has been awareness across the society to do something urgently to the suffering first nation people. Some even undertake some dangerous missions to get ease of their guilt feelings. It may be remembered that the early settlers using their guns pushed the first people to the remote reserves and usurped their lands. In the recent years in Canada the churches have taken upon themselves the social r4esponsibility of going to the rescue of the Native people. They have expressed their solidarity with the Native People and supported their land claims. This new faith- and-justice movement took off in Canada at the end of the sixties. This new movement began at the grass roots. The theme of this new social gospel movement as has been pointed by Gregory Baum is "God demanded justice in society" (67). It should not be construed that this movement is a new one. It has been in Canada from the close of the nineteenth century as well, but in a low key. In the dark years of the Great Economic Depression, it exerted political pressure and involved in the creation of the radical political party, the Cooperative Commonwealth Federation (CCF). But at that time the Church of Canada did not take note of it. But now there is a tremendous awareness and the Canadian bishops are willing to listen to the victims of society, much to the puzzle and chagrin of the major White community.

As Gregory Baun observes in his article, "The New Social Gospel in Canada":

> They (the bishops in Canada) were inspired by the radical position adopted by many Third World churches and supported by John Paul II's recent encyclicals (68).

The Canadian Catholic bishops have published many pastoral messages clarifying their stand on radical commitment to social justice in Canadian society. It has everything that can go into making "a Canadian liberation theology" (Baum 68). The bishops' documents stress the historical situation of the modern Canadian society:

> We live in a world that oppresses at least half of the human race and this scandal threatens to get worse [....] The present social and economic order fails to meet the human needs of the majority of people
>
> (cited in Baum 68).

Concomitantly, it widens the chasm between the rich and the poor and the elite and the non-elite and the Native and the settler major White. One of the key sentences that the bishops constructed expresses how deep their sense of commitment to these unfortunate brethren is:

> We stand in the biblical tradition of the prophets of Israel where to know God is to seek justice for the disinherited, the poor, and the oppressed
>
> (Baum 68).

It is in consonance to this thinking and social commitment that we find Heather Rose in the play in reference dedicating herself to do her little mite to help alleviate the suffering of the Natives. As the saying goes, in compassion and solidarity, people find God.

Just as we have body-centred theories, the Native-centred theories have also come up increasingly reiterating the need to recognise their legitimate aspirations. In feminist theories, it is a known fact that women's bodies have achieved a universal negative significance, to quote M. Nourbese Philip:

> Bodies which have become palimpsests upon which men have inscribed and re-inscribed their texts (12).

Just as genuine female experience was out of texts a few years ago, the genuine experience of the first people too had been out of the imagination of artists, but now just as women have plenty of feminists to champion their causes by writing about their subordination and the need to break their architectural fortresses raised by men for their selfish ends, authors like George Ryga, Sharon Pollock, and Wendy Lill right now bring out their first hand experiences of the first people in their works of diverse genres.

That the first people naturally confine themselves in their reserves is not because they don't want to mingle with the outside world, but because they are invariably targeted to all sorts of humiliation. There are also increasing catechism against the white marrying the Metis, because the native is a "neechi" which meant "dirty Indian" (Christine Welsh 57), something to be ashamed of. Even children born out of White and Native union "even masqueraded as French or even Hawaiian, depending on who asked" (Christine Welsh 57). As Christine Welsh, who is born out of mixed parents, confesses in her article, "Women in the Shadows: Reclaiming a Metis Heritage", "I lived in mortal terror that the truth would get out" (57). Howsoever the Natives cover their identity, their Native background seems to be written all over them[1]. The Indians in the reserves lived together, not because of their cultural ties but because they were poor and they had no means to build a good house. They were poor and that's why they lived in cramped quarters. They had no jobs. They had no today and no tomorrow. Nurse Rose like the majority White had no occasion to taste or smell poverty. She was going to witness it for the first time in the reserve Snake Lake. All her romantic notions about the reserve is gone blasted when she first encountered the Indians in the reserve. She saw with her eyes that:

> An Indian reserve is not a nine-to-five place. Not a September-to-June place. It's a hanging-around place
>
> (Rose 179).

Only in the 1960's the Natives woke up from their stupor and as a result there was "a new pride in native identity among Native people across Canada".[2] (Christine Welsh 58). They slowly started coming out of the thick web of denial, shame, bitterness, and silence.

Heather Rose has gone to the reserve much against her inner fears because she felt a genuine bond of compassion and respect for the Canadian Dalits. Never even once she has displayed any contempt for their native heritage. Though it is a lonely struggle, she takes the cross upon her shoulders, and never entertained the question of going back. She has to undergo all sorts of hardships in the reserve. More than the Natives, it is her own tribe that gives her a lot of difficulties. See how the black-marketer Ramsay tempts her:

> Why don't we be [...] friends? Hmmmm? It's hard living on an Indian reserve. Your friends in the South forget you, your magazines never come. People hear every word you're saying on the radiotelephone so you can't be intimate with someone a long way away. Everyone will talk about you, even laugh at you. I'll get to the point that you even think the ravens are laughing at you, and when that happens, come and see me. Old Ramsay will give you a shot of stamina (177).

The Natives are not in the habit of leaving any letters, or diaries or wills so that the present/future generation could reconstruct their story. Historians have seldom recorded their voices. Though some European traders have left behind some notes about the historic encounter between the First Nation's men and the Europeans, they haven't had anything to say about the First Nation's women who struggled hard with their men folk, for "women were the strength, the backbone of aboriginal society" (Christine Welsh 61). Such early first nations women were nameless and faceless though they served their new husbands (the European traders whom they married) well and taught them the skills needed to survive in what the Europeans regarded as a wilderness, and it was their genuine companionship that made life bearable for the early European traders who had left behind their kith and kin (wives too).

With the heavy inflow of European immigrants into Canada in the late nineteenth century, they usurped the land of the Metis, land that had been the home of Indian and Metis people for generations. The Indians were confined to reserves, and the Metis had lost their land and their way of life. As Christine Welsh retraces their history writes:

> The Metis resistance that had begun at Red River in 1870 and ended at Batoche in 1885 resulted in the dispossession of the Metis people, and they found themselves relegated to the road allowances and the margins of Canadian society. In the dark years that followed very few Metis people spoke about being Metis and there was widespread denial of Metis identity among generations of Metis who survived that troubled time and grew up in its aftermath. While most Metis people were not subjected to the brutal suppression of language and identity that the Indian people experienced in the residential school system, they were nonetheless made to feel ashamed of their heritage and many Metis came to see assimilation to the 'white ideal' as the only way to escape desperate lives of oppression and grinding poverty (64).

Interestingly, ironically too, not only the Natives get our sympathy but the Nurse Rose too. Her situation is in no way better than the reserve communities. She gets help from nowhere. Neither the government nor the private entrepreneur has any concern for the reserve-dwellers. As women are more concerned about ecological damages caused by the insensitive male, Wendy Lill does not fail to give vent to her feelings in the play. The industrial waste from the nearby paper plant owned by a white industrialist contaminates the Snake Island. Even the fish in the lake:

> were full of chemicals [...], the wild rice didn't grow since the government put in the hydro dam. And it was hard to

> keep your kids clean when there wasn't enough money for proper sewage
>
> (Rose 176).

It is still a puzzle how Nurse Rose was drawn to the North. She remembered someone had told her: "You're going to kill yourself [...]" (177). It was more "like a firefly to light" (*Rose* 173). Determined to serve the reserve people, she was going in a Dakota plane. She felt, in her monologue:

> I was going down, down, downward into another place, another time, falling through a rabbit hole into a green and silver world below. I was Alice in Wonderland (174).

Landing she felt as if her heart would fall out and she would die on the spot. The place had virtually nothing—no medicine, no food, no warm clothes. When she ploughed through the previous Nurse Bunny's medical records, she understood that the Indian Jobit Loon:

> died of shaking [...] Moonias Turtle died of exposure. [...]. Entire bottom end of reserve has diarrhoea. Toilet backed up. Closed early (174).

The twenty-one year old Heather Rose's monologue gives us a glimpse of the other excruciating situation in the reserve. There was no light. It was "black night. There were no street lights" (175). Heather Rose was dismayed at this and was wondering:

> Were there animals out here in the darkness? Bears, wolves, moose? Were there Indians out there? My patients? Was there a world outside in the shadows waiting for me? (175).

The despicable condition of the natives is brought out without any sentimentality by the reporting of the Nurse. Heather Rose's first patient was Camilla Loon. She came for treatment with her daughter Naomi. To Heather Rose:

> Camila's face was like a worn old leather purse without coins. And when she opened her mouth, soft little noises came out, like coos from a dove. Her wooden leg was hurting her (175).

The Nurse had never seen such an old prosthesis. She felt that Camilla needed a new set of false teeth. As the Indians were the poorest of the poor, naturally they had no confidence to look at any outsider on the face. Accordingly, Camilla too was looking at the top button of Heather Rose's uniform "as if it had some mysterious power over her" (175). In spite of many handicaps, the Indians didn't seem to mind them, for Camilla and Naomi were laughing the whole day. The visiting Nurse liked both the mother and the daughter. She had an "overwhelming urge to hug each one of them" (176). She wanted to learn their culture and she wanted to teach her Western culture to the Indians.

Prior to her trip to the reserve, Heather Rose thought that she knew all the problems of the Indians when she attended an orientation camp. She shared some of these with the Red Indian chief, Chief Red Sky. The chief seemed to know that the Nurse had already ordered for artificial limbs and false teeth. But he knew that the truth was very bitter; to the White the Indians were just unwanted animals and nobody would care to send medicines and apparatuses to them; they were "pushing the Indians off the road as they barrel from place to place" (176).

That the White who choose to serve the Indian community in the far away reserves soon forget their good intentions and become lethargic, wayward and pleasure-loving is brought out in this play by the author. Wendy Lill seems to dismiss the prevalent notion that the Indian men are different from white men; they smell different, and that they have warm skin and that they are better in bed. She does so by presenting it through the character of the legendary teacher Annadora, who was taking quite a number of Indian boys to her room after school hours to have sex with them. As the report goes, when the Chief Red Sky came to know of this, he ordered that Annadora should not teach their children any more. Interestingly, as the text shows, "the Indians actually carried her down to the dock and shoved her on the plane" (177). Wendy Lill also points out how mindless the white become when they go to such reserves. Invariably their sole objective seems to be to make a quick buck doing all sorts of unlawful activities like bootlegging, black-marketing, high profiting and cheating. Ray and Ramsay are such insensitive type of people in the play. It is men like Ray who throw cold water on the good intentions of Nurse Rose. The playwright also seems to show how bad the sanitary condition is in the reserve:

> [...] It's kind of hard to stay clean when there's shit floating up your water intake pipe"(177).

Communication with the outside world is also not a comfortable thing. The Nurse asks:

> 'Why the hell can't they get decent telephones in the North (185).

Wendy Lill repeatedly brings out in the play that the reserve is a god-forsaken place. There were even gunshots outside the trailer of Heather Rose. On such occasions, the Nurse would be lying in the dark "waiting for the end [...]. It wasn't a nightmare. It was the real thing" (179). Even the church was not a consolation to the Nurse, because the shooting was heard only from the church and the church sat there "like a scared hapless, toothless face against the cold autumn sky" (179). In fact, every now and then the Natives got restless and there would invariably be a big shoot-up on such occasions. So the Nurse was even scared to go to Church. People stayed indoors and prayed in private. Heather Rose could never comprehend how any one would shoot from the Church. She was very much wary about the Indians. She wanted to help them out from their troubles, but nothing seemed to be working out the way she wanted. To her there was no cooperation from the Indians. She was not happy with their drinking, their fights, and their weekends when hell would let loose. The only cheery sight was the airplane, which brought in a kind of possibility. Heather

Rose also felt total government apathy to welfare measures. Even the basic needs of the Indians were not supplied on time. Artificial legs for amputated legs were sent to other reserves by mistake. The departmental policy was to send dentures only once in four years to the reserves "so that they wouldn't be filling orders every time an Indian got drunk and dropped [...]" (183). Though the journals present the Indian culture colourful, in reality, "they are poorer, sick, unhappy, uneducated, [...]. Good photo opportunities" (185). In their gatherings sometimes there would be music and drum beating especially whenever they celebrate winter festival. But invariably Heather was drummed out. And on those occasions she would feel sad to be an outsider.

Many a time, Heather Rose felt that she was trapped. Sometimes dreaming would bring in temporary relief to some persons. But even such a fantasy-luxury deserted the Nurse. The city-bred young woman even fantasised that she was going to be raped and scalped by an Indian. She felt that she was a funny little mouse. She was also constantly tempted to sleep with Ramsay the store-man. He goaded her to drink so that she could forget about her worries. Ramsay tried to get her for him like he got the "sweet city woman" (181) Annadora. Heather Rose boldly resisted not only his temptation but also his sexy words, "Shut up! Shut up!" (181). Realising her helplessness, the Nurse very often cried. It gave her some relief. She was not like the high-paid white officers coming through to help the Indians. In her words:

> Flying in and out, in and out, in and out, consulting on this, consulting on that, flashing their million dollar smiles, stalking about the reserve from plane to community hall, to band office, to plane to community hall, to band office, to plane, with their Indian friends, being helpful and advisory, then back in the air. Once a month old Blue Eyes came and went, his tan always the same. Perfect (182).

It is awfully surprising to see the Indians stand mute most of the time before the Nurse. They do not even know to wipe their bleeding noses. They do not know how to say 'Thank you' when someone does some nice things to them. But instead Rose says, "[...] I get silence. Dark eyes. Secrets. Why is that?" (183). Unable to bear it any longer she has been drinking for the last couple of weeks. She finds it too difficult to stay there sober. In her monologue we hear, "[...] I have fallen apart. Completely apart"(185). Every day invariably dawns with some sad news or other. Her native companion, the talkative Naomi, who is in love with the native Clarence Loon is once brought to the community hall with yellow fluid all over her face. She has obviously drunk gasoline. Heather Rose feels Naomi's heart and finds that she is sinking. Her eyes are closing. Heather could only command, "Naomi. Hey! It's spring. Rise up! You're supposed to RISE UP!" (186). Two thousand years ago, when Jesus Christ found Jairus' daughter dead, he comforted the:

> Weep not; she is not dead, but sleepeth [...]. And he put them all out, and took her by the hand, and called, saying, Maid, arise. And her spirit came again, and she arose straightway [...]
>
> (St. Luke 8: 52-55).

But when Heather Rose commands Naomi to rise, there is no response. She has also no effective drug to combat the poison. And Naomi's heart stops. Heather Rose looks for help outside but there is only darkness everywhere. The occupation of Heather Rose is really hard.

Wendy Lill's play tells us how the Natives have been surviving in spite of their terrible experiences. They do so primarily by their resourcefulness, adaptability and courage, especially by the womenfolk. Even though there is plenty of pressure to give up their native heritage and get themselves assimilated, they have been quietly struggling to keep themselves alive mostly by the affirmation of their strength, courage, and resilience. So it is a celebration of survival and survival is the greatest challenge that they have before them. They cannot afford to hate their survival. The literature of the Metis/Native/conscientious White and other artists has one important theme: the theme of survival/continuance. The play in reference is also about it. Heather Rose shares her excruciating experience with us, because she doesn't want the legend of herself spill into silence[3]. Writers like Emma La Rocque want the Natives/Metis remember this always:

> For our words and music and images are testaments to the remarkable fact that we are still here—that we have survived near-annihilation and that we continue to resist—and though they necessarily give voice to our pain, they also express our vision for the future, and in so doing they become tools for healing, for empowerment, and for change
>
> (cited in Christine Welsh 66).

One could imagine how the first nation people would carry their experiences to the subsequent generation if one reads through Ray Bradbury's science fiction *Fahrenheit 451*, and the film version of it in 1966. Francois Truffaut made the film as an elegy on the book culture. The authorities in the film burn all the books not for being pornographic or revolutionary but simply being books. Truffaut depicts a group of isolated rebels who, as Kalidas Misra shows in his article, "Theory at the End of the Millennium":

> [...] despaired of preserving physical books, reinvented the ancient art of memorising. They dedicated themselves to committing whole volumes to memory, so that the classics can be transmitted to succeeding generations by word of mouth. His film's most vivid image is a group of volunteers walking in circles in the snow reciting their book aloud (263).

The foundations of a culture are kept alive by the study of texts. As Hiren Gohain points out in the article "Criticism in Crisis: Politics of Pedagogy" the study of texts "makes for community and for understanding" (272). We read and understand texts as historical beings with a past and a future. Texts like *The Occupation of Heather Rose*, Jeannette Armstrong's poems[4] as well as her other works, Robertson Davis's *At My Heart's Core*, George Ryga's *Indian*, and *The Ecstasy of Rita Joe* to name a few can not be dismissed as pure imaginative exercises. They certainly carry the true experience of the first nation people.

Lill's play cannot be easily brushed aside as "whites in the wrong places". Much like Lill herself, her central character Heather Rose is deeply concerned about community, especially the marginalised of Canada and she wrestles with how to effect and invoke changes to create a better world for everyone. Lill's play focuses on particular and localised incidents of social injustice, but these chosen incidents, along with the manner in which she crafts them within her play, speak to a broader audience and transcend the specific issues. Along with Sharon Pollock, Joan MacLeod, Linda Griffiths, Margaret Hollingworth, and others, Wendy Lill's socially conscientious plays have been instrumental in giving a strong place and voice to women playwrights in Canada. If there is one thing these women authors have in common, it is a commitment to and fascination with plays.

The Canadian national literary canon is a malleable commodity frequently shaped and reshaped by changes and the appearance of new authors. Till yesterday, the Canadian male author had not much difficulty in entering the school or the university curricula. It was mostly due to the gender factor and his academic connections. Though the Canadian women authors have been marginalised for long, in the beginning of the third millennium, it looks now that they have come in a big way and they cannot be ignored in the Canadian canonical domain. In other words, the Canadian literary elite is no longer the exclusive zone of the male; it includes an equal number of women too. Seeing the prolific outpourings of the women authors these days, and the quality of literary pieces, it looks that the publishers, the media, and the academy have to give way to them; otherwise they will push aside the canonical gatekeepers and occupy a decent space for them. Now no one can say like Nathaniel Hawthorn who made an attack on women authors in 1854, using the stinking expression, "damn'd mob of scribbling women" (cited in Carole Gerson 149). No doubt at the time of Nathaniel Hawthorne, American literature was "masculine culture" (cited in Carole Gerson 149) and the woman writer who entered the American literary history was considered as an enemy. In Canada too, till very recently the male dominated the literary scene; and even in academic circles, the male-dominated academy rejected female gentility. Now of course things are different, and though the generic difference is not ruled out exclusively from the academic institutionalisation of the reading choices, women authors don't remain ghettoised. Plays like *The Occupation of Heather Rose* will help their authors create new paradigms of canon formation. This is mandatory because Canada happens to be a culturally pluralistic society and so a traditional view of Canadian literature may not help and therefore only a cross-culturally pluralistic approach alone will help form the Canadian canon of literature.

Notes

1. The children born out of the White and Metis parents are contemptibly referred to as half-breeds. See how Pique, the daughter of Morag Gunn in Laurence's *The Diviners* is humiliated by a guy who teased her in school: "Aw come on, don't give me that shit—you know half-breed girls can't wait to get fucked by any guy who comes along" (447). For publication details, please see Works Cited.
2. It may be noted that in the same period in India too, the marginalised people like the Dalits woke up to a new awareness and boldly came out with their identity. Slogans like "Don't be ashamed to be a Dalit; raise your head and proclaim boldly that you are a Dalit" were very common then.
3. "The legends of ourselves/ spill into silence" is a beautiful line found in Eli Mandel's poem "In My 57th Year".
4. My article, "*Words Are Memory*: Readings into Jeannette Armstrong's Select Poems" deals at length about Armstrong's efforts at unearthing and delineating the experience of the first nation people in her poems. The article is published in *Littcrit,* No. 57, Vol. 30, June 2004, 84-95.

Works Cited

Baum, Gregory. 'The New Social Gospel in Canada'. *New Contexts of Canadian Criticism*. Eds. Ajay Heble, Donna Palmateer Pennee and J.R. (Tim) Struthers. Ontario: Broadview Press, 1996, 67-77.

Carole, Gerson. 'Anthologies and the Canon of Early Canadian Women Writers'. *New Contexts of Canadian Criticism*. Ed. Ajay Heble, Donna Palmateer Pennee and J.R. (Tim) Struthers. Ontario: Broadview Press, 1997, 146-167.

Filewod, Alan. 'National Theatre/ National Obsession'. *New Contexts of Canadian Criticism*. Eds. Ajay Heble, Donna Palmateer Pennee and J.R. (Tim) Struthers. Ontario: Broadview Press, 1996, 15-23.

Gohain, Hiren. 'Criticism in Crisis: Politics of Pedagogy'. *Theory and Praxis: Curriculum, Culture and English Studies*. Editors. Prafulla, C. Kar and Kailash C. Baral and Sura P. Rath. Delhi: Pencraft International, 2003, 269-274.

Kar, Prafulla, C. and Kailash C. Baral and Sura P. Rath. Editors. *Theory and Praxis: Curriculum, Culture and English Studies*. Delhi: Pencraft International, 2003.

Laurence, Margaret. *The Diviners*. Toronto: McClelland & Stewart Inc. 1995. (Originally Published in 1974.

Leitch, Vincent, B. *Cultural Criticism, Literary Theory, Poststructuralism*. New York: Columbia University Press, 1992.

Lill, Wendy. *The Occupation of Heather Rose. Modern Canadian Plays*. Vol.II. Editor. Jerry Wasserman. Vancouver: Talonbooks, 1994. (Third Edition).

Luke, *St. The Gospel According to St. Luke. Holy Bible*. Cambridge: Cambridge University Press, (n.y.p).

Misra, Kalidas. 'The World Beyond the Book: Theory at the End of Millennium'. *Theory and Praxis: Curriculum, Culture and English Studies*. Editors. Prafulla, C. Kar and Kailash C. Baral and Sura P. Rath. Delhi: Pencraft International, 2003, 258-268.

Philip, Nourbese M. 'Who's Listening? Artists, Audiences, and Language'. *New Contexts of Canadian Criticism*. Eds. Ajay Heble, Donna Palmateer Pennee and J.R. (Tim) Struthers. Ontario: Broadview Press, 1996, 1-14.

Welsh, Christine. 'Women in the Shadows: Reclaiming a Metis Heritage'. *New Contexts of Canadian Criticism*. Eds. Ajay Heble, Donna Palmateer Pennee and J.R. (Tim) Struthers. Ontario: Broadview Press, 1996, 56-66.

2

"Articulating the Inarticularable Horror": A Study of Beckett's *Waiting for Godot*

— K.S. Anish Kumar

The mid-twentieth century English drama opened a new epoch in the history of English literature with its own distinct way of representing human condition of the time. In fact the plays of the time (and other literary works as well) clearly depicted man as an isolated individual who often feels himself as the sojourner to the world. He is not just deprived of illusions but "his is an irremediable exile" as Camus puts it. Man's irrational, purposeless and helpless condition names the human predicament of the post-war period as absurd. M.H. Abrams in his text *A Glossary of Literary Terms* outlines the common elements of writing of this period that represented human condition as "essentially and ineradicably absurd (...) reject realistic settings, logical reasoning or a coherently evolving plot (1).

It is worthy to note that one cannot easily avoid the strong influence of foreign writers on English writings that depicted the absurdity of life. Alfred Jary, Franz Kafka, Brecht are the most influential writers. Edward Albert Beckett's contribution is the most important influence after Brecht. His writings remain not only a benchmark to absurd writings but also implicitly announce the beginning of postmodern condition, according to Ihab Hassan.

Beckett's writings continue to question rational thinking, goal setting, identity and there by bring to light absurdity of life. In the structural level also he considerably deviates from the drama of the past—a drama which contains a well–constructed stage, a well-defined plot and a definite climax—and as G.J.V. Prasad remarks in his introduction to *Waiting for Godot* (here after referred to as *Godot*):

> The plotless plot and characterless characters then are subject to a serious of senseless and, thus, their actionless actions.
>
> (*Godot* XVI)

In fact, this "structureless structure" of the play leads Andrew K.Kennedy to call the play 'anti-play'.

Beckett seems to suggest to the readers that the world now is "beyond repair". One cannot deny the fact that man has already done enough damage to humankind and hence people live within their own world of uncertainties. *Waiting for Godot* is the true description of the human condition of post-war period with all its follies.

The play was staged several times in several countries and hence attracted many audience irrespective of locale, for it touches a slice of their own life. For instance Andrew K.Kennedy writes in his essay entitled 'Action and Theatricality in *Waiting for Godot*' how the play has captured the attention of prisoners:

> It is not surprising that fourteen hundred convicts of San Quentin penitentiary responded enthusiastically to a performance of Beckett's play (in 1957)—completely strange yet meaningful to them. They could draw on their own experience of waiting, the empty kind of waiting where "nothing to think about" is a permanent threat, and every happening offers both a promise and a disillusioning repetition of the daily round. (16)

Apart from this strange kind of audience reception the critical reception to the play was also laudable. In fact, critics continue to concentrate on every aspects of the play starting from the structure to the thought content of the play. It is worthy to note that *Waiting for Godot* seems to evade all assumptions about the play.

The play remains a testimony of Beckett's style that he discovered after World War II. It is this play which popularised him as a playwright of "new theoretical aesthetics" which focus mainly on the marginalised position of men of the time and their distorted psyche duly represented by the two tramps namely Vladimir and Estragon.

In the play 'nothing happens again' though ordinary reader may assume that there are a lot of repetitions. The repetition of certain words and incidents may lead him to arrive at such conclusions but these apparent repetitions do create commendable vibrations when he goes beyond the denotative level ; the changes that occur are presented through the tramps. For instance the dead willow of the first act has leaves in the second act. Throughout the play Pozzo continues to be the master of Lucky but in the second act a major change is then brought to the notice of audience: Pozzo is blind and Lucky is dumb.

All the "actionless actions" happen while tramps are waiting for Godot. (They are not sure about the name also for Godot is not a name.) The play *Waiting for Godot* opens with a startling idea of uncertainty. Estragon says, "Nothing can be done," soon after giving up trying to take off his boot. This existential condition is obvious throughout the play for their existence itself is a struggle but they find happiness in togetherness. Vladimir says, "Together again at last! We'll have to celebrate this: But how? Get up till I embrace you". Their togetherness provides them with a momentary pleasure though their life is miserable. For instance, the following dialogue aptly reveals the true condition of one of the tramps, Estragon:

> *Vladimir* : (Hurt, coldly) May one enquire where his Highness spent the night?
> *Estragon* : In a ditch.
> *Vladimir* : (Admiringly) A ditch! Where?
> *Estragon* : (Without gesture) Over there.
> *Vladimir* : And they didn't beat you?
> *Estragon* : Beat me? Certainly they beat me.
> *Vladimir* : The same lot as usual?
>
> (*Godot* 1)

The dialogue "The same lot as usual" reflects the condition of the tramps and the inexplicable horror of their survival. The dialogue "I resumed struggle" also brings to light the existential position that man has to resume in his struggle for he has nothing to resume and they knew that "nothing can be done."

Estragon and Vladimir engage in conversation—one making fun of the other, passing instructions (as Estragon says "you might button it (fly) all the time")—merely to pass time.

Vladimir : Ah yes, the two thieves. Do you remember the story?

Estragon : No.

Vladimir : Shall I tell it to you?

Estragon : No.

Vladimir : It'll pass the time (Pause). Two thieves, crucified at the same time by our Saviour. One—

Estragon : One what?

Vladimir : Our Saviour. Two thieves. One is supposed to have been saved and the other... (He searches for the contrary of saved) .... damned

(*Godot* 4)

These dialogues offer Beckett's speculation on the age old idea of being saved. The line "one of the thieves being saved" reminds one of the Christian theology in which one of the thieves who was crucified along with Jesus was saved. The interaction between Christ and the two thieves are recorded in Luke in the *Bible*. One spoke on behalf of Christ and other offended him. The man who spoke on his behalf said, "Jesus, remember me when you come into your kingdom". He receives assurance from Christ, "today you will be with me in Paradise". In fact, he was saved from going to hell.

It is worthy to note that most of the time in the midst of their conversation. (Beckett seems to violate the actual tone and content of conversation by fragmenting the pattern with rise / fall or fall / rise one reminds the other of waiting. To pass time they narrate not only stories but discuss about "hanging themselves" and it becomes comical, for they discuss who should hang himself first and they never hang themselves. To Camus committing suicide is a way to surrender to the absurdity of the world. They postpone the act of committing suicide by leaving the decision to Godot. Actually they are not sure of the name, for Estragon asks "His name is Godot?" and Vladimir replies, "I think so" and later they mistake Pozzo for Godot. This again adds more intensity to uncertainty for they are not sure about his arrival, and it appears that the tramps may or may not identity him.

The other two characters, Pozzo and Lucky, are presented in contrast to Estragon and Vladimir for the former pair maintains master-slave relationship instead of an inter-dependency of the latter. It appears that the master-slave relationship might have resulted as a matter of habit too. Some of the critics associate Pozzo with the image of God. G.J.V. Prasad in his introduction to the text opines:

> Pozzo (....) is almost a God—substitute one who gives Lucky a sense of purpose, a place in the world order. (....) Pozzo is precisely that Vladimir and Estragon fail to recognize him, just as many Jews failed to recognise Jesus Christ.
>
> (*Godot* XXIV)

Prasad's idea of equating Pozzo with the image of Jesus Christ is again debatable, for Pozzo treats Lucky merely as a slave and Lucky always appears with a rope passing around his neck. Lucky also carries a heavy bag, a folding stool, a picnic basket. In fact, Lucky (a paradoxical name for a slave) acts according to his commands, and Pozzo is not seen as kind hearted like Jesus Christ. He uses words like 'Pig', 'hog', 'whip' to refer to Lucky. In addition to this, Pozzo takes him to a fair to sell him. This clearly indicates he likes to get rid of him for he is of no use to him. Hence, it seems that Pozzo may not be the image of Christ for Christ has mercy on least important beings on earth as reflected is W.B.Yeats's *The Ballad of Father Gilligan*:

> He who is wrapped is purple robes
> with planets in His care
> Had pity on the least of things
> sleep upon a chair. (45—48)

In fact God sends an angel in Gilligan's image to help Gilligan in his old age. This shows the generosity and kindness of Christ. Contrary to this Pozzo never appreciates nor helps him. Lucky is depicted not only as a symbol of suffering but also a man of creative thinking, though he is physically tied to his master, Pozzo. His long speech in the play is highly philosophical which concentrates mainly on the life of human beings on this earth. He highlights the idea that all human beings are left with the uncertainty of death. As many of them are entrapped in invisible nets, Lucky is entangled in a net and hence thinks only on command. Beckett tries to suggest that modern man is entangled in a net of issues and hence everybody views the world according to his perception but everybody strives hard to exist. One should remember that it is also a speech that violates the most famous peace-making philosophical speeches like the lectures of Dr. Radhakrishnan (On earth one family) or Einstein. Jeffrey Nealon in his essay 'Samuel Beckett and the Postmodern: Language, Games, Play and *Waiting for Godot*' rightly remarks:

> Beckett directs Lucky's long monologue against the popular notion that philosophy's job is to restore unity to man's learning, a job which philosophers can only do by recuperating some metanarrative which links together all moments in human history, within a single, continuous metaphysical system. Lucky's think, though, is a narrative that disrupts and deconstructs all notion of universal, ahistorical, consistent meta-narrative—all Godots.
>
> (*Godot* 47)

At the end of the Act I like a messiah in Greek plays a boy comes and tells the tramps, "Mr. Godot told me to tell you he won't come this evening but surely tomorrow" (44) Vladimir is very curious to know about Godot and his activities. He also tells him that to assure him that he did see them. The two tramps appear to be satisfied by the boy's response and hence decide to wait for Godot. Vladimir rightly says, "He said Godot was sure to come," and from this statement one can easily understand that Estragon and Vladimir will wait for Godot. They will wait by killing time. In fact, waiting comforts them and gives them "the illusion that they are doing something which is meaningful." Angelie Multani rightly observes:

> Waiting helps the tramps into a sense of security—they are fine with waiting as long as that is what they have to do. It is the absence of waiting that makes them insecure.
>
> (*Godot* 128)

It is worthy to note that waiting is not a physical activity but a mental activity. Their painful waiting is often equated by some critics with slow crucifixion. James L.Calderwood remarks it as a "self erasing non-activity". Estragon's and Vladimir's attitudes are very close to the modern life in which people wait for things that are not clear to them. They may think that God will at last save them from suffering as the tramps wait for salvation. Both Estragon's and Vladimir's pointless and meaningless waiting brings to light the horror of existence. In fact they fill the void of their existence also with their timely dialogues and temporal excitement and often they talk for the sake of talking.

> *Estragon* : What am I to say?
> *Vladimir* : Say, I am happy.
> *Estragon* : I am happy.
> *Vladimir* : So am I.
> *Estragon* : So am I.
> *Vladimir* : We are happy.
> *Estragon* : We happy (silence). What do we do now, now that we are happy?
> *Vladimir* : Wait for Godot.
>
> (*Godot* 51)

Again and again the audience and reader of the play are compelled to ask, "Are they really happy?" They appear to be happy sometimes in a dream (an escape from reality), and sometimes one induces the other to pretend to be happy as Vladimir does but most of the time they engage is meaningless dialogues. Through the disconnected dialogues like these Beckett seems to bring to light the absurdity of life and the irrational behaviour of the people of the post-war Europe.

The tramps often decide to go but never make a move, for they are tied by an inescapable act of *Waiting for Godot*. Godot's unseen presence in the play not only works as a catalyst but also as a reactant.

Estragon : Let's go.
Vladimir : We can't.
Estragon : Why not?
Vladimir : We're waiting for Godot.

(*Godot* 59)

Estragon and Vladimir are entrapped in repetitions of life and they live in a 'timeless zone' for the actions happens not in a specific place. The stage can be everywhere. Pozzo, a time conscious man, in the beginning enters into the timeless zone in Act II. His systematic life and materialistic living has come to an end for he has become blind. He says, "I woke up one fine day as blind as Fortune". He adds, "The Blind have no notion of time. The things of time are hidden from them too" (*Godot* 79). Beckett uses a capital letter 'F' in order to give a stress to the word 'Fortune'. The question one intends to ask is, "Is blindness a fortune?" To Pozzo blindness appears to be fortune for the world is full of sufferings and he was (in the beginning) preoccupied with the routine and is always conscious about time but now he feels liberated.

The boy comes again and informs them that Godot will come tomorrow. They again decide to stay back for Godot's arrival. Once again they discuss about hanging themselves but this time they postpone hanging telling, "We'll hang ourselves tomorrow. (Pause) Unless Godot comes" (*Godot* 87)

Estragon : And if he comes?
Vladimir : We'll be saved.

(*Godot* 87)

Vladimir's words compel the readers repeatedly to speculate about Godot. Is he a God? or Godlike? Is he referring to the second coming of Christ? Throughout the play Beckett tries to create an abrupt picture of Godot through the words of Vladimir or his questions to the boy or his answers to Estragon. Vladimir, a highly dynamic character in the play, appears to be very curious to know Godot, his character and his appearance (to identify if he comes). Vladimir's first encounter with the boy reveals the mysterious character of Godot.

Vladimir : You work for Mr.Godot?
Boy : Yes, sir.
(—)
Vladimir : Is he good to you?
Boy : Yes, sir.
(—)
Vladimir : He must be fond of you.
Boy : I don't know, sir.
Vladimir : Does he give you enough to eat?
(The boy hesitates) Does he feed you well?
Boy : Fairly well, sir.

(*Godot* 44-45)

The second meeting of the boy in the play with Vladimir happens in Act II and brings out the appearance of Godot which some say resembles Jesus Christ.

Vladimir : (Softly) Had he a beard, Mr.Godot?
Boy : Yes, sir.
Vladimir : Fair or ... (he hesitates) .... or black?
Boy : I think it is white, sir.
(Silence)
Vladimir : Christ have mercy on us!

(*Godot* 85)

It is again left to the audience / reader to find out who is Godot. In fact Beckett never clearly describes Godot and Vladimir's interaction can be also viewed as his mental picture of Godot. The boy's answer is abrupt and not clear. Soon after the enquiry Vladimir's prayer, "Christ have mercy on us", is suggestive and symbolic, for Godot may be the son of God, Jesus Christ. Vladimir assumes that if they see him they will be saved. His answer's to Estragons question also provide us with a hint of Godot's character.

Estragon : And if we dropped him? (pause)
If we dropped him?
Vladimir : He'd punish us.

(*Godot* 86)

In yet another place in the play he again answers the question of Estragon.

Estragon : And if he comes?
Vladimir : We'll be saved.

Vladimir's answers clearly reiterate the idea that both the tramps wait for salvation. They want to be saved by Godot as one of the thieves was saved by Jesus Christ. Beckett never attempted to answer the question, 'Who is Godot?' and purposely leaves it to the reader. Angelie Multani identifies Godot as a source of comfort and God:

> Godot may represent nothing but vague promises, supplications, entreaties, or he may represent food, warm and dry place to sleep in and a roof over their heads (.....) He may be a God or he may be nobody (....) a goal, an objective
>
> (*Godot* 129)

At the end of each act Beckett purposely writes, "They (the tramps) do not move", suggesting that they continue to resume their immobile condition.

Beckett through this tragicomedy continues to assert the existential position of man by criticising the rationalistic attitude of man. In fact the play seems to reflect the condition of Satre's protagonist in his novel *Nausea,* "Every existing thing is born without reason prolongs itself of weakness and dies by chance" (qtd in Gupta 36).

Vladimir's observations of life clearly present not only the absurdity of life but also remain as evidence of existential condition. He says, "one is what one is and the essential does not change" (*Godot* 14). Pozzo also comments on the sordid reality of life. To him:

> The tears of the world are a constant quantity. For each one who begins to weep somewhere else another stop. The same in true of laugh.
>
> (*Godot* 25)

G.J.V. Prasad in his introduction to the play remarks:

> Our life in a laugh, the more the pity. It is in the fusion created of this understanding the coexistence of laugh and the tear
>
> (*Godot* XX Viii).

It is the laughter and suffering that govern the tramps who make this play a tragicomedy. Beckett's understanding of the haunting reality is reflected through Estragon also..

> *Vladimir* : Where else do you think? Do you not recognise the place?
>
> *Estragon* : (Suddenly furious) Recognise! What is there to recognise?. All my lousy life I've crawled about in the mud! And you talk to me about scenery!
>
> (*Godot* 52)

When Vladimir and Estragon talk about removal of boots and when Vladimir asks Estragon to pull on his trousers, the audience burst into laughter. It is worthy to note that though the play *Waiting for Godot*, is published with a sub-title 'A Tragicomedy in Two Acts', it contains more tragic elements than comic ones, and it also leads any researcher to treat the 'comic elements' of the play as black humours of modern plays. Beckett skilfully portrays the modern mind with all its distortions and perversions. In fact, he articulates the horror that exists in everybody's life. It seems that Beckett tries to reiterate the idea that sufferings are unavoidable in life and man's logical thinking miserably fails before the absurdity of life. Every articulation of the absurdity of life ends is an inarticulable horror. Angelie Multani rightly remarks:

> The main difference between the tramps and us in that they know they are playing games while waiting and we remain unaware.
>
> (*Godot* 132)

In this play the mystery of the identity of Godot is the essence. If we once know who is Godot the sense of mystery is lost and the play has no charm. The characters want some help or some rescue from him. But Godot seems to be a mirage. That is what makes this play all the more engrossing.

Works Cited

Abrams, M.H.*A Glossary of Literary Terms*. Banglore: Prism Books Pvt Ltd, 1993.

Albert, Edward. *History of English Literature*. New Delih: Oxford University Press, 2009.

Beckett, Samuel. *Waiting for Godot: A Tragicomedy in Two Acts*. London: Faber and Faber, 1956. Ed.G.J.V.Prasad. India: Dorling Kindersley Pvt, 2010 (Third Impression).

Calderwood, James L. 'Ways of Waiting in *Waiting for Godot*' in *Waiting for Godot and Endgame*. (New Casebooks) Ed. Steven Connor. London:The Macmillan Press Ltd, 1992. (29-43).

Gupta. U.P.Ed. *Jean—Paul Sartre: The Mastermind of Awareness*. Delhi: Vijay Goel, 2008.

Kennedy, Andrew K. 'Action and Theatricality is *Waiting for Godot*' in *Waiting for Godot and Endgame*. (New Casebooks) Ed.Steven Connor.London: The Macmillan Press Ltd., 1992. (16-28).

Multani, Angelie. '*Waiting for Godot*: The Games that people play". *Waiting for Godot*. London: Faber and Faber, 1956. Ed.G.J.V.Prasad. India: Dorling Kindersley Pvt, 2010 (Third Impression) (120–133).

Nealon, Jeffrey. 'Samuel Beckett and the Postmodern: Language Games, Play and *Waiting for Godot*'. *Waiting for Godot and Endgame*. (New Casebooks) Ed.Steven Connor. London: The Macmillan Press Ltd., 1992. (44-54).

Yeats. W.B. 'The Ballad of Father Gilligan' in *Harmony*.Ed.Biyot K.Tripathy. Chennai: Oxford University. Press. 1981.

3

The Oppressed Femininity and the Unlearnt Masculine Strategies in *The Tower*

— V. Kadambari

> "Thinking again", the Duchess asked with another dig of her sharp little chin. "I've got a right to think," said Alice sharply for she was beginning to feel a little worried. "Just about as much right", said the Duchess, *"as pigs have to fly"*.
>
> —*Alice in Wonderland*

Hal Porter's (1911-84) *The Tower* published in 1963, was first produced in London, Hampstead Theatre, 1962. The seven times winner of Commonwealth Literary Fund fellowship received very little critical consideration, maybe due to the production of Osborne's *Inadmissible Evidence* and Edward Albee's *Who's Afraid of Virginia Woolf* alongside. The few lines that were dedicated to him in the dailies were officious and offending in their conciliatory tone. To add to one's surprise, the home production too received no recognition. While plays by Alan Seymour Smith, Douglas Stewart and Patrick White were again and again seen, appreciated, analysed and applauded, Porter's contribution to serious drama went out of reading and performance quietly unnoticed.

Set in the year 1850 in one of the early settlements, Hobart Town, Australia, the play *The Tower* proceeds to destroy the tower of lies built by the early immigrants and patriarchs. The play analyses at one level the fact as to how the convicts and gentlemen knighted by the British monarchy can easily exchange places. On a different plane it deals with feminist issues, and throughout one recognises the voice of the dramatist protesting through his characters, the colonialist's attitudes, the bourgeoise values, and the patriarchal indifference to female sensibilities.

The scene is Hobart Town, Tasmania, one of the early settlements in Australia. When the play opens we find Amy, the daughter of the house engaged in decorating the room and getting ready for the arrival of the new wife of her stepfather. Edwin, her stepfather's adopted son is also with her looking at the Port through his opera glasses. Amy is in her wheelchair, due to an accident, we are told, from which she is recovering slowly. We learn from her conversation with Megan, the servant-maids that a tower is being built to establish Rodney's reputation in Hobart Town. It has, however, already spoilt the façade of the palladian house. The aunt, Hester also joins her in arranging the flowers on the table and at the same time talks about the stepmother, her own brother Rodney, who is the step father of Amy. Hester warns Amy to be careful in revealing her emotions. Sir Roland and Lady Haviland soon join them along with Perry, a local young man, who is in the service of the British government and is in love with Amy. Amy is pregnant with her father's convict slave Knight's child and we learn through their conversation that Amy is determined to have the child and have Knight too though she has not yet come of age. Thus, the first Act introduces all the characters, their conflicts and is as Capone Giovana neatly sums up:

> *The tower* is both construction and corruption, and flooding back with the symbol, comes the sense of ubiquitous corruption and falsity. Indeed, all the characters are false in one way or another. Sir Rodney is not really Amy's and Edwin's father. Amy is not really Rodney's daughter, since she is the daughter of his second wife, born from her previous marriage. Edwin is not really Rodney's son, since he is the son of Marcus Knight. Hester is not really Amy's aunt since, as Rodney's sister, she has no blood ties with Amy, and was only a friend of Amy's dead mother. Marcus

> and Amy are not really parents, since their child will never be born. Lady Haviland is not really Amy's mother, nor are Amy and Edwin really siblings. (*The Tower* 165)

The second Act proceeds to unravel the plot further after Amy had told her father the distressing truth about her pregnancy and seeks his permission to marry Knight. The Act begins with a conversation between Aunt Hester and Amy which soon is joined by Lady Haviland. There is little that is common among the three, and the hatred between Amy and Lady Haviland is made obvious. The young man Tom Perry who arrives with the intention to seek the permission of Sir Rodney to propose to Amy is sent after her to the Tower where she has gone to cool herself. Perry returns soon shocked and dismayed because his proposal has been turned down by Amy. He leaves abruptly after disclosing Amy's refusal to Sir Rodney; Amy herself arrives and reveals her mind and condition to Sir Rodney and Aunt Hester, much to the shock of both. She leaves to fetch the burning torch from the tower and Aunt Hester returns to her room. We find Sir Rodney following Amy to the tower and in a highly economical scene that follows, we are told about Amy's death, and a careful introduction of Edwin with his opera glasses, helps us realise the uneasy truth about Amy's death—not an accidental fall, but a meticulously planned murder.

Act III opens in a mourning house, with Lady Haviland insisting on Amy's death to be a suicide and Sir Rodney talking about the funeral with much relish as an event graced by people of rank in Hobarts' Town. Tom Perry is made to believe by Sir Rodney that Amy's refusal of him was only a whimsical way of saying 'yes'. But his tower of lies is not kept up for long. Edwin and Knight make him accept the truth in the end. Edwin's impressive narration of a brawl that he witnesses on the deck of the ship through his opera glasses is metatheatrical. Sir Rodney is made to realise that his act of pushing Amy down the tower has a witness in Edwin. Knight too for his part makes him realise that both of them—the settler and the convict have the same weakness. While Knight's itch for wealth led him to prison and to deportation, Rodney's led him to a new colony. The play ends with Edwin as the master of the occasion urging

Rodney to accept that Amy's death was no accident, and on the note that the tower of lies cannot for a long time be stable.

Porter's *The Tower* is a reaction against community and family. Amy wants to destroy the tower of lies built by Sir Rodney the patriarch around himself. She protests against the falsity in him. In a scene where Rodney tries to prevail upon her to marry Perry, we find Amy saying:

> You make me more weary than I already am. You skirt the truth because you cannot live on truths. You live on lies, you live in a tower of lies. Permission, you say, your permission. It's a delusion, a lie of your conception, and you've the power to grant permission of that sort. I am not an employee of yours or a borrowed convict I'am not an assigned servant to whom you are God (*The Tower* 278).

But Rodney equates what Amy calls lies to civilisation and progress—a patriarchal construct certainly and chastises her:

> That is your name for social realities, for the truth of civilisation and progress. I would not be stripped of these, and shall not. You are dangerous to them, and to my peace of mind. Since you've not learned reasonable behaviour and the way of the moral world, it will be taught to you. (282)

The patriarchal arrogance of Rodney is defied by Amy and Hester too. Speaking of being almost a prisoner at her father's house inspite of not stealing anything, Amy recollects memories of her mother and remarks bitterly:

> *Amy* : He doesn't remember her... he keeps no memories or mementos of her save the ring he took from her fingers and the money he married her for.
>
> *Aunt H* : Amy he is my brother.
>
> *Amy* : He is no one's brother, no one's father, no one's husband. He loves nothing but himself and his advancement, his schemes andambitions, his plotting for a knighthood, his acres and warehouses and hideout tower.

Aunt H: He is a man... You cannot understand what dreams men have for themselves!...how could any woman understand the foolishness of men? Does she need to?...You will never understand. I've known him since we were children. He stole my top. He tore my scrapbooks. He was often odious. He was sometimes charming. To fathom his passion for worldly powers ... la, 'twas impossible. Men are men; their dreams are not the dreams of females. I do know that he desired a son... it was too patent...more than warehouses and knighthoods and the highest tower in Hobart Town. (249-50)

And Amy points out Patriarchy's greed to accumulate and its ways of achieving it.

Amy : ...He will have Edwin a facsimile. The horrid little wretch is already dissimulating and ruthless...Edwin like papa will garner possessions, power, false honours. Oh he is not to be trusted. Edwin will have his tower, too. (251)

Edwin does have his tower in the end in the most adept manner. The play records masculine assessment and dismissal of women. Rodney has no time to lend his ears "to female arguments", when his young wife wants to talk to him about Hester. While Aunt Hester tries to talk to Amy in favour of Perry, she is cut short by Rodney with a curt statement, "Don't interfere in matters in which you can have neither power nor experience" (279) because it is he who has inherited from Amy's dead mother the right to advise her, to look after her best interests and to plan her future and "to guard you from the consequences of your own immature and headstrong actions." (279). His talk with Perry about proposing to Amy is very matter of fact.

Rodney : I know from my own experience, that wifely devotion, female elegancies, all that a married woman is...oh, all these virtues are immeasurably enhanced by a decent fortune. (274)

When Hester asks him if he is aware of his young wife's hatred for Edwin he dismisses it:

> Hate is an absurd word, a woman's word. Edwin is a child. If necessary—I repeat, if necessary—he can be taught... Should need arise, I'll teach him what is—well—what is of most value. He knows quite enough for the moment: that he'll be my heir, that he is my son. Little else concerns him or me. 'Tis no concern of yours, and little concern of my wife's. She has her duties. Edwin's character is not one of them. He is my son, not hers. (298)

And he teaches the first gendered lesson when Edwin questions him about Amy's funeral:

Edwin : Did you shed tears of deep sorrow sir?

Rod : Men do not shed tears, Edwin. Tears are for the gentler sex. Men sternly conceal whatever anguish they feel and go on doing what has to be done in life. The sun doesn't cease to shine when someone dies; the duties of the living towards the practicalities of life do not cease when death takes away someone they love. (300)

and he makes this speech soon after killing Amy. And about Hester's leaving for England, he comments:

Rod : Tis a sudden decision and her own wish. Women's decisions are often sudden and more often absurd. Yet I'm convinced that this one of your aunt's is ...better. What do you think?

Edwin : I agree with you. Tis better—much better so.

Rod : Why?

> *Edwin* : She will be at a loss without Amy. And…oh dear, I think I'd better not say the other.
>
> *Rod* : I've asked you to. And—remember/—you always tell me the truth? Eh?

And in response to Edwin who says that Aunt Hester and Lady Haviland do not love each other, he comments:

> *Edwin* : You've found out early that women rarely like each other… out of idle jealousy and sheer female vindictiveness… (300)

Eagleton, points out:

> The woman is both 'inside" and "outside" of the male society, both aromantically idealised member of it and a victimised outcast. She is sometimes what stands between man and chaos, and sometimes the embodiment of chaos itself. This is why she troubles the neat categories of such a regime, blurring its well-defined boundaries. Women are represented within male-governed society, fixed by sign, image, meaning, yet because they are also the "negative' of the social order there is always in them some thing which is left over, superfluous, unrepresentable, which refuses to be figured. (*Literary Theory* 190)

Hal Porter's women fit this observation and refuse to be figured. But so do the men who govern the world of Tower.

Feminisms shares certain aims whatever may be the specific agendas:

1) To challenge the biological determinism that says that men are superior to women. Feminism contends that power is not genetic.
2) To assert the importance of self-determination for women, individually and/or collectively.
3) To change the position of women in social, political, cultural and emotional spheres in some way. It is the third aim which needs to include masculinity to strengthen its strategies.

'Masculine', the *Oxford English Dictionary* defines as, "the appropriate excellences of the male sex, manly, virile, vigorous and powerful". The last three words represent definable, if predictable, attributions whereas 'manly' throws us back tautologically upon the word masculine—what is manly is masculine and what is masculine is manly—and it is equally open to stereotypical preconceptions. Helen Cixous's definition may also be remembered in this connection—a set of hierarchical binary oppositions with the male representing Culture rather than Nature.

However, what is quite interesting is that the configuration of the masculine remains a function of the particular conceptual construction of male identity in any play at any given time. Femininity that is situated on a lower level in this hierarchical binary oppositions has been analysed, discussed, rewritten, subverted, etc. till the last decade of the previous century, from the centralised notion of victimisation. Oppressed femininity protested, challenged and rebelled. Amy is no exception. She will not wait anymore. Quite interestingly, the year in which the play is set is 1850 and back at home in England and in other nations women had started their protestations against their status in society and at home and seeds have been sown for the Women's League of Rights. Amy, twenty and heiress to an ample endowment, has a convict for a lover. She wants to marry him and she is pregnant with his child. She is tired of waiting:

> *Amy:* I've been waiting too long. I seem to be always waiting. And I've been standing too long... Bu I fear I've waited too long and have been standing too long... and shall stand no more. (242)

She will marry Knight even before she is of age. She has thought and has arrived at a decision. It is her body that has been enjoyed by Knight. "It is my body. There's no blood of papa's in it." She goes ahead, discloses her secret and informs her decision, turns down Perry's proposal, lets Sir Rodney know that she knows his secret—about Knight's son being his adopted son. More than everything, she tells patriarchy to its face that she is aware of the web of lies constructed to tower over everything else and made to look normal and true. The challenge does not go unanswered. A very age old simple solution closes a chapter of threat. At this juncture one cannot but wonder why intelligent and independent thinking women go wrong in their lives. Literature has any number of examples: Bathsheba, Jane Eyre, Isabel Archer, the list is endless and continuous.

A number of people active in the movement against violence against women during the last decade of the previous century have tried to find answers for this worrying situation and been accusing feminism which has presented women as victims. The various writers admonish feminists to break this habit. Christina Hoff Sommers (1994) advised feminists to be content to enforce equality rather than complain of women's plight: Naomi Wolf (1993) urges women to learn to use power; Camille Paglia and Katie Roiphe (1993) ask feminists to stop blaming men for women's individual sexual discontents or mistakes; and Rene Den Field (1995) asserts that feminists are actually sexual conservatives in disguise. Such authors recommend that feminists acknowledge women's individual agency and encourage women to "take responsibility" for their particular situations. The most obvious defense against these insists on the real victimisation of women and calls these criticisms "backlash" against accurate exposures of masculinist domination. Harriet Holter, a pioneer Scandinavian sociologist, when toying with the idea of mainstreaming even as early as in the 1970s observed:

> The main investigations of women's roles need to be, supplemented by studies of men's roles. Or rather, the roles of both sexes should be, considered... The relative neglect of men's roles by social scientists is probably, in part, a reflection of the fact that it is women, not men, who complain most about the bases of role differentiation. It is also probable that social scientists make the common assumption that men constitute the norm with which members of the deviant sex, women should be, compared. (16-17)

Indeed, men's roles and thought pattern should be studied assiduously. Edwin teaches Amy the first lesson in diplomacy which she never learns. When the latter is annoyed about the new wife's arrival, Edwin tells her:

> *Edwin* : *Soyez calme, ma'mselle.* Edwin is calm. He is as crazy as you to see this step-mamma. But calm. You see. I am calm.
>
> *Amy* : You are dead to feeling. You are too immature and shallow to have emotions.
>
> *Edwin* : Am I? She is as much my mystery as yours. Yet I am calm, as adopted sons must be calm. As step daughters should also be.
>
> *Amy* : I am a calm stepdaughter.
>
> *Edwin* : You gammon to be so...and unsuccessfully.
>
> *Amy* : I am calm. I am calm.
>
> *Edwin* : If this be your calm, I advise you to amplify it. For now...very, very soon...you will have not merely your old familiar step-papa but a brand new step-mamma. In a feathered bonnet she's on her way to make you doubly a stepdaughter. (245)

When Amy is ready to disclose her secret and to face her father saying, "I no longer care too deeply about danger", Knight warns her to take care, and that "there is no reason for us to walk boldly and recklessly into trouble....Amy, we must be patient. In another year you will be of age. Be wise. It will be madness not to wait...He has other weapons" (253-55). But Amy in her frustration accosts Sir Rodney in his tower after refusing Perry's offer:

> *Amy* : You lent him [Perry] the confidence and elation. You lent it because you planned a return of advantages to yourself. But the hand you gave him permission to ask for was not yours to barter....Permission, you say, your permission. It's a delusion, a lie of your own conception that you've the power to grant

> permissions of that sort. I am not an employee of yours or a borrowed convict; I'm not an assigned servant to whom you are God. (278)

It is to be noted that the play was produced in the year 1962, a time when women had not learnt the strategies and were frustrated about the oppressions. Patriarchy continued to keep the tower of constructs in tact. All precautions were taken to "ensure the tower's utter safety" and women who were like "*querulous ghosts*" were not allowed to wander free and destroy it. Rodney will not have Amy stay in Hobart town to set it talking about her amorous relationship at a moment when he is waiting for further advancement in his status and Amy would strip him of his tower of lies.

> *Rodney* : I repeat you are crazed. Why should you imagine that I—that any human being except yourself-would wish to be stripped of what you call a tower of lies. That is your name for social realities, for the truth of civilisation and progress. I would not be stripped of these, and shall not. You are dangerous to them and to my peace of mind. Since you've not learned reasonable behaviour and the way of the moral world, it will be taught to you.
>
> *Amy* : The way of that world I'll not be taught....I should rather die...The waters of the Estuary are deep. The tower is high. (282-83)

Rodney does not want to listen to her any more and does not want to "know no more of your mischief and hysteria and false ideas than I do". Amy gets killed since she would not remove herself. She loses her life as she would not listen to the strategies of masculinity to outwardly remain calm, to take care of oneself by understanding that prudence is better part of valour and to not be frank for there is a "place and time" even for truth. Money and power are as much important to Edwin and Knight as it is to Rodney. Oppressed femininity in its frustration fails to learn these masculine strategies for its success. But then, what kind of success and to what end is a question that is yet to be explored.

Works Cited

Capone, Giovanna. 'Hal Porter, The Tower and the Quintessence of Porterism' in *Australian Literary Studies* 1991, Vol 15.2, pp. 162-73.

Eagleton, Terry. *Literary Theory: An Introduction*. Minneapolis: University of Minnesota, 1983.

HG Kippax. Introduction, *Three Australian Plays*. Australia: Penguin, 1963.

Holter, Harriet. *Sex Roles and Social Structure*, Oslo, 1970.

4

Humour and Pathos in the Plays of Wole Soyinka

— Ashish Gupta

Soyinka was born into a Yoruba family, specifically, a Remo family in Isara-Remo on July 13, 1934. His father was Christian Clergy, Canon SA Soyinka (aka "Teacher pupa" (light skinned teacher). He received primary school education in Abeokuta and attended secondary school at Government College, Ibadan. He then studied at the University College, Ibadan (1952–1954) where he founded the pyrates confraternity (an anti-corruption and justice seeking student organisation) and the University of Leeds (1954–1957) from which he received an First class honors degree in English Literature. He worked as a play reader at the Royal Court Theatre in London before returning to Nigeria to study African drama. He taught in the Universities of Lagos, Ibadan, and Ife (now Obafemi Awolowo University, Ile-Ife). He became a Professor of Comparative Literature at the then University of Ife in 1975). He is currently an Emeritus Professor at the same university.

In the plays written and produced in the early 1960s, Soyinka showed his ability to project traditional Nigerian themes and stories through English instead of Yoruba. He was recognised as a dramatic poet and skilled dramatic craftsman. The plays dealt with a great diversity of theme—from the farce of *The Trials of Brother Jero,* to the romanticism of *The Lion and the Jewel,* to the tragedy of *The Strong Breed.* Soyinka was concerned with universal problems, and his plays examined town life, a retrograde countryside, and the ambitions of the "new" Nigerians. After studying in Leeds, England, he returned to Nigeria to edit literary journals, teach drama and literature at the university level, and found two theatre companies. His plays, written in English and drawing on West African folk traditions, often focus on the tensions between tradition and progress. Symbolism, flashback, and ingenious plotting contribute to a rich dramatic structure. His serious plays reveal his disillusionment with African authoritarian leadership and with Nigerian society as a whole. His works include *A Dance of the Forests* (1960), *The Lion and the Jewel* (1963), *The Strong Breed* (1964), *Death and the King's Horseman* (1975), and *A Play Of Giants* (1984). He has written several volumes of poetry; his best-known novel is *The Interpreters* (1965). A champion of Nigerian democracy, he was repeatedly jailed and exiled. In 1986 he became the first black African to be awarded the Nobel Prize for Literature.

Soyinka then left Africa to study drama at Leeds University in England under the influential British critic and professor G. Wilson Knight. While in London he also worked as a reader at the Royal Court Theatre, where his first play, *The Invention,* was staged in 1957. One of Soyinka's few explicitly political plays, *The Invention,* explores in satirical fashion the consequences for the South African apartheid government of the sudden destruction of skin pigment in its entire black population. Horrified at their inability to distinguish black from white, the government assigns the nation's scientists the task of restoring the visible differences on which apartheid is based.

In 1960 Soyinka triumphantly returned to the University of Ibadan as a Rockefeller research fellow in drama, and he commenced serious study of Nigerian folklore. His arrival was marked with productions at the Arts Theatre in Ibadan of two of his early plays, *The Swamp Dwellers,* which had been given a student production in London in 1958, and *The Lion and the Jewel. The Swamp Dwellers* is a verse tragedy depicting the manipulation of a community of poor, superstitious swamp farmers by greedy religious leaders. *The Lion and the Jewel* is a comedy that warns against reckless modernisation and strives to demonstrate that some of the old values ought not to be thoughtlessly abandoned. These two productions established Soyinka as a literary figure of serious consequence in Nigeria.

A Dance of the Forests is one of the most recognised of Wole Soyinka's plays. At the time of its release in 1960, it was an iconoclastic work that angered many of the elite in Soyinka's native Nigeria. Politicians were particularly incensed at Soyinka's prescient portrayal of post-colonial Nigerian politics as aimless and corrupt. Despite the deluge of criticism, the play remains an influential work. In it, he espouses a unique vision for a new Africa, one that is able to forge a new identity free from the influence of European imperialism.

A Dance of the Forests is regarded as Soyinka's theatrical debut. In it, he unveils the rotten aspects of the society and demonstrates that the past is no better than the present when it comes to the seamy site of life. He lays bare the fabric of the Nigerian society and warns people as they are on the brink of a new stage in their history; indpendence.

A Dance of the Forests presents a complex interplay between gods, mortals, and the dead in which the ideal goal is the experience of self-discovery within the context of West African spiritualism. The living have invited two glorious forefathers to take part in a feast and celebration—the "Gathering of the Tribes." The god Aroni, however, explains in the prologue that he received the permission of the Forest Head to select instead "two [obscure] spirits of the restless dead": the Dead Man and the Dead Woman. Perhaps the best example of the juxtaposition of the past and present was in *A Dance in the Forest.* Three guilty persons were lured into a deep woodland where they were confronted with their spirit counterparts from the past. Selfishness, dishonesty, and lust were personified as elements in all societies—past and present. It was at this time that he founded his influential amateur theatre group, the 1960 Masks, dedicated to forging a new Nigerian drama. This drama was to be written in English but draw its inspiration from the ceremonial performance traditions of Africa—religious festivals, pantomime, and traditional music among them. Most of the members of the group were teachers or civil servants who lived either in Ibadan or in Lagos, one hundred miles away; they frequently conducted rehearsals over the phone or in the Land Rover that carried Soyinka and the company from one city to the other.

The Masks' first major production was Soyinka's *Dance of the Forests,* which had been commissioned from him for the Nigerian independence celebrations of October 1960. Despite the festive occasion, Soyinka seized this opportunity to warn his fellow Nigerians of the dangers of repeating the violence and opportunism of their past and of romanticising it at the expense of the present. In *A Dance of the Forests,* the tribes assemble for a great festival during which the 'egungun' are ritually summoned. The people expect their ancestral spirits to be as heroic and noble as they are in legend, and they are shocked to discover that the petty meanness of the ancestors rivals their own bickering.

However, by 1960, Soyinka had received the Rockefeller Research Fellowship from his alma mater in Ibadan, and returned to Nigeria. In March he produced his new satire *The Trials of Brother Jero*, which established him as Nigeria's foremost dramatist. One of his most recognised plays, *A Dance of The Forest*, a biting criticism of Nigeria's political elites, won a contest as the official play for Nigerian Independence Day. On 1 October 1960, it premiered in Lagos as Nigeria celebrated its sovereignty. Also in 1960, Soyinka established an amateur ensemble acting company which would consume much of his time over the next few years: the Nineteen-Sixty Masks. In addition to these activities, Soyinka published various works satirising the "emergency" in the Western Region of Nigeria, as his Yorùbá homeland was increasingly occupied and controlled by the federal government. This had usurped the democratically-elected, Yorùbá-based Action Group (AG) political party by installing the 'Nigerian National Democratic Party' (NNDP), an amalgamation of conservative Yoruba interests backed by the largely Northern-dominated federal government. The increasingly militarised occupation of the Western Region eventually led to inequilibrium in power, placing the more left-leaning Action Group and the Igbo-centric

'National Council of Nigeria and the Cameroons' (NCNC) in tenuous positions, as national politics began catering exclusively to more conservative interests. This imbalance eventually led to a coup by military officers under Major Kaduna Nzeogwu.

With the money gained from the Rockefeller Foundation for research on African Theatre, Soyinka bought a Land Rover and began travelling throughout the country as a researcher with the Department of English Language of the University College in Ibadan. In an essay published at this time, he criticised Leopold Senghor's "Négritude" as a nostalgic and indiscriminate glorification of the black African past that ignores the potential benefits of modernisation. "A tiger does not shout its tigritude," he declared, "it acts." In December 1962, his essay *Towards a True Theatre* was published. and he began working for the Department of English Language at Obafemi Awolowo University in Ibp□. Soyinka discussed current affairs with "negrophiles," and on several occasions openly opposed government censorship. At the end of 1963, his first feature-length movie emerged, *Culture in Transition*. In April 1964 *The Interpreters,* "a complex but also vividly documentary novel", was published in London. That December, together with other scientists and men of theatre, he founded the Drama Association of Nigeria. This same year he resigned his university post, as a protest against imposed pro-government behaviour by authorities. A few months later, he was arrested for the first time, accused of underlying tapes during reproduction of recorded speech of the winner of Nigerian elections, but he was released after a few months of confinement, as a result of protests by the international community of writers. The same year he also wrote two more dramatic pieces: *Before the Blackout*, the comedy *Kongi's Harvest*, and a radio play for the BBC in London called *The Detainee.* At the end of the year he was promoted to headmaster and senior lecturer in the Department of English Language at Lagos University. Soyinka's political speeches at that time criticised the cult of personality and government corruption in African dictatorships.

April 1965 brought a revival of his play *Kongi's Harvest* at the International Festival of Negro Art in Dakar, Senegal, where another of his plays, *The Road,* was awarded the Grand Prix. In June, Soyinka produced his play *The Lion and The Jewel* for Hampstead Theatre Club in London.

The Lion and the Jewel is a satire on the contemporary system. Baroka (bah-ROH-kah), the "Bale" of Ilujinle, the "Lion" is the title of the play. This village chief is sixty-two years old, very proud, deceptive, and cunning. His attempt to win the village belle, Sidi, through deception is the central focus of the play. The Bale manipulates the other characters by feigning sexual impotence. Sidi (SEE-dee), the village belle, about eighteen years old, is very pretty and coquettish. She distracts the young schoolteacher, Lakunle, attracts a travelling photographer who wants her picture to be in a magazine, and passively flirts with the Bale, unaware of the Bale's vast experience in romance. Sidi is tricked into making love with the Bale at the end of the comedy. Lakunle is a young, "modern," and stylishly dressed liberal. He is, in fact, a conservative who pretends to be interested in social revolution; his real concern is for Sidi or any other available young woman in the village. Lakunle's supposed platonic love for Sidi is no match for the Bale's cunning and experience, and Lakunle proves to be a poor adversary. Sadiku, is the primary wife of the Bale. One of her principal jobs is to woo younger wives for the Bale. She convinces Sidi that the young woman should marry the Bale by telling her that the Bale is old and that Sidi will have the honor of being the senior wife of the new Bale. The favourite, is the Bale's present young woman. She tries to please him, but she is informed by the Bale that she has no time to improve her affection because he is taking a new wife. She represents another conquest by the Bale. The surveyor is an outsider who is planning to build a road through the village. He is easily bought off by the Bale, who offers gifts if he will build the road in another place, thus preserving the land and the traditions of his people.

Soyinka's plays range from comedy to tragedy and from political satire to the theatre of the absurd. He has combined influences from Western traditions with African myth, legends and folklore, and such techniques as singing and drumming. Like other major Nigerian writers, including Elechi Amadi, Chinua Achebe, John Okigbo, John Pepper Clark and Cole Omotso, Soyinka was educated at the University College of Ibada. In 1954 he moved to England, where he studied English literature at the the University of Leeds, receiving his B.A. in 1959. During this period he started study of the work of Eugene O'Neill and wrote two plays, *The Swamp Dwellers* and *The Lion and The Jewel*, a story of a foppish school teacher and a old African chief competing for a young village woman. Both of the plays were staged in London.

> What I boast is known in Lagos, the city
> Of magic, in Banagry where Saro women bathe
> In gold, even in smaller towns less than
> Twelve miles from here.
> SIDI: Well go there. Go to these places where
> Women would understand you.
> If you told them of your plans with which
> You oppress me daily. Do you not know
> What name they give you here?
>
> (*The Lion and the Jewel*)

In 1965 Soyinka was arrested by the Nigerian government, accused of forcing a radio announcer at gunpoint to broadcast incorrect election results. His arrest sparked a protest campaign by PEN, the international writers' organisation. Such influential American authors as Norman Mailer and William Styron called for his release. No evidence was ever produced by the police to prove the allegation, and Soyinka was released after three months. Today it is commonly assumed that the election was rigged.

In 1967 Soyinka became the chairman of the Department of Theatre Arts at the University of Ibadan, but in August of that same year he was once again arrested—this time during Nigeria's civil war, to which Soyinka was implacably opposed. Nigeria, a country roughly twice the size of the state of California, is occupied by people speaking hundreds of different languages. In 1967, after several military coups, 30,000 members of the Ibo tribe were slaughtered in the North, where the Hausa-Fulani tribe dominated. More than a million Ibos fled to the east, where they declared the independent Ibo state of Biafra. Federal troops then went to war against Biafra. Soyinka lived on the federal side of Nigeria and his own Yoruban tribe supported the federal cause, but he defied those loyalties and set about organising Nigerian intellectuals to lobby for a ban on arms sales to both sides. His peaceful initiative failed, however, because he was immediately arrested. Though he was never formally charged, a faked confession released by the government in October indicated that he was being accused of assisting the Biafrans in their attempt to overthrow the government. Ironically, the government specifically accused the pacifist Soyinka of supplying weapons to the rebels. Soyinka spent two years as a political prisoner at the Kaduna Prison facility, mainly in solitary confinement. When his jailers vaccinated most of the prisoners against the deadly disease meningitis, Soyinka was passed by. In addition, he was not allowed medical attention when he developed vision problems. He was refused access to reading and writing materials, but manufactured his own ink and began keeping a prison diary and writing poetry on cigarette packages and toilet paper. Every time a letter or poem was miraculously smuggled from prison, the international press seized upon it both as an important literary event and as welcome evidence that he was still alive. Soyinka was released in 1969 and left Nigeria, not to return until after a change of government in 1975.

Soyinka's Nigeria was a country in transition, attempting to mould itself out of a variety of tribal cultures and a turbulent European colonisation. Soyinka did not romanticise his native land, nor was he willing to see African culture as a flat symbol of primitiveness. He was as willing to charge Nigerian politicians and bureaucrats with barbarity and corruption as he was to condemn the greed and materialism of the West. These attitudes were even more prevalent after his second incarceration on the trumped up spying charges. His work took on a darker and angrier tone. When he was released from prison in 1969, he left Nigeria and did not return until the government changed in 1975. His prison diary, published in

1972, *The Man Died: Prison Notes of Wole Soyinka,* was a fragmented and grim account of the days he spent incarcerated, often in chains. Along with his verses that captured the essence of his prison experience, *The Man Died* provided invaluable context for his subsequent imagery in his works.

The Strong Breed (1964) is a highly symbolic play. It tells the story of Eman, who lives in a strange village and has to sacrifice his life in order to save the village. Sunma, who is in love with him, tries to convince him to leave the village before the new years festival begins at night, because she knows that it is strangers who are normally used as carriers to cleanse the village from its sins. Eman refuses to leave with the last vehicle of the day passing through the village. Sunma despises her village as she feels that it is quite evil, she doesn't agree with its cultural practices. She rebels against her father, Jaguna, because of this. Unfortunately, she lacks the moral strength of Eman therefore doesn't bring much change to the village. Sunma is mentally isolated from the rest of the village and wants to leave it. She works for Eman in his hut which he uses as a staffroom and clinic. She doesn't understand why Eman does not want to leave the village. She vents her anger out on Ifada as she feels that it is Ifada who is distracting Eman's attention from her. Eman comes from the line of strong breeds that are used as carriers.

The play is marked with flashbacks between Eman's past and the present where he sees images of his father and his dead wife Omae. He had left his village for twelve years in search of a new destiny but had to go back, because as his father said, they were born to be carriers and he could not flee from his destiny. Omae who was his childhood sweetheart had waited for Eman to come back all those years while living in his father's homestead. Eman had left the village soon after his circumcision and told Omae to wait for him. Omae died during child birth as all the females in the lines of the strong breed do and Eman left his village again.

In the new village, he is a teacher and a healer, but the villagers don't appreciate what he does, since he is a stranger. He tries to rehabilitate Ifada who is a young boy who suffers from an incurable disease. Ifada is a stranger and the villagers attempt to use him as the carrier but Eman chooses to take his place instead. There is also a sick girl who symbolises evil, who refuses to go to Eman's 'clinic' for healing though it is free. She carries around an effigy that she is going to sacrifice during the festival so that she can be cured. She is an insensitive person as she uses Ifada as suits her. She says, "You have a head like a spider's egg...." Eman flees from the village elders as he is going to be sacrificed and has to be chased around the village for most part of the night. The sacrifice has to be carried out before midnight for it to effectively cleanse the villagers before the New Year begins. Finally, the elders decide to set a trap for Eman. They know that he is thirsty and will head for the river; they dig a hole and cover it with twigs. Sure enough, Eman goes to the river and falls into the trap, ultimately fulfilling his destiny as a carrier even though he is in a strange land. Eman has been portrayed as a type of Christ because he is both a teacher and healer and sacrifices his life to an insensitive village. Eman's father was also a carrier and sacrificed his life.

Death and the King's Horseman is considered by many to be among the best of Wole Soyinka's plays, which number more than a dozen. In awarding Soyinka the Nobel Prize for Literature in 1986, the Swedish Academy drew special attention to *Death and the King's Horseman* and *Dance of the Forests* (1960) as evidence of his talent for combining Yoruban and European culture into a unique kind of poetic drama. *Death and the King's Horseman* play tells the story of Elesin, the king's horseman, who is expected to commit ritual suicide following the death of the king, but who is distracted from his duty.

The story is based on a historical event. In 1946, a royal horseman named Elesin was prevented from committing ritual suicide by the British colonial powers. Soyinka alters the historical facts, placing the responsibility for Elesin's failure squarely on Elesin's shoulders, so that he might focus on the theme of duty rather than of colonialism. The play is well known in the United States, frequently anthologised in textbooks as an example of African drama for students and teachers who are increasingly curious about the literature of other parts of the world. Because of its mingling of Western and Yoruban elements, and because of the universality of its theme of cultural responsibility, *Death and the King's Horseman* is seen as a good introduction to African thought and tradition. While it is frequently read, however, the play is seldom performed outside of Africa. Soyinka himself has directed important American productions, in Chicago in 1976 and at Lincoln Center in New York in 1987, but these productions were more admired than loved. Although respected by critics, Soyinka's plays are challenging for Westerners to perform and to understand, and they have not been popular successes.

As *Death and the King's Horseman* opens, Elesin Oba walks through a Nigerian village market at the close of the business day. He is followed by an entourage of drummers and praise-singers, and as he makes his way through the market he talks with the praise-singer Olohun-iyo about "the other side" and about the importance of "this day of all days." Apparently, Elesin Oba is enjoying his last day on earth; at night he will go to join his "great forebears." The women abandon their work of putting away the goods from their stalls and come to flirt with Elesin, who is obviously a great favourite and well known for his sexual prowess and his many conquests.

Much of the dialogue is written in rhythmic free verse. Elesin dances, and chants the story of the Not-I bird, a bird who fails to fulfil his duty. In an exchange with the crowd, laced with Yoruba proverbs, Elesin promises that when the time comes to fulfil his duty he will not delay. Led by Iyaloja, the mother of the market, the women dress Elesin in their richest clothes and dance around him. Suddenly he is distracted by the sight of a beautiful woman whom he has never seen before. Although she is already engaged to someone else, Elesin demands that he be allowed to take her to bed before he dies. Because Elesin is at the threshold between life and death, he cannot be refused. Iyaloja warns him not to be deterred from his duty, and not to bring trouble on the people who will remain. Then, as the other women prepare the young woman to be Elesin's bride, Iyaloja leaves to prepare the bridal bed. In the concluding part, during the same evening, at the home of the district officer, Simon Pilkings, a British officer stationed in the British colony of Nigeria. Simon and his wife, Jane, are listening to a tango, dancing in the shadows. Amusa, a Nigerian working for the British as a native administration policeman, arrives and is horrified to see that Simon and Jane are dressed in the clothing traditionally worn for the *egungun* ceremony, costumes sacred to members of a local religious cult. Simon has confiscated the robes from the cult leaders, and he and Jane plan to wear them to win a prize for best costume at a fancy-dress ball the British are holding that night. Although Amusa is a Muslim and not a part of the cult, he respects the clothes and will not speak to Simon until he has removed them.

Like many African cultures, the Yoruba have a fundamental belief that life is a continuum. The dead are not forgotten; the ancestors are honoured and cherished as guides and companions. The not-yet-born are also cherished, and new babies may in fact be ancestors returning to physical life. The most highly charged moments in the lifecycle are the moments of transition from one type of existence to the next that is, the passage into the physical world during birth and the passage into death. Elesin's responsibility as king's horseman is to enact the transition from life into death in a ritual manner, to remind the entire community through his death that life is a continuum. *Death and the King's Horseman* has been recognised from the beginning as an important work, but its critical reputation has been somewhat different in Nigeria than in Europe and the United States. Westerners have almost universally praised the play, and the Swedish Academy drew special attention to it in awarding Soyinka the 1986 Nobel Prize for Literature. Within Nigeria and within the community of Africans on the political left, however, some critics have quarreled with the play's political messages.

Soyinka became a vocal critic of Negritude, accusing politicians of using it as a mask for autocracy. His increasing use of polemic against social injustice and his demands for freedom coincided with the military takeover in Nigeria and the later drifted toward civil war. Soyinka's best-known essays *Myth, Literature, And The African World* were published in 1976. He has been one of the most outspoken critics of the concept on, Negritude, which have been associated with Léopold Senghor, the writer and former President of Senegal.

Soyinka sees that *négritude* encourages self-absorption and affirms one of the central Eurocentric prejudices against Africans, namely the dichotomy between European rationalism and African emotionalism."A tiger does not shout its tigritude," Soyinka said, "it acts." In his essay 'Reparations, Truth and Reconciliation' (in *The Burde Of Memory, The Muse Of Forgiveness*, 1999) Soyinka defends the idea, that the West should pay reparations for crimes committed against African people. "Reparations... serve as a cogent critique of history and thus a potent restraint on its repetition." Let we understand the concept of 'Negritude'.

According to the concept of the African philosopher Senghor, the term "Negritude" offers the most articulate analysis of African way of thinking, which is distinct from, but in no case inferior to, European mode of thinking and experience. According to Abiola Irele, Senghor's concept of Negritude remains:

> The most comprehensive and coherent effort of reflection upon African situation. [Abiola Irele 393]

At the beginning of the written tradition of African philosophy, the concept of Negritude not only articulated the existing ideas and concepts but it left wide scope for further speculation in African philosophy.

As a philosophical paradigm, the impact of Negritude was so wide and deep that it has been termed by critics as the 'movement' in African philosophy. E. C. Eze remarks:

> with the discovery of Bantu Philosophy in Africa and the emergence in the United States of the Harlem Renaissance—with its philosophers and intellectuals: Alain Locke, Claude Mackay, W.E.B. Dubois and others—

> where Africans in the Diaspora were already engaged in the critic of African colonialism and the racism of the New World, a third movement in the history of African philosophy was born negritude.[Emmanuel C. Eze 11]

The notion of Objective Negritude suggests that the intuitive reasoning of African people, though distinctive from the discursive reasoning of the West, has some elements of universality as it exists in diverse cultures supported by oral traditions. This twofold classification of Negritude is attempted to prove that it is both particular and universal at the same time. The major contribution of the theory of Negritude to African Philosophy and culture is that it successfully addresses the central question of African situation, that is the identity of blacks in the modern day world. Hence, Negritude signifies that African identity is distinct yet it is not opposed or contradictory to other similar identities. It is not a narrow philosophical dogma; it encompasses the whole complex of civilised values—cultural, economic, social and political, which sustain and characterise black people.

A Play of Giants is set in the 'Bugaran' Embassy in New York, where several of Africa's most ridiculous tyrants have gathered. A sculptor is immortalising them, but they are hard to set in stone — for one, because of their constant concern about their countries collapsing (or leadership falling into other hands), especially in their absence. The three figures (Gunema, Kasco, and Kamini), and the fourth who joins them (Tuboum) are readily recognisable: as Soyinka explains:

No serious effort is made here to hide the identities of the real-life actors who have served as models for *A Play of Giants*. They are:

> *Benefacio Gunema:* Macias Nguema (Equitorial Guinea)
>
> *Emperor Kasco:* Jean-Baptiste Bokassa (Central African Republic)
>
> *Field- Marshal Kamini:* Idi Amin (Uganda)
>
> *General Barra Tuboum:* Mobuto Sese Seko (Congo/Zaïre)

Kamini, the host, is the central character, and *A Play of Giants* focuses in particular on this abomination that was Amin. The play offers some Western sycophants and apologists—notably Gudrun, a Scandinavian journalist, and Professor Batey—as well the Secretary General of the UN and, eventually, representatives of the two then-superpowers, the US and USSR. Most of the figures are caricatures, the play itself a satire that spares no one.

The African leaders are shown in their complete absurdity—power-mad men with no concept of politics, economics, or diplomacy. The Chairman of the Bugaran State Bank tries, for example, to explain that merely printing more currency will not solve the country's financial problems, and winds up spending most of the play with his head held down in a toilet. Among the leaders' biggest problems: how to keep their entourages from abandoning them, especially while they're abroad (i.e. where associates can flee and escape retribution).

The domestic collapse of their countries, far away, is nevertheless mirrored in the events in the embassy, Kamini abandoned by those he thought loyal to him, but still meting out arbitrary (in)justice and holding everything (or at least what's left) together by sheer terror, his unpredictability and irrationality forcing everyone to treat him with care. Some of the leaders' delusions are amusing, and some of their power-plays chilling; sadly, Soyinka did not have to invent much to paint these caricatures: this is, more or less, how these men were and what they did. There's little introspection from these leaders, though Kasco does observe:

> Power comes only with the death of politics. That is why I chose to become emperor. I place myself beyond politics. At the moment of my coronation, I signal to the world that I transcend the intrigues and mundaneness of politics. Now I inhabit only the pure realm of power. I fear, *mes amis*, all three of you have chosen to remain in the territory of politics. But — is it choice? Or are you trapped?

Kamini is shown as a charismatic charmer. He doesn't really fool anyone, but for their various reasons everybody puts up with (or kowtows to) him. Meanwhile, the Americans and Russians are presented as cynical Cold War realists, indifferent to the plight of the African people and nations, as long as their interests are served.

All in all it makes for good if ugly fun, but the humour isn't really sharp enough and the satire simply too broad and simplistic to make it a truly satisfying play. These are easy targets, and while Soyinka savages them well enough he does so with little finesse. Since the stories—and the foolishness of all those who put up with these tyrants—are well-known, there's limited novelty here. The lesson has been taught many times before, even if it still hasn't been learned, and *A Play of Giants* is successful only in depicting it once again, rather than actually dealing with it.

Soyinka's political speeches at that time criticised the cult of personality and government corruption in African dictatorships. When civilian rule returned in 1999, Soyinka returned to a hero's welcome back in Lagos, Nigeria. He accepted an Emeritus Professorship at Ife (now Obafemi Awolowo University) on the condition that the university bar all former military officers from the position of chancellor. Soyinka is currently the Elias Ghanem Professor of Creative Writing at the English department of the University of Nevada, Las Vegas and the President's Marymount Institute Professor in Residence at Loyola Marymount University in Los Angeles, California, US. The future of African literature seems to be bright. The new writers have given ample evidence that they can take African literature to greater heights by appropriating techniques from their ethnic cultures and inspiration with the writers like Soyinka, which will enable them to propagate the cultural heritage of the continent and construct and deconstruct the new possibilities.

The fact that Wole Soyinka has lived to write so much about the African experience is a miracle. Throughout his long and productive career, Soyinka's politics have placed him in danger repeatedly. His upbringing reflected both African and Western influences, and the conflict and interaction between these two forces would occupy much of his writing, particularly in the play

Death and the King's Horseman. Through drama, poetry, essays, and autobiographies, Soyinka has documented not only the struggles of his homeland of Nigeria but of the African continent as a whole. His works earned him the Nobel Prize in Literature in 1986, and he used the occasion to highlight the plight of fellow activist Nelson Mandela. Soyinka's life has been so full of intrigue and accomplishment that he has published several memoirs in which the hardships of the African nation overlap with his own personal evolution. His Nigeria was a country in transition, attempting to mold itself out of a variety of tribal cultures and a turbulent European colonisation.

Soyinka did not romanticise his native land, nor was he willing to see African culture as a flat symbol of primitiveness. He was as willing to charge Nigerian politicians and bureaucrats with barbarity and corruption as he was to condemn the greed and materialism of the West. These attitudes were even more prevalent after his second incarceration on the trumped up spying charges. His work took on a darker and angrier tone. When he was released from prison in 1969, Soyinka left Nigeria and did not return until the government changed in 1975. Soyinka's prison diary, published in 1972 *The Man Died: Prison Notes of Wole Soyinka* was a fragmented and grim account of the days he spent incarcerated, often in chains. Along with his verses that captured the essence of his prison experience, *The Man Died* provided invaluable context for Soyinka' subsequent imagery in his works.

Works Cited

Abiola Irele, "The Negritude Debate", in Albert Bernard ed. "European Language Writing in Sub-Saharan Africa" Vol.1, Akademia Klado, Budapest, 1986, p.393.

Biodun Jeyifo.(ed.) *Conversation with Wole Soyinka*. University Press of Mississippi (Jackson, MS), 2001.

Emmanuel C. Eze, "Post-Colonial African Philosophy", Oxford Blackwell publishers, 1997, p.11.

Five Plays (Includes The Lion and the Jewel, The Swamp Dwellers, The Trials of Brother Jero, The Strong Breed and A Dance of the Forests), Oxford University Press, 1964.

Nikosi Lewis. *Postmodernism and Black Writing in South Africa*. ed. Derek Attridge and Rosemary Jolly Cambridge, C.U.P. 1998.

Myth, Literature and the African World. (essays), Cambridge University Press, 1976.

Soyinka,Wole. *The Lion and the Jewel*. Oxford University Press, 1962.

_______, *A Dance of the Forests*. Oxford University Press, 1962.

_______, *Death and the King's Horseman*. Norton, 1975.

_______, *A Play of Giants*. Methuen, 1984.

_______, *The Man Died: Prison Notes*. 1972, Arrow Books, London,1985.

http://nobelprize.org/nobel_prizes/literature/laureates/1986/soyinka-bio.html

http://www.princeton.edu/main/news/archive.

www.wikipedia.com

www.learner.org

5

Vijay Tendulkar's *Ghasiram Kotwal*: A Study of Power Dynamics in the Aesthetics of History

— Bhagabat Nayak

Vijay Dhondopant Tendulkar's *Ghashiram Kotwal* (1973) is a landmark creation in the history of modern Indian drama. It deals with power as a subjective force in human life that victimises and dehumanises people. In the duality of individual's scheming nature, power can help the beginning of a golden age or it can start a reign of terror in Orwellian sense. Tendulkar makes the play a critique of power politics and its dehumanising effect. In intellectual debate, controversy, and confrontation of ideas he analyses the dynamics of power in human conditions and its effect in individual's existential reality. As a dramatist of enormous social conscience and radical attitude he has the anger against individual's hypocrisies, social inequalities, gender discrimination and hollowness of social institutions.

> In the theatrical presentation of power dynamics his piercing social commentary entertains while simultaneously making us aware of our hypocrisies.
>
> (Ramnarayan 5)

In his seasoned journalistic experience, explosive expressions, articulation as a thespian and a consummate artist he has sensitised most of our socio-political tensions in his plays. His *Ghashiram Kotwal,* regarded as a literary classic, earned him international fame. The play presents the pathetic tale of a power-hungry man. Like the great political philosophers in history Tendulkar believes that absolute power corrupts absolutely and it causes a spiritual bankruptcy among the people. He estimates human beings as the characters in Mickey Mouse on certain hypothesis and projects their kin fight for survival in his plays.

He informs Gouri Ramnarayan in an interview:

> In this battle one mouse kills another. Many mice gang up... and end up ruthlessly destroying one another... as a sort of blind justice. (Madge 168)

In the mapping of his protagonist's struggle for power in a historical parenthesis he projects the human condition in oppression, torture, agonies, anger, revenge and self-assertion with universal connotations. With the fusion of power in individual's ambition he presents its Frankensteinian effect. His dramatic *modus operandi* reveals moral degradation, social degeneration and spiritual regression of Maratha society of the late eighteenth century Peshwa Empire in particular and power greedy individuals in general. The themes of sexuality, treachery, hypocrisy, violence and revenge for power expose the savagery in human nature. Giving an aesthetic touch to history in artistic exuberance he focuses how man is caught like a helpless fly in the cobweb of power.

The play deals with the issues of political, moral and ethical corruption of a definite period in Indian history. Tendulkar attempts to introduce ideological possibilities, modernist and avant-gardist features in the play. Gowri Ramnarayan rightly says:

> Tendulkar tells his story and leaves it to us to decide how to grapple with the questions he raises. (5)

In dramatisation of the historical context he projects hypocritical Nana Phadnavis, the Chief Minister of the Peshwa; the greedy and decadent poona Brahmins who were living like the parasities by offing power and wealth of the Peshwa; and a shrewd Kanauj Brahman (at the apex of Brahminical society)

Ghashiram who met his end while attempting to outwit the Poona Brahmins. *Ghashiram Kotwal* was considered a politically provocative play like his *Sakharam Binder* and *The Vultures*. It was under the Supreme Court injunction, legal consorship and unofficial pressure for being accused of his ill-motivated intrusion into the life of Nana Phadnavis and Poona Brahmins.

> For Tendulkar 'History' is the vehicle of rational self-consciousness through which the incomplete human spirit progressively acquires an improved sense of its own totality. (Gandhi 105)

For him history is less a determinate pattern in the power dynamics of Peshwa's representative and Brahminic hierarchy.

> The play depicts historiography... a form of narration conditioned by the narrator's own prejudices and preoccupations, and so itself a kind of rhetoric or fiction. (Eagleton 197)

In 'idealist historicism' Tendulkar portrays the Poona Brahmins and a Kanauj Brahmin in their 'indigenous racism', political actualities, historical and natural advantages. Looking back into history he frames his plot with "Nana Phadnavis, the eighteenth century ruler of Pune, who tries to create a puppet for his own little games, only to realise that he has given birth to a monster who may swallow him up"; and looking at least a decade ahead, "The play predicted with terrifying accuracy, the Indira Gandhis—Sant Bhindranwale dance of death, 11 years in advance of the events" (Karnad 65).

Power is the central theme of the play interpreted in the aesthetics of history. Whether Tendulkar has distorted history or has delineated it by deglamourising the great Maratha hero and the Brahmin community of Poona is debatable. In fact, the playwright intends to attack a corrupt and pretentious society with its contemporary issues like violence, treachery, sexuality, hypocrisy, greed and immorality. Tendulkar likes to project how "Real power is purchased at a price of certain submission" (Eliot 28) but while handling power one should be farsighted, ethical and tactful. Power often shuns ethics but ethics always goads power to keep it on the right track. Without ethics power becomes destructive both to the ruler and to the ruled. In the power dynamics one can manipulate it for his rise but application of ethics in it helps for good governance.

> Power can be used in ethical terms (which) do not serve only to express feeling. They are calculated also to arouse feeling, and so to stimulate action. (Lillie 313)

Both Nana and Ghashiram assert power without ethics, values and morals. If morality is made for man, not man for morality then the greatest danger to morality is posed by power which a person enjoys in different forms. Power is a great catalyst. It changes human personality. In power dynamics a friend can be a foe and vice versa. In power dynamics friendship, loyalty, enemity, alliances and betrayals are common. In the plot of the play Tendulkar instrumentalises power for one's rise and fall. He desires power to be servile to a person, not a person to be servile to power. In power politics Nana needs Ghashiram, and Ghashiram needs Nana; but in the shifting game of power, it is only a temporary adjustment that Nana exploits as long as necessary and can drop unceremoniously the moment it has served its purpose (Bandopadhyay iv). If Ghashiram craftily becomes a demon with power and victimises the Poonites then Nana outwittingly betrays him in power politics as it becomes a deciding factor for his destiny.

In the hierarchy Peshwa rules at the centre of his empire. But Nana and Ghashiram rule in the periphery. While Nana is Peshwa's 'Other' (with capital 'O' 'Other' refers to the centre of the power for his contribution and sacrifice) and Ghashiram is Nana's 'other' (with small 'o' 'other' indicates his servility and loyalty) then the latter serves the former his in subordinate position. Their assessment of power is historically subjective and existentially objective in human situations. In the fictional presentation of historical situation and assesment of characters Tendulkar makes a tight-rope walking between history and contemporaneity. On the one hand he portrays Nana's licentiousness and Ghashiram's mad desire for revenge on the other. Both of them are capacited and charged with power at certain variations. Ghashiram, the poor Brahmin from Kanauj had come to Poona for making his fortune. As Poona was the prosperous capital of the Peshwas and centre of Brahminic domination during the late eighteenth century Poona citizenry included the Vedanta scholars, vaidya doctors, linguists, astrologers, pious Brahmins from Tanjore, Rameshwaram, Kumbakonam and Benaras. All had their solidarity with the Poonaites who were religious minded and believing in spiritual sanctity. But the Brahmins of Poona as portrayed were greedy, narrowminded, vulgar, boisterous, ungovernable and capricious. Like many others Ghashiram had come to Poona with his wife and daughter in search of an employment and had joined as a servant in courtesan Gulabi's house.

Nana Phadnavis, the Chief Minister of Peshwa and the shrewd administrator of Maratha Empire was worshipped as the omnipotent power. History reveals that Nana was the Chancellor of the Peshwa from 1778 to 1800. During this crucial time when foreign powers were trying to destroy the Maratha identity Nana Saheb could keep the Maratha empire in tact due to his political statesmanship and strategy. His leadership, courage, political astuteness after Narayanrao Peshwa's murder kept the British, Nizam, Siddi, Tipu and the Mughals at bay. The credit of Nana is well observed from his cautious steps in administration, politics and diplomatic relationship with his hostile neighbours. His power and glory had convinced his enemies to say, "Nana says—the Peshwai obey.... There's only one Nana / The rest are na-na-na" (30). They knew that "Jabatak Nana tabatak Poona"—Poona is safe as long as Nana was alive. The Marathas in particular and Indians in general regard Nana a national hero. This does not mean that this heroic personality had no vices. He is beatified for his wisdom, moderation of Maratha administration, honesty and efficiency. While he is appreciated for his supreme contribution to the Maratha Empire, historians criticise his attempt to control his master Sawai Madhavarao Peshwa and competition with Mahadaji Sindhe. Tendulkar presents this eighteenth century hero in the contemporary perspective. Locating the plot in the antiques of history Tendulkar assesses this finest administrator and greatest patriot with certain human weaknesses. He has deconstructed the historical myth and the cult hero with a very sensitive touch to his morality. He attacks the sociology of Poona and historical realism of the period. This is the reason why he is accused of damaging the Maratha political and cultural pride in the play by forming a "Vulnerable spot in the Maharastrian psyche" (Gokhale 81).

Tendulkar transforms the historical realism into his contemporary social realism. For this he has been commented as a neo-realist. Noted historian, S. Madhav Pagdi does not find any historical accuracy in the portrayal of Ghashiram Kotwal, the police commissioner of Nana nor in offering of his daughter to Nana. There was no such redlight area as Bavannakhani. Tendulkar's emphasis on these facts are not the findings in his exploration of Maratha history rather they are the historical distortations for the aesthetic perfection of art for art's sake. Historian G.S. Sardesai mentions in his *New History of the Marathas* (Vol-II) that Ghashiram Savaldas, a Brahman from the north was appointed as the prefect of Poona on 31 August 1791. In contrast to S. Madhav Pagdi's view, he mentions that Ghashiram had become very autocratic after winning the confidence of Nana Phadnavis. Being an outsider this Brahmin had created a reign of terror in Poona in the name of administration. To his misfortune he had dug up his own grave when he arrested 35 Brahmins and put them in a small cell out of whom 21 died of suffocation. As the matter was reported to Peshwa by a land owner the incident was supervised. Although Ghashiram explained that the Brahmins had died due to opium poisoning the authority was not convinced. This incident had created a hue and cry in the empire of Peshwa. Nana had ordered for his arrest and handed him over to the people to be stoned to death.

Tendulkar's intention is not to distort history. In his view the names like Nana and Ghashiram are beyond time and space. In many societies there are many Nanas and many Ghashirams. He is concerned with the social injustice and individuals' disillusionment with power. While the historians idealise this national hero in praise of his political strategy, shrewdness and patriotism, Tendulkar universalises him just by fictionalising his vices in human situations. His intention is not to attack the great national hero nor to insult the hero worshipping nature of Indians but to project hypocrisy, treachery, immorality and decadene of human values in great human personalities by cooking the facts in historical kitchens. He has not rewritten history but has deconstructed history in aesthetics.

With the voice of a thespian and soul of a social critic he defends his position in the 'introduction' to the play:

> Although based on historical legend, I have no intention of commenting on the morals, or lack of them, of the Peshwa, Nana Phadnavis or Ghashiram. The moral of this story, if there is any, may be looked for elsewhere. (iv).

Tendulkar does not believe in all existing ideologies, nor he desires to make art for propaganda, nor announces any message but expresses a profound urge in the play out of historical curiosity. Portraying a power-hungry man's pathetic tale in his survival strategy and existential suffering he makes the play a literary classic. Commending Tendulkar's ideological and political references Samik Bandyopadhyay observes:

> Ghashiram has been attacked on peripheral counts rather than on its basic assumptions. Tendulkar has been criticised for showing Nana Phadnavis, a cult hero, in an unsavory light. But the play is not really about Nana—who was the Peshwa's Chancellor. (iii)

His intention is to expose the weakness of our great leaders who have often made life miserable for the masses. In the analysis of these power-seekers, one of the authentic critics on Tendulkar's plays Manoj Bhise says in an interview with V.M. Madge:

> Ghashiram is seen as a pawn in the game of power politics, the play becomes a metaphor or an allegory of power-hungry people in all walks of life—social, political and even educational. There are Ghashirams and Nanas everywhere. This makes the play a brilliant expose of power-brokers, of realpolitik, in fact. (146)

In the play Tendulkar is more concerned with the human frailty in power. He believes that a power-wielded person succumbs to violence, revenge, sexuality and gratification of his sensual pleasures. He makes the play "a study of power game" in which the characters become pawns to power and they suffer from gender bias, sexual perversion and unbrahmanical activities. In realisation of this Urbashi Barat rightly remarks :

> Tendulkar responded... pointing out that *Ghashiram Kotwal* was not meant to be a historically accurate account of Nana's or Ghashiram's character or rule over Poona. Whether or not the dramatist has indeed misrepresented these two men (or the Poona Brahmins) is not the moot point. What is important is that he has examined the very contemporary issue of the relationship between power and gender in patriarchy in a historical setting with historically recognisable characters. This makes his political statementabout the nature of power much more than just a matter of contemporary interest (100).

Tendulkar was intending to write on the psyschology of the great manipulators of power like Nana and Ghashiram in history. He universalises the existential aspects of the historical persons in our regional, cultural, sectarian, casteist and sexual politics. Keeping the Maratha history in mind he presents Maratha Kings, Peshwas, caste hegemony of the Brahmins; Nana's alliance with the British, Nizam and Tipu; the role of Sindhes, Holkers and Bhonsales in Maratha politics; their internal suspicion and external hostilities excellently. He has explored the aspects of musical dance drama and folk-theatre. He also focuses on revenge, feminist, psycho-analytical and tragic elements; class and caste oppression and marginalised human status in the play. The play illustrates his idea of power politics, in which to have ambition is a virture but to be ambitious in obsession with revenge is a crime and it invites one's fall. This idea of power-politics had a spurt with the sudden rise of Shiv Sena in Maharashtra politics. Tendulkar marked how ambitious people can win power by becoming the tormentors of humanity. He had observed how the Sena activists in ambition and vengeance had created terror and destruction in Maharashtra against which even the Communist Politburo can not dare to protest. Thus, with the Shiv Sena activity providing the impetus he gave a brilliant exposure to his characters—Nana and Ghashiram in real politik. He writes in a very confessional and affirming tone:

> The hungry dogs got transformed into ferocious tigers and the government began to fear them. When I saw this, I felt the urge to use this theme in a play and as I traversed backwards in history, I noticed that this was a repetitive pattern—such individuals and parties had been created through history. Hitler was one such example. I felt that using a contemporary personality, party or setting would limit my scope. When I was exploring further and further into the past, the idea of Ghashiram and folk theatre came to my mind (*Lokprabha* 23).

Over this political provocation he presents the historical game of power politics with a universal connotation in the play. In an interview with Gowri Ramnarayan he says:

> The play takes place at the fag-end of the Peshwa period when the East India company had established its power. The incident involves an uneducated outsider, Ghashiram, who comes to Pune, uses his native intelligence and the lure of his own daughter on the womaniser Nana Phadnavis (the Peshwa Prime Minister) to climb the power ladder. Actually, he is being used as a tool by professional politicians. His immorality and sadism grow to such monstrous proportions that, upon the demand of the Brahmins of Pune, the upstart is stoned to death.
>
> The inspiration for the play was a topical situation. I was working for *Loksatta* when the first major riots were launched in Bombay by the Shiv Sena. Bal Thackeray seemed an ordinary man, not at all the sort of person who would indulge in daredevilry. The middle-class boys who followed him were not demons. In that particular situation they acquired power, abused it and spread terror. I sensed that terror in my newspaper office. We were not free to write anything about Shiv Sena. If the title "Senapati" was not prefixed to Thackeray's name in a report, a morcha would be taken out with burning and looting.

> Actually, the Shiv Sena was deliberately fuelled by the ruling party to establish a force against the masses. Then came Krishna Menon and his election campaign when the Shiv Sena was pitted against the communists. You can see the similarity between the Ghashiram incident and this event to which we were all witnesses. (170-171)

In ideological possibilities, and artistic aesthetics the playwright gives a naturalistic and humanistic touch to the human condition and historical situations. The progressive Dramatic Association (PDA) of Poona had its pressure to censor his satirical portraiture of Nana, the cult hero and the culture of Poona Brahmins. The Shiv Sena claiming the play vilified a Maratha hero, tried to stop it from being sent abroad. But it was smuggled out with the help of the then Chief Minister Sharad Pawar, and went onto win global acclaim. The playwright says about this in an interview with Shrish Pai and Priya Tendulkar:

> The form I used for Ghashiram has limitations. That is why I have not written another play in the form. (174).

Tendulkar projects how authority, sexuality, revenge, violence and Brahminism have devastated the city of Poona, the symbolic location of Brahminism. He projects that spiritualism is the essence of Brahminism but in Poona's socio-cultural environment it is lost in the shadows of hypocrisy, brutality, inhumanity and scheming nature of men. Sensuality and brutality have replaced spirituality in the minds of the people. Here women have become the wretched of the earth. They have become voiceless, disempowered and victimised in the power dynamics of patriarchy and state authority. They are used as toys for men's sexual appetite. In grotesque parody he projects that the Brahmins do not go to temples but to prostitutes. They do not prefer 'Kirtan' but 'lavanis' and erotic dances. They visit Bavannakhani, the red-light district of Poona, the Mathura, the garden of Krishna. For them Nana appears as the embodiment of power who visits this garden for amorous dalliances with numerous gopis. But under Gulabi's mohini charm Poona looks powerless. When Haridas sings abhang, Nana sits silently ogling at the beautiful women in the audience. The Brahmins perform 'Kirtan' and 'lavani' on the story of Vishwamitra and Menaka. The chorus sings and dances in place of lord Ganapati and the repetition of "Ganapati Bappa Morya" astounds the place in supplication to the deity. The Brahmins are more involved in backbites in their complex likes and dislikes. They are the victims of their self invented intra-conflicts, class consciousness and compete to win the favour of Nana. In the power politics of Poona Brahmins, Ghashiram feels isolated. He is an internal diaspora in pan-Indian situation, who fails to earn a cohesive solidarity with the Poona Brahmins for his unbrahminical appearance, rhetoric and fresh nativisation. In the 'identitarian' power politics and superiority complex of native Brahmins Ghashiram suffers from the horrors of psychological subjugation. In the rhetoric of their blame of lacking the native Brahminic inwardness he enjoys his "dreadful secondariness" (Said 207). He is humiliated in their power dynamics that causes his "self-subalternisation" and promotes the motive for revenge. He observes:

> Power is employed and exercised through a net-like organisation. And not only do individuals circulate between its threads; they are always in the position of simultaneously undergoing or exercising this power. They are not only its inert or consenting target; they are also the elements of its articulation. In other words, individuals are like vehicles of power, not its points of application. (Foucault 98)

Ghashiram thinks that 'power' is the metaphor of success by which he can have his physical conquest over the Poonites. He believes that the insult that has wounded him can only be subsidised by having power, a mask for conquest with his indigenous intelligence. He observes Nana's change of mood when the song changes from "abhang to 'lavani.' He marks Nana's weakness for his sixteen year young daughter Gauri at the time of her bowing down to the idol of Ganapati.

Ghashiram knows Nana's terrible weakness for women. People call him,"Nana of the Nine Courts, Nana of the wealth and power." He finds him visiting the place of Gulabi with a

'Silver handled walking stick' in one hand and a 'garland of flowers' on his wrist. While Gulabi dances erotically and her sari and hair get dishevelled Nana 'ogles' and 'leers' at other women. They feel uncomfortable and adjust their saris. Even the worshipping of Ganesha means nothing for him. The sacredness of the occasion of Rangpanchami is demeaned for his sensuality. He looks at Gauri, the pretty girl unblinkingly and accosts her:

Nana : (Voice of lust) Child, What do you want? All your dreams, this Nana will fulfil. (He puts a hand on her shoulder. She pulls back). Oh, don't be shy. This is our house. This is a private hall. No one will see. No one in Poona today has the audacity to watch the great Nana Phadnavis!

Girl : He will see.

Nana : He will see? Who?

Girl : (Points to Ganapati) He.

Nana : That idol of holiness? That all holy Ganapati? The maker of God? Look, he has two wives. One on this side, one on that side. If you sit on our lap, he won't say anything about that! (18-19).

Others are busy in supplicating the deity in the din of drum and shehnai. But observing Nana's lecherousness Ghashiram makes up his mind to use his dearest daughter as a sexual bait to hunt power from Nana. Nana's accidental bruises of his foot offers Ghashiram the scope to exploit the situation. He immediately offered his back to Nana to rest his foot for further treatment. Ghashiram's servile manner establishes:

> The connection between lechery and power is made obvious as Ghashiram places the injured foot on his back, a striking visual image of the humiliating flattery and the supplicatory posture that the powerless must adopt in order to achieve power themselves.(Barat 97).

Holding Nana's injured slippered foot in his hand he says:

> In my hands has fallen grace!
> All here envy me my place.
> This is a gift to last me all my days (10).

Ghashiram's loyalty and devotion is out of sycophancy which impress Nana very much. For Ghashiram's gratefulness he offers him a pearl necklace as reward. To Ghashiram's misfortune Gulabi claims that she exactly deserves the reward and snatches it away from him. Gulabi's men throw him out of her house. He is humiliated by them. Homeless he strands hungrily in the city. This existential situation compels him to join the line of Bahmi'ns who wait to receive gifts from the Peshwa in the 'Dakshina' ceremony. He finds that the Brahmins try their best in flattery to win the favour of Nana. They quarrel with one another belittling their position. They steal their fellow beings' 'dakshina'. In selfishness, narrow religious pride and power politics they try to overcome others. Ghashiram marks their intolerance, jealousy, selfishness, opportunistic attitude and running after worldly pleasures.

Tendulkar presents the 'Dakshina' ceremony a mockery of the Brahmins of Poona perhaps not for their hard earning of wealth but for depending on other's grace and narrow exploitation of religious faith. Although the ceremony carries some religious implication and establishes the purity of mind, it has no sign of virtues, spirituality, honesty and tolerance due to the nuisance of Brahmins. Nana watches how eagerly the Brahmins grab the gifts and fight among themselves like dogs. They are so selfish that when Ghashiram joins them in the line he is thrown out mercilessly. The native Brahmins accuse him of not resembling like a Brahmin and falsely accuse him of stealing other's coffer. He is beaten and handed over to the soldiers who put him in the prison.

Ghashiram appeals in despair :

> I didn't steal, I swear to god. I didn't. I'm not a thief. I am from Kanauj. I'm a Brahman. I've been here two weeks. I came here to find my fortune and lost my reputation. How did it happen? What will happen to my wife? To my daughter? What will they say when they hear of this?" (116).

After few days he is released from the prison with a warning to go away from Poona. This reveals:

> The anarchy in Poona incorporates the universal. The illegitimacy and the impropriety of the law could be at any place, at any time. The treatment of Ghashiram at the hands of Gulabi, the Brahmans and the police could be happening to any one who is incapable of shielding himself, even today (Sharma 26).

The native Brahmins' humiliation awakened in him a vindictiveness for revenge. Now he takes a firm decision to stay in Poona and pay the Poonites in their own coin. He says:

> I'll show my strength. It will cost you! Your good days are gone! I am Kanauj Brahman, but I've become a shudra, a criminal, a useless animal. There is no one to stop me now, to mock me, to make me bend, to cheat me. Now I am devil. You've made me an animal, I shall be a devil inside. I'll come back like a boar and I'll stay as devil. I'll make pigs of all of you. I'll make this Poona a kingdom of pigs.Then I'll be Ghashiram again, the son of Savaldas once again. (17)

Now Ghashiram has a self-willed metamorphosis in his personality. He became an opportunist, a schemer and a Machiavelli of Poona politics and tried his best to exploit the best possible advantages by destroying the ego of native Brahmins. Universalising Ghashiram's spatial sufferings Tendulkar expresses how a person's existential socio-political situations make him good or bad.

Tendulkar projects the decadence of Brahminic aristocracy. In order to project the decadence of a dominating caste or class in a society he focuses on the Brahmins in Hindu society. He presents how Bavannakhani has become the Mathura for the Brahmins of Poona where they make Rasleela with the street prostitutes. They have lost their glory of wisdom in spirituality, and remain busy in sexual overtures and licentious behaviour.

Presenting their status in the play he writes:

> The Brahmans have lost themselves in Bavannakhani and the Brahman women are at home; they stay at home...the Brahmans have lost themselves in the cemetery, in Kirtan; the Brahman women are sentenced to solitary confinement. (8)

While the Poonaites assert their superiority in native pride, Ghasiram offers his dearest daughter Gauri to Nana as a "luscious peach" (35) to gain power. He commits a henious crime by surrendering his daughter to satisfy the sexual appetite of Nana. This causes Ghashiram's violation of patriarchal ethics by compelling his daughter for prostitution. For the betrayal of faith between the father and child B.S. Naikar rightly remarks:

> He commits the tragic crime of sacrificing his own daughter's virginity for attaining some kind of power from Nana. (Sharma 105)

He succeeds to exploit Nana's sexual weakness for his logical advantage receding from ethical path. In his blind urge for power he tells to Nana, "if the hunter is ready, the prey will be found" (19) and "if order is given, this servant will bring her" (20). Revenge is a mad desire which he prefers at the cost of his daughter's virginity. He knows that Nana is frustrated and craving for his daughter's tantalising youth. He tries to exploit the situation by asking Nana, "All right sir, to shut people's mouth, make me the Kotwal of Pune".

> Nana : No! Send her. I'll make you the Kotwal. When will you send her?
>
> Ghasiram : After I have the order, signed and sealed, in my hand.
>
> Nana : Bastard. You've got me in a narrow pass.
>
> Ghashiram: Yes, the narrow pass of my only daughter (24).

Nana makes Ghashiram the Kotwal of Poona. Kotwalship will delegate some power to Ghashiram. He accepts the evil side of power and steadily becomes mischievous, arrogant in behaviour and vindictive by nature.

Neela Bhalla rightly opines:

> There is good and bad power. Good power leads to leadership and guidance. Bad power leads to authoritarian dominance, coercion and tyranny. The driving power can be attributed to the singleness of motivation. (Madge 132)

He used power for personal aggrandisement very cunningly with the brain of a Machiavelli and body power of a Nazi Hitler. He became a totalitarian and gained complete control over the city. He introduced endless restrictions on the Poonaites and humiliated them. He crushed them mercilessly and caused a lot of inconveniences. His ruthless manner and absurd behaviour made the people restless and desperate. His tyrannical rule made the city 'desolate' and brutish. Now "Gauri orders, Nana does, Ghashiram rules" (37). The people of Poona used to tremble at the mention of his name.

The effect of power on Ghashiram is marked with his motive of haunting malignity. He took revenge on the Poona Brahmins without compunction. Tendulkar projects his disturbed mind as under:

> Now he's in my hands... Oh my daughter... the beast (then yells at the audience). Oh you people. Look ! I've given my beloved daughter into the jaws of that wolf! Look, look at this father? Putting his heart's child up for sale. Look at him, eating her like a peach... spit on me... Look, look. But I will not quit. I shall make this Pune a Kingdom of pigs. (22)

He orders men and women to stay at home at night. His imposition of strict rules reached the height of absurdity. With his order

> Prostitutes' lane was desolate.The chasing of women was halted /Pimps turned into beggars./Counterfeit coins were worthless. (27)

He draws the impression to remain moral in an immoral world is both difficult and meaningless. He supports his action with the logic, "You've made me an animal, I'll be a devil inside" (27). He fails to realise that an individual's logic is often not supported by reasons. This is the reason why he enforces law on the Poonaities not in his sub-ordinate's capacity but as per his personal whims. He straightens the "whoremongers, fuckers" and imposes "severe corporal and capital punishment" (46) on them.

He implements rules to preserve the social values by checking sexual promiscuity. In the name of sound administration he inflicts unspeakable misery on the life of common people. He fails to differentiate between essential and moral. He imprisons innocent people returning home at night on the suspicion that they might be the whoremongers. He suspects even a real permit as a counterfeit one when a dead body is taken for cremation. His irrationality comes to limelight when a woman complains to Nana:

> My husband and his brother have been arrested by the Kotwal's soldiers. My father-in-law died. They won't let them hold the funeral. The permit is real, but they call it counterfeit. Sir—the corpse has been lying in the cremation ground since morning. The dogs are gathering. Sir, please, give us justice. (32)

He extracts false confessions from a Brahmin in a theft case and orders his men to put hot iron balls on his palms when he denies to his crime. Ghashiram does not react when he curses:

> I did not steal, I did not steal. I did not steal, O Ghasiram. You have tormented a poor innocent Brahman. You'll die without children. You yourself will endure torment greater than mine. You'll die a dog's death grinding your heels in the dirt. (36)

Nana changes his mistresses like usable commodities. When Nana gets ready for his seventh marriage Ghasiram finds how his "heart's child" is discarded by Nana. Gouri dies a miserable death in the street due to the possible abortion forced upon her. Her death as an unwed mother affects Ghashiram's reputation. The insult of the Poona Brahmins was a perpetrated one but the loss and shock due to Gauri's death is a quite befitting one due to his blind urge for power to take revenge. Ghashiram's sin is balanced with retribution. In anger and remorse he threatens Nana and asks about his daughter's fate. Nana reminds him philosophically:

> Ghasya, how much more will you grieve? Now be calm. Whatever happened, protocol should not be forgotten. Don't you forget that. Whom do you stand before? First you must bow. Now—bow—That's right. Good. We acknowledge your loyalty. By our favour, you have become Kotwal. We are pleased with that. (44)

Further, Nana reminds Ghashiram about the temporality of life:

> The body will burn....Death is without meaning....Life too is without meaning. No one belongs to any one. No one is anyone's daughter. No one is anyone's father. In the end, only oneself belongs to oneself. Life is like a dance of four days' charm. One must do one's duty. That is enough. I am the Chief Minister. You are the Kotwal. These are our duties. So go, go to your. (45)

In Nana's consolation, warning and encouragement he felt depressed and harassed. He became more vindictive and sadistic. In anger and highhandedness he committed a great blunder. He arrested some Brahmins who had mistakenly entered into his garden to pluck fruits and put them in a small unventilated cell. This caused the death of twentytwo Brahmins. A landlord, Sardar Phakade who was dead against Ghashiram reported the matter to Peshwa. The magnitude of the blunder was so powerful that he could not satisfy the authority.

Nana, the shrewd "political fox" (Dharan 122) apprehended danger to his name and position. He understood the psyche of agitating Brahmins and Peshwa's mood from his summoning. He ordered Ghasiram to death. In public hatred, self-humiliation and terrible psychosis Ghashiram tells the angry mob:

> I danced on your chest but I wasted the life of my little daughter. I should be punished for the death of daughter. Beat me. Beat me. Heat me. (54)

Ghashiram is stoned to death. He meets his retribution with a lesson that he who negates the moral order of the universe gets neglected by it ultimately. He violated his power both in patriarchal and state authorities. It is only for cruelty, vindictiveness, sycophancy and sadism he sacrificed his daughter and spoilt himself for the position of Kotwal. With Ghashiram's death Nana addresses the crowd lightheartedly:

> Use a thorn to take out a thorn. That's great. The disease has been stopped. Anyway, he was no use any more. (63)

He cheers the crowd:

> The demon Ghasya, who plagued all of us, has met his death. Everything has happened according to the wishes of gods. The mercy of the god is with us always. We have commanded that there be festivities for three days to mark this happy occasion.(65-66)

Urbashi Barat rightly remarks, "Gauri's father who re-enacts Shiva's tandav over the city of Poona which comes to an end with his own destruction" (95) like that of Bhasmasura in Indian myth.

In the power dynamics and sexual politics women become the worst sufferers in the hands of men. They are treated as the subalterns who can not speak for their rights. Although they play very important role in men's psyche; and in the construction of family and society they are neglected and commodified. Women become the victims of men's sexual politics. The wives of the Brahmins are neglected by their husbands, Gauri is almost sold like an animal with her father's desire for power, and Gulabi sells herself as a sexual object for her existence. In gender consciousness they are treated as voiceless animals. They are used as objects and an economic class. They depend on others for their sustenance and survival. Tendulkar is serious for their suffering in patriarchal authority. They are defined, codified and marginalised by men. In man's power dynamics a woman is vulnerable to rape and assault. In the name of love, marriage and conjugal life they are exploited through marital rape, forced sexual overtures and subordination. Their names are given to signify beauty, strength, grace and wealth. But before achieving the virtues in reality they are reduced to dust. Gauri's name mythically signifies the power of Shakti, the mother goddess but she is rendered powerless. In the portrayal of Bavannakhani the playwright not only expresses the status of women but also discloses the hypocrisy of men. Tendulkar is solemnly focuses on the male perception on women:

> Women are the gifts which men exchange between each other... they are gifts; not givers. They have no significant power or influence within a system, which is controlled by men and works to their benefit. Men, not women, have the power to determine the value of women in the exchange and the meanings associated with them. (Greene 7)

In the power politics of men, women are treated as an oppressed and humiliated class. Expressing the unpleasant truth about women's issues and women's questions he presents their subjugated status in their sexuality, maternal longing and desire for building family. The play reveals Tendulkar's heartfelt desire to remove the age-old tradition that culminates in many unmitigated mental disturbances and uneasiness.

The play is a revenge tragedy. Ghashiram is the tragic hero. Desire for revenge is the greatest flaw in his character. While Nana is unscrupulous in his blind lust, Ghashiram has a maimed conscience. Ghashiram's selling of Gauri to Nana for Kotwalship and Nana's desire to fulfil his caranal pleasure with a daughter like girl lacks ethical implicit. As Michael Henchard sells his wife and daughter in his patriarchal authority under the influence of wine in Hardy's *Mayor of Casterbridge*, Ghashiram bargains his daughter with Nana for power with a maimed conscience. He desires to energise himself with power with a hope of achieving Midas touch but before enjoying it his daughter is turned to a corpse.

Like Marlow's Dr. Faustus he has sold his soul (daughter) to the devil (the incarnation of power) Nana in the hope of enjoying power. His reactions and actions against the Brahmins of Poona appear to be hypothetically logical because he was humilited, abused and tortured by them. But it goes beyond reasons when the benevolent Kotwal ruled like a malevolent murderer.

As Shakespeare's Shylock, the Jew who revolted against the Christians:

> If you prick us, do we not bleed? If you tickle us, do we not laugh? If you poison us, do we not die? And if you wrong us, shall we not revenge?... The villainy you teach me I will execute... (*The Merchant of Venice* Act III, Sc-I, ll. 53-60)

Ghashiram protests against the wrongs done to him in history. Instead of correcting the wrongs he commits the greater wrongs to punish the Brahmins of Poona. He commits more sins than the sins committed to him. His metamorphosis from Savaldas to Kotwal could have brought a change in the heart of Brahmins of Poona, but in revenge motive he dragged them to a hellish world where he himself ended his life. He could not properly assess his position in a new socio-political environment and took a wrong decision in the crucial hour of his life. One can view that in Ghashiram's survival strategy violence is immanent.

> And it gets tinged with—as the psychiatrist would diagnose it-the psychopathic. It carries the impress of an empty interpersonalworld and a maimed conscience. (Nandy 1)

In historical curiosity, individual's existential complexities, ideological ardour and spiritual bankruptcy, Tendulkar explores how his protagonist works in moments of adversities in life. He believes that power is a great catalyst that changes the nature of human beings and promotes the cause of violence.

As Gouri Ramnarayan comments, "he leaves it to us to decide how to grapple with the quesions he raises" (5) on power that makes an individual selfish, intolerant and vindictive.

Works Cited

Barat, Urbashi. 'Gender and Power in *Ghashiram Kotwal*'. *VijayTendulkar'sGhashiram Kotwal*. Ed. Vinod Bala Sharma. New Delhi: Asia Book Club, 2001.

Bhalla, Neela.'*Ghashiram Kotwal* : Text and Sub-text'. *Vijay Tendulkar's Plays: An Anthology of Recent Criticism*. Ed. V.M. Madge. New Delhi : Peneraft International, 2007.

Dharan, N.S. '*Ghashiram Kotwal*: Tendulkar's Thesis on Power Politics'. *Vijay Tendulkar's Ghashiram Kotwal*. Ed. Vinod Bala Sharma. New Delhi: Asia Book Club, 2001.

Eagleton, Terry. *Literary Theory: An Introduction*. New Delhi: Doaba Publications, 1996.

Eliot, T.S. *Murder in the Cathedral*. London: Faber and Faber, 1938.

Foucault, M. *Power / Knowledge: Selected Interviews and Other Writings 1972-1977*. Ed. Colin Gordon. Hertfordshire: Harvester Press, 1980.

Greene, Gayle & Coppelia Khan. 'Feminist Scholarship and the Social Construct Women'. *Making a Difference: Feminist Literary Criticism*. Ed. Gayle Greene and Coppelia Khan. London: Methuen, 1985.

Gandhi, Leela. *Postcolonial Theory*. New Delhi: OUP, 1998.

Gokhale Shanta. 'On *Ghashiram Kotwal*'. *Ghashiram Kotwal* by Vijay Tendulkar. Calcutta: Seagull Books, 1999.

'Interview: Vijay Tendulkar in conversation with Gowri Ramnarayan'. *Vijay Tendulkar's Plays*. Ed. V.M. Madge. New Delhi: Pencraft International, 2007.

, 'Interview with Shirish Pai and Priya Tendulkar'. *Natak Ani Mee*. Thane: Dimple Publication, 1997.

Karnad, Girish. 'The Tumultuous Prophet'. *Outlook*. Vol. 48, No. 22, June 2, 2008:

Lillie, William. *An Introduction to Ethics*. New Delhi: Allied Publishers Limited, 1967.

Naikar, B.S. '*Ghashiram Kotwal* : A Tragedy of Power'. *Vijay Tendulkar's Ghashiram Kotwal*. Ed. Vinod Bala Sharma. New Delhi: Asia Book Club, 2001.

Nandy, Ashis. 'Breakfast With Evil'. *The Hindu Literary Review*. September 2, 2001.

Ramnarayan, Gouri.'Theatre'. *The Hindu Magazine*. Vol. 127, No. 39, October 3, 2004.

Said, Edward. 'Representing the Colonised : Anthology's Interlocutors'. *Critical Enquiry*. Vol. 15, No.-2, 1989.

Sharma, Vinod Bala, ed. *Vijay Tendulkar's Ghasiram Kotwal*. New Delhi: Asia Book Club, 2001.

Tendulkar, Vijay.*Ghashiram Kotwal*. 'Introduction' by Samik Bandopadhay and Trans. Jayant Karve and Eleanor Zelliot. Calcutta: Seagull Books, 1999.

______, Vijay. *Lokprabha*. Diwali, 1991. (Trans. by Kalindi Deshpande),

6

The Craftsmanship of Girish Karnad as a Dramatist

— Megha Trivedi

Girish Karnad is an eminent personality in the world of Indian Writing in English. He has been highly praised as a playwright, poet, actor, director, critic and a translator. He has bestowed Indian Drama with his dramatic skills and technical experimentations. His plays have received outstanding recognition. They have been frequently performed in Europe and in America. His plays have the rich flow of inspiration ever flowing in the variety of myths and folklore. They attempt to discover the ambiguous and less known myths with the focus on Indian values and its cultural ethos. He writes:

> The energy of folk theatre comes from the fact that although it seems to upholdtraditional values, it also has the means of questioning these values of making them literally stand on the head. The various conventions-the chorus, the mask, the seemingly unrelated comic episodes, the mixing of human and non human worlds –permit the simultaneous presentation of alternative attitudes to the central problem.
>
> (Karnad: *Three Plays* 14)

Karnad has focused on several themes in his plays and has observed folk theatre from a different perspective. He made it as a vehicle of intellectual learning. His plays subjugate the predicament of modern man through symbols and folktales. He has used the Indian myths with the view of exposing the absurdity of modern life with all its wonderful complexities and eternal struggles. He has made courageous innovations and experiments in his plays and has presented combination of various ideas and emotions in the background of myth. He has always preferred to narrate old tales from a remarkable new perspective. He has not just retold and reinterpreted the narratives from the past but has also given it a new eye of contemporary relevance. Aparna Dharwadkar observes:

> Karnad employs traditional Indian narrative materials and modes of performance successfully to create a radically modern urban theatre.
>
> (Dharwadkar 355)

His plays attempt to revolutionaries social structure for a better renewed social system by merging the myths with reality and the past with the present.

He along with Vijay Tendulkar, Badal Sircar, Rakesh Mohan has succeeded in making Indian theatre global by making drama contemporarily significant and by focusing on intricate cultural structure of India.

According to Karnad:

> My generation was the first to come of age after India became independent of British rule. It, therefore, had to face a situation in which tensions implicit until then had come out in the open and demanded to be resolved without apologia or self justification: tensions between the cultural past of the country and its colonial past, between the attractions of western modes of thought and our own traditions, and finally between the various visions of the future that opened up once the common cause of political freedom was achieved. This is the historical context that gives rise to my plays and that of my contemporaries.
>
> (Karnad 3)

Yayati (1961) was the first play of Karnad as a playwright and the later was written *Tuglaq* in 1964. Subsequently, he published *Hayavadana* (1971), *Angumalinge* (1977), *Httina Hunja* (1980), *Naga Mandala* (1988), *Tale Danda* (1990) and

Agni Mattu Male (1995). He wrote all the plays in Kannada which were later translated into major languages including Hindi. He has received many prestigious awards including the Padmashree in 1974 and the Padmabhushan in 1992.

R. K. Dhawan states in *Girish Karnad: The Man and the Writer*:

> Girish Karnad is the foremost playwright of the contemporary Indian Stage. He has given the Indian theatre a richness that could probably be equated only with his talents as an actor, director. His contribution goes beyond theatre. He has directed feature films, documentaries and television serials in Kannada, Hindi and English, and has played leading roles as an actor in Hindi and Kannada art films, commercial movies and television serials. He has represented India in foreign lands as an emissary of art and culture.
>
> (Dhawan 13)

Karnad found the myth of *Yayati* (1961) from the *Mahabharata*. The play revolves around the central character of Yayati—a King who was cursed with old age during the prime time of his life. He goes on pleading different people, "will you take my old age" but was accepted by none other than his son, Puru. Thus, Puru becomes old in the prime of his life while Yayati regains his youth. The play highlights conflicts between family hopes and personal aspirations. Karnad was facing the similar conflict in his personal life which he realised while reading the Myth of Yayati in the *Mahabharata*. R.K. Dhawan has summarised this particular incident in the life of Karnad:

> When Karnad was preparing to go to England amidst the intense emotional turmoil, he found himself writing a play. One day as he was reading the *Mahabharata* just for fun, he read the story of Yayati. It clicked his mind. He started writing. It came as a play. He suddenly found he was a playwright and a Kannada playwright at that. This was so sudden and so natural. The play was in Kannada, the language of his childhood. And the theme of Yayati was taken from ancient Indian Mythology. While the theme and language was typically native. The play owed it's from,

> not to numerous mythological plays he watched but to western playwrights whom he had read. While the subject matter was purely native and traditional, the form and structure were essentially western.
>
> (Dhawan 3)

Karnad came across a situation of identity crisis on both social and personal level. He received a scholarship to study abroad but belonged to a conservative traditional family where going and staying abroad was an infrequent phenomena. He has expressed his feelings on the same in the 'Introduction to *Three Plays*':

> Should I at the end of my studies return home for the sake of my family, my people and my country, even at the risk of my abilities and training not being fully utilised in what seemed a stifling claustrophobic atmosphere, or should I rise above such parochial considerations and go where the world drew me?
>
> (Karnad 2)

Talking further about Yayati, in one of the Interviews with Rajendra Paul (1971), Karnad has stated:

> I was excited by the story of Yayati, this exchange of ages between the father and the son, which seemed to me terribly powerful and terrible modern. At the same time, I was reading a lot of Sartre and the Existentialist. This consistent harping on responsibility which the Existentialists indulge in suddenly seemed to link up with the story of Yayati.
>
> (Karnad 54)

The originality of Karnad lies in identifying the motivational forces retrieved from the experience of Yayati, his attachment towards life, its pleasures and at the same time drawing the attention of the readers towards the tawdriness of Yayati's won life.

Yayati turns towards renunciation at the end of the play by realising the importance of performing one's own duty and accepting responsibilities. He admits:

> Dear son, sensual desire is never quenched by indulgence any more than fire is by pouring ghee in it. I had so far heard, and read about this. Now, I've realised it: no object of desire–corn, gold, cattle, and women- nothing can ever satisfy the desire of man. We can reach peace only by a mental poise that goes beyond likes and dislikes. This is the state of Brahman. Take back your youth and rule the kingdom wisely and well....We should wash our sins by doing penance in the forest. I have spent my youth in this city but will spend my old age in the forest.
>
> (*Yayati* 82-83)

Karnad retold the myth of Yayati as a satirical drama of disappointment, ineffectiveness and bereavement. He has derived his structure from the Greek tragic playwrights like Jean Anouilh, Jean-Paul Sartre and American dramatist Eugene O' Neill. He has presented a conflicting nature of human relations. Yayati is a representative of a modern ordinary man who is constantly in search of peace. He is dissatisfied in spite of having everything in his life. It presents a psychological elucidation of human being, a crucial conflict of man, his limitations, faults and the continuous struggle he is involved in.

In *Hayavadana* (1971), Karnad has used the myth of the transposed heads. *The Transposed Heads* by Thomas Mann has been the source of inspiration for Karnad's *Hayavadana*. Kirtinath Kurkoti in 'The Introduction to *Hayavadana*' has said:

> The plot of *Hayavadana* comes from *Kathasaritsagara*, an ancient collection of stories in Sanskrit. But Karnad has borrowed it through Thomas Mann's retelling of the story in *The Transposed Heads*. The Sanskrit tale, told by a ghost to an adventurous king, gains further mock heroic dimensions in Mann's version. The original poses a moral problem while Mann uses it to ridicule the mechanical conception of life which differentiates between body and the soul. He ridicules the philosophy which holds the head superior to the body. The human body, Mann argues, is a fit instrument for the fulfillment of human destiny. Even the transposition of heads will not liberate the protagonists from the psychological limits imposed by nature.
>
> (Kurtoli V)

Hayavadana opens with the myth of Lord Ganesha. He has been worshipped as a destroyer of incompleteness who himself is elephant headed and is incomplete.

> O Elephant headed Herambha
> Whose flag is victory
> And who shines like a thousand suns.
> O husband of Riddhi and Siddhi,
> Seated on a mouse and decorates with a snake.
> O Single-masked destroyer of incompleteness,
> We pay homage to you and start our play
>
> (*Hayavadana* 1)

The story reveals the triangular love story between Devadatta, Padmini and Kapila. The play highlights a psychological conflict faced by Padmini and also depicts a quest for Identity and a feeling of incompleteness. Devadatta is an insecure husband who is convinced of his wife fondness and love towards his handsome friend Kapila. He also saw an inclination of Padmini, his wife towards Kapila. He observed:

> No woman could resist him- and what does it matter that she's married? What a fool I've been. All these days I only saw that pleading in his eyes stretching out its arms, begging for a favour. But never looked in her depth.
>
> (*Hayavadana* 26)

Frustrated Devadatta beheads himself convinced of his wife's love for Kapila. Kapila takes his own head as well after learning the dreadful deed of his friend and with the terror that he will be held responsible for his murder. He screamed of terror:

> You've cut off your head! You've cut off your head! Oh my dear friend, my brother, what have you done? Were you so angry with me? Did you feel socontempt on me-such abhorrence? No, Devadatta, I can't live without you. Devadatta, my brother, my father, my friend....
>
> (*Hayavadana* 30)

Karnad has employed a fine combination of traditional Indian Folk and Modern Western drama in *Hayavadana*. Padmini too thought of ending her life and pleaded in front of goddess Kali. She utters out of agony:

> Oh God! What's this? Both! Both gone! And didn't even think of me before they went? What shall I do? What shall I do? Oh, Devadatta, what did I do that you left me alone in this state? Was that how much you loved me? And you, Kapila, who looked at me with dog's eye—You too? How selfish you are—How unkind! What shall I do now—where shall I go? How can I go home?
>
> (*Hayavadana* 31)

She decides to kill herself. Goddess Kali takes pity on Padmini and asks her to follow her instructions:

> Put those heads back properly, attach them to their bodies and then press that sword on their necks. They'll come up alive.
>
> (*Hayavadana* 32)

Padmini took the advantage and committed a postmodern contravention. She mixes the head of Devadatta and Kapila by placing Devadatta's head on Kapila's body and Kapila's head on Devadatta's body. They came back to life. Padmini rejoiced for having the mix of Devadatta and Kapila as her husband. Gradually she gave birth to a baby boy with a physical deformity.

Devadatta slowly started loosing his muscular strength and his strong body. Padmini was disappointed:

> What happened to you these days? You sit at home all the day. Never go out. You've forgotten all your swimming and sports?
>
> (*Hayavadana* 49).

Meanwhile, Kapila was in the forest and regained his muscular strengths and his attractive body.

Padmini finds succour in the final act of Sati after Devadatta and Kapila fight in the forest and kill each other with the feeling of deception and disenchantment. Karnad has signified the importance of body in one's identity in the *Hayavadana*. According to Jacob George:

> Karnad's trend-setting play *Hayavadana* strikes a significant note by exploring the dramatic potential of the ancient Indian Myth Legends and folk traditions.... The play revolves around the myth of Lord Ganesha which operates at several levels.
>
> (George 213)

Karnad has blended different issues like love, individuality and sexuality with folk background and has also provided us a glimpse of the past as well as its significance to understand the modern world.

The noted dramatist has been remembered for his several plays and one of his outstanding works is *Naga Mandala* (1988). Girish Karnad says in the 'Preface'to *Naga Mandala*:

> It is based on two oral tales from Karnataka which I heard several years ago from Professor A.K. Ramanujan.

The significance of the role of Cobra in the play is indicated by the sub title *Play of Cobra* given by Karnad.

According to Santosh Gupta *Naga Mandala: A Story of Marriage and Love*:

> *Naga Mandala* is a powerful portrait of the agony and anguish faced by both Men and Women in their development into adult roles and social adjustment in a society where the individual is given little space for self development, awareness and independence as a being.
>
> (Gupta 249)

Appana in the play is a young man with both the parents dead, always used to keep his wife Rani in a locked room in his village. She was devoid of all the happiness and pleasure which a wife aspires for. Appana kept a strict view on Rani and she was not allowed to speak or even smile at the outsider. The play starts with the introduction of Rani:

> A young girl.... Her name ... it doesn't matter. But she was only daughter, so her parents called her Rani. Queen... Queen of the whole wide world. Queen of the long tresses.... For when her hair was tied up in a knot, it was as though a black king Cobra lay curled on the nape of her neck, roil upon glistering coil. When it hung loose, the tresses flowed, a torrent of black, along her young limbs, and got entangled in her silver anklets.
>
> (*Naga Mandala* 6)

Naga, a snake god, associated with Lord Shiva appears to save Rani. Naga helps Rani to overcome the suppression and humiliation she was facing at the hands of Appana. Naga enters her house from the drain in the bathroom and takes the shape of Appana. He tries to give all the happiness whenever they meet. Naga enjoys her company and beauty. She becomes pregnant and was offended by her real husband on her swallown belly. He screams:

> Aren't you ashamed to admit it, you harlot? I locked you in, and yet you managed to find a lover! Tell me who it is. Who did you go to with your sari off?
>
> (*Naga Mandala* 33)

Appana questions her chastity but was later proved by the virtue of the snake trial that the village elders put before her. Appana, after that was sorry for his deeds. He says:

> Forgive me. I am a sinner. I was blind.
>
> (*Naga Mandala* 40)

Rani gets her husband back and enjoys a blissful life. Naga, the snake, wanted to have a final look at Rani. He visits Rani, her husband and her son when were fast asleep. Naga presses Rani's hair to his body, ties a loop and throttles himself to death. When Rani combs her hair on the next morning, a dead cobra falls to the ground. It was later cremated by her son as Rani knew that the Naga was the real father of her son. Naga once again appears in the play at the end and was allowed by Rani to live in her tresses forever.

Karnad has used numerous symbols in the background of a folk tale, which includes flames, snake, avatars, performance of extraordinary ordeals, cremation of the dead snake, and the background chorus. *Naga Mandala* demonstrates the outstanding quality of well reminiscent images and concepts surpassing pragmatism to create a thought-provoking feeling on the readers.

Tale-Danda (1990) is a revolutionary play by Girish Karnad. It focuses on socio, political and religious shortcomings in the society. It deals with a historical event which took place before eight hundred years in the city of Kalyan, the rise and fall of Sharana movement and the issue of Hypergamous marriage- a marriage of Brahmin with the untouchables. Karnad mentions in the 'Preface' to *Tale Danda*:

> I wrote *Tale Danda* in 1989 when the 'Mandir' and "Mandal' movement were beginning to show again how relevant the questions posed by these tinkers were for our age. The horror of subsequent events and the religious fanaticism that has gripped our national life today have only proved how dangerous it is to ignore the solutions they offered.
>
> (Karnad: Preface to *Tale Danda* 1)

Tale Danda represents subtle psychological forces. It opens various remarkable and disruptive evils prevailing in our ancient and medieval culture. The plot of the play is the marriage of a Brahmin girl with an untouchable boy which resulted into violence and bloodshed in the city of Kalyan. The word *Tale Danda* means death by beheading. 'Tale' is Head and 'Danda' is Punishment. Karnad in the 'Preface' explains:

> Offering one's head, either on completion of our vow or in penitence, was a common practice in the medieval Karnataka... During the two decades, in AD 1168, in the city of Kalyan a man called Basavanna assembled a congregation of poets, mystics, social revolutionaries and Philosophers. Together they created an age unmatched in the history of Karnataka for its activity, courageous questioning and social commitment.... They believed in the equality of sexes and celebrated hard, dedicated work. They opposed caste system not just in theory but also in

> practice. This last act brought down upon them the wealth of the orthodox. The movement ended in terror and bloodshed.
>
> (Karnad: Preface to *Tale Danda* 1)

Tale Danda deals with the evils prevailing in the society in the name of caste, creed and marriage as an institution. The play throws light on the superficiality and deformity existing in the so called laws framed by the Hindu religion. It focuses on the need to re-frame, re-evaluate and re-write the laws for the betterment of the society. Bijjala, the king of Kalyan is a barber by caste. He and his forefather have tried all the ways and means to shed their caste. Bijjala utters:

> For ten generations my forefathers ravaged the land as robber barons. For another five they ruled as the trusted feudatories of the emperor himself. They married into every royal family in sight. Brided generations of Brahmins with millions of cows. All this so they could have the caste of Kshatriya branded on their forehead.
>
> (*Tale Danda* 14)

There is a constant caste consciousness in Bijjala. He further explains:

> A man's caste is like the skin on his body. You cannot peel of the skin, whenever the new skin appears people recognise the skin-the same old skin-same old caste-Kshatriyas, Rajputs, Untouchables, herdsmen—This is the special trait of this earth.... I am sixty two... in all these years...The only people whose eyes did not have the shadow of my caste are Sharanas, Basavanna and his People.
>
> (*Tale Danda* 24)

Bijjala has a rich court with great scholars and philosophers. His officer Basavanna, a great poet philosopher, brings together all the great and intelligent people and tries to promote equality in the city of Kalyan. All the great people together shed their caste and became the devotee of Lord Shiva and called themselves Sharanas. To them, caste was insignificant. Their gracious mutiny ends with the marriage of a Brahmin girl—

Kalamati with Sheelavanta, a Panchama boy which later resulted into the war between Sharanas and the conservative Hindus at Kalyan.

Karnad has questioned the concept of untouchability prevailing in the Hindu Society. He comments on the caste system derived from the Hindu Myth associated with four Varnas: Brahmin origins from the mouth of Brahma, Kshatriya from the arms, Vaishyas from the thighs, and Shudras from the feet of Brahma. He has challenged the social system which suppresses the downtrodden in the name of caste. He does not provide any solution to it but raises it to the level which makes it the epitome of caste discrimination. It exposes the adverse consequences which culminates in the tribulations existing in the Indian Society these days.

Karnad's *The Fire and The Rain* (1995) revolves around a seven-year fire sacrifices planned to persuade the God of Rain-Indra to send rain. The sacrifice is to end the destructive annoyance of famine. The play involves the universal subject of Love, Jealousy and Loneliness as it sweeps towards an unanticipated conclusion. The play is originally written in Kannada titled *Agni Mattu Male*. According to Karnad:

> 'Agni' is the Sanskrit word for fire. And, being a Sanskrit word, it carries, even when used in Kannada connotation of holiness, of virtual status, of ceremony, which the Kannada word for fire (benki) does not possesses. Agni is what burns in sacrificial altars, acts as a witness at weeding, and is lit at cremations. It is also the name of the god of Fire.
>
> (*The Fire and the Rain* 63)

The plot of the play is about two sages, Bharadwaja and Raibhya, and their sons. Raibhya was chosen as a Royal Priest in spite of Bharadwaja who was equally endowed with deep spiritual pre-eminence. Paravasu is the eldest son of the great sage Raibhya. He has forsaken all worldly pursuit, his wife, Vishaka, and his brother, Arvasu, for the fire sacrifice which he has performed for seven long years. The fire sacrifice was to mollify the gods and get rain for the drought-ridden land. His dignified position as a Chief Priest of the sacrifice created dispute and hatred within his own family, from his father Raibhya to his cousin Yavakri.

Yavakri was Paravasu's cousin as well as his opponent. He was the son of Bharadwaja. He had the grievance against the world that his father did not receive the respect and appreciation which was his due. He returns home after ten years of meditation, armed with the boon of eternal knowledge bestowed upon him by the Lord Indra. Yavakri wanted to take revenge at any cost. He made a penance and gained knowledge as the boon from Lord Indra. Yavakri is the central character in the play. The Myth of Yavakri is borrowed by Karnad from Mahabharata.

Karnad says:

> *The Myth of Yavakri* (or Yavakrita) occurs in chapter 135-38 of the *Vana Parva* (Forest Canto) of *The Mahabharata*. It is narrated by the ascetic Lomasha to the Pandavas as they wander across the land during their exile. I have met Sanskrit scholars who were aware of the existence of the myth: it is easy to lose track of a short narrative like this in the tangled undergrowth that covers the floor of that epic.
>
> I first came across the story of Yavakri and Paravasu, while still in college, in C. Rajgopalachari's abridgment of *The Mahabharata*. That Rajaji, confronted with the stupendous task of abridging the world's longest epic to about four hundred pages, should not have discarded this seemingly peripheral tale is a tribute to his sensitivity and judgment. It was fortunate for me that Rajaji did not do so, for the moment I read the tale, I knew it had to be turned into a play. For the next thirty-seven years, I struggled with it, trying to fit all the ramifications of the myth within some sort of a manageable shape.
>
> (Preface to *The Fire and the Rain* XI)

Girish Karnad has effectively employed all the dramatic devices to give *The Fire and The Rain* a productive meaning. Karnad has used mythology as a source to discover the hidden connotation of the compound life, a modern man and woman is forced to face. Karnad in *The Fire and the Rain* brings into light the conflict between two brothers. He says:

> The myth can be seen as expressing a deep anxiety which informs the whole of Indian mythology the fear of brother destroying brother. This fear branches out fully and nakedly in *The Mahabharata* where the bonding of brothers within the Pandava and Kuru clans is as close as the enmity between the cousins is ruthless and unrelenting. In *The Ramayana* the fraternal bonding in the Raghu family.
>
> Rama and his brothers-expresses other facets of the same anxiety with the betrayal of surgriva and vibhishana (interestingly in the cause of the ethically correct side) marking the counter points. The story of Arvasu and Paravasu fascinated me as unusual variant of this Indian obsession with fratricide and it seemed logical too that Yavakri should be their cousin through the Mahabharata does not explicitly say so, I cannot remember, when I decided to incorporate the Indra-Vitra legend in my plot, but years later, while rereading the original version, I was astonished to find that right at the beginning of the tale of Yavakri, Lomasha mentions that the whole story took place on the banks of a river in which Indra had bathed to cleanse himself of the sins of killing Vitra! One of the fascinating aspects of dealing with the myths is their self reflexivity.
>
> (*The Fire and the Rain* 68-69)

Tughlaq, the play, was first written in Kannada in 1964 by Girish Karnad and was later translated into English. The play highlights the Sultanate era of fourteenth century but has equally gained contemporary significance. According to Girish Karnad:

> My subject was the life of Muhammad Tughlaq, a fourteenth century Sultan of Delhi, certainly the most brilliant individual ever to ascend the throne of Delhi and also one of the biggest failures. After a reign distinguished for policies that today seem far-sighted to the point of genius, but which in their day earned him the title "Muhammad the Mad" the Sultan ended his career in blood sheds and political chaos. In a sense, the play

> reflected the slow disillusionment my generation felt with the new politics of independent India, the gradual erosion of the ethical norms that had guided the movement for independence and the coming to terms with cynicism and real politik.
>
> (Karnad 27).

Tuglaq, the play, highlights the attempt of Muhammad-bin-Tuglaq to shift the capital of India (from Delhi to Daulatabad) and the change of currency system which resulted in catastrophic consequences because of its futility for the people in his kingdom. He dreamt to build an empire which will be envy of the world. The play portrays the gradual downfall of the Sultan Tuglaq. Karnad writes:

> What struck me absolutely about Tuglaq's history was that it was most contemporary.The fact, here,was the most idealistic, the most intelligent King ever to come on the throne of Delhi... and one of the greatest failures too. And within a span of twenty years this tremendously capable man had gone to pieces. This seemed to me both due to his idealism as well as shortcomings within, him such as his impatience, his cruelty his feeling that he had the only correct answer. And I felt in the early sixties India had also come very far in the same direction—the twenty years period seemed to me very much a striking parallel.
>
> (Karnad 2)

The play reflects a conflict between the ideal and the real, the old and the new. The Old represents the orthodox Muslims who do not support the ideologies of sultan Tuglaq, while the young represents the young people who stand with sultan and his ideologies about unity and equality of any caste and creed. The action of the play begins with:

> *Old Man:* God, What's this country coming to!
>
> *Young Man:* What are you worried about, grandfather? The country's in perfectly in safe hands-safer than any you've seen before.
>
> (*Tuglaq* 1)

The 'safe hands' referred by the young man symbolises the safety which the young man identifies in the regime of sultan Tuglaq. The view of Tuglaq was far beyond his age. He believed in equality where the Hindus and Muslims lives like brothers. In the Introductory speech he stressed:

> My beloved people; you have heard the judgment of the Kazi and seen for yourself how justice works in my kingdom-without any consideration of might or weakness, religion or creed. May this moment burn bright and light up our path towards greater justice, equality, progress and peace-not just peace but more purposeful life.
>
> (*Tuglaq* 3)

Tuglaq had killed his father and his brother for the throne. He decided to shift the capital from Delhi to Daulatabad and received severe criticisms from the people. One of the critical observations is as follows:

> Third Man: This is tyranny, sheer tyranny! Move the capital to Daulatabad! Such things never happened in his father's days. May his soul rest in peace. Now he's got his father's throne. He isn't happy with that and ...
>
> (*Tuglaq* 52)

The play describes the psychology and the ideology of a great emperor in the Indian history. The character of Tuglaq is full of paradoxes. He was unable to foresee the emotional attachment of people towards their native land when he thought of shifting the capital from Delhi to Daulatabad. Tainted politics and corruption in his kingdom resulted in desperation and destruction of his kingdom. Jawaharlal Nehru in *Glimpses of World History* viewed Tuglaq as:

> He (Tuglaq) was a most learned and accomplished man both in Persian and Arabic. He has studied Philosophy and Logic, even Greek Philosophy. He knew something of Mathematics and Science and Medicine. He was a brave man, and for his times quite a paragon of learning and a wonder. And yet, and yet, the paragon was a monster of cruelty and seems to have been quite mad! He came to the throne by killing his own father. He had fantastic notions of conquering Persia and Chine.
>
> (*Glimpses of World History* 214)

Karnad in disguise of Tuglaq has touched upon sensitive socio-political problem like communalism. The focus is on Contemporary India and its politics with interesting story, intricate plot, complex symbolism, subtle irony, copious satire and by the use of theatrical conventions. The play explores the paradox of the idealistic sultan. The treatment given to the play is not Historical though the story is derived from History. P. Bayapa Reddy has highlighted the theatrical skills employed by Girish Karnad in Tughlaq. He says:

> Tughlaq experiments with a verity of theatrical techniques to create visual and auditory images, thereby producing the desired dramatics effect on the stage. By employing a variety of theatrical devices –spectacle, quick shift of scenes, blackout—he tries to control the movement of the play and its impact on he audience. Spectacle refers to all the visual aspects of production, scenery, costume, make-up and the business and the movement of the actor....the very appearance of Tughlaq in his striking costume adds a lot to the element of spectacle in the play.
>
> (Bayapa Reddy 153).

The wide use of the native themes and techniques in his plays presents a picture of the intrinsic national identity. The plays of Karnad serve varied functions like providing directions, amusement, happiness, harmony and moral upliftment. He attempts to present the joys and sorrows in human life through different gestures and dramatic techniques. This made him one of the foremost playwright on the contemporary Indian stage. He struggled to break the illusions of the theatre and has forced the audience to respond rationally to the action of his plays. He tried to interpret history in terms of the present and vice versa by exploring some basic human emotions and sentiments. All his plays are enriched with infinite variety, tantalising portrayal of characters and emotional, spiritual and intellectual appeal that captivate audience.

Works Cited

Ananthamurthy, U.R. 'Introduction', *Tuglaq*. New Delhi: Oxford University Press, 1972, p. vii

Babu, Sarat. M. "The Concept of Chastity and *Naga- Mandala'* in Jaydipsinh Bodiya (ed.), op.cit., 248.

Bayapa Reddy. 'The Theatrical Representation of history : Girish Karnad's *Tughlaq', the plays of Girish Karnad Critical Perspective*, (ed.) Jaydipsinh. New Delhi: Prestige, 1999.

Dhawan, R.K., 'Girish Karnad: The Man and the Writer' in *The Plays of Girish Karnad: Critical Perspectives,* (ed) Jaydipsingh Dodiya, New Delhi: Prestige Book, 1999. p.15.

Dharwadkar, Aparna Bhargana. 'Introduction' *Collected Plays: Tuglaq, Hayavadana, Bali: The Sacrifice, Naga Mandala* (Play with a Cobra). Vol. One.

Dhanavel, P. *The Indian Imagination of Girish Karnad.* New Delhi: Prestige Books, 2000.

George, Jacob C. 'Myth as Fulcrum; Lord Ganesha as Dramatic Presence in *Hayavadana'*. in *The Plays of Girish Karnad: Critical Perspective.* (ed) by Jaydipshingh Dodiya, New Delhi: Prestige Books, 1999, p.213.

Gupta, Santosh. '*Naga Mandala*: A Story of Marriage and Love', *The Play of Girish Karnad: Critical Perspectives.* (ed.) Jaydipsingh Dodiya. New Delhi: Prestige Books, 1999. p. 249.

Karnad, Girish. *Three Plays: Naga Mandala, Hayavadana, Tuglaq*. Delhi: Oxford University Press, 1998. p.3

_______. *Hayavadana*, Chennai: Oxford University Press, 2000.

_______. *Naga Mandala*. Delhi: Oxford University Press, 1997. p.6

_______. *Tale Danda*. Delhi: Ravi Dayal Publisher, 1993.

_______. 'Notes', *The Fire and the Rain.* Delhi: Oxford University Press, 1998.

_______. 'Introduction to Three Plays'. *The Plays of Girish Karnad—Critical Perspective.*(ed.) Jaydipsinh Dodiya. New Delhi: Prestige, 1974 p. 21-37.

Kurtkoti, Kirtinath. 'Introduction' to *Hayavadana*, op.cit., p.V.

New Theatre Quarterly, Vol. XI, No. 44. November 1995, p. 362.

Nehru, Jawaharlal. *The Glimpses of World History.* New Delhi: OUP, 1982.

Paul, Rajendra. 'Girish Karnad Interviewed'. *Enact,* No. 54 (June 1971), n.p.

http://southasiaconference.wisc.edu/yayati.htm

http://www.ithaca.edu/fleff/blogs/south_asian_spaces/indianness_and_girish_karnads_plays

7

Gender Politics in Mahesh Dattani's *Tara*

— Lata Mishra

A folk song from Uttar Pradesh describes best the position of women in Indian society. The various aspects of preference for a son in India reveal a complex nexus of cultures, religions, traditions and economics. An attempt is made to approach the gender aspects dealt with, in the text of Mahesh Dattani's *Tara* through Kate Millett's *Sexual Politics*— that theorises the relationship between sex difference and sexual politics. The work seeks to address the impact of the material bases of sexual difference upon sexual politics. Millet is more interested in exploring the ramifications of sex difference in relation to the economic and political sphere. For her sex difference may produce differences in consciousness. But these differences are seen as historically set revelation of oppressed consciousness. Theorists like Millet, Juliet Mitchell or Beauvoir consider that dominating section or males of the society have throughout history treated sexual difference with repressive results for women. The main aim of these writers is to theorise how and in what ways sexual difference is positioned in the field of power relations, as politics; and how these relations might be changed, once the long oppressed women understand it.

Within a theoretical framework Millet defines politics as an *unequal* system of power relations. She views patriarchy as both a universal and basic system of political oppression. With this attitude Millett theorises how various power stıuctures in different societies produce varying levels and kinds of sexual oppression. Sexual politics is a system that is perpetuated by the necessity of women's consent to and participation in their own oppression. Kate Millet in *Sexual Politics* states that 'sex' is a biological construction and 'gender' is a social construction. This clearly implies conventional conditioning stereotype of the gender roles in society. Usually man and woman do not change roles and if they do they face strong opposition and lose opportunities for selfpromotion and mental growth. Even feminine and masculine qualities are compartmentalised.

Literature is a social institution in which the concrete outlook of humanity receives its expression. Indian writing in English has made its notch in multitudinous human concerns in the hands of a great number of Indian writers. Indian English drama is written with social consciousness, experiencing the crises and tensions of the struggling classes and their protests. Theatre has always been one of the most powerful media of sensitisation and social communication in India. Communal violence and conflicts arising out of caste, religious, and gender identities have found a unique resonance and representation in post-Independence Indian theatre. There is a deep concern for the exploited masses, a longing for freedom from the clutches of age-old burden and a search for newer paths that would lead the masses away from unjust existing social system.

Theatre reveals many salient aspects of urban violence by the staging or enactment of violence. These dramatists await a society with equal rights, privileges and opportunities for all. Their revolt against the social, political and economic problems is, in fact, a quest for an ideal society. They try to create a social awareness among the common people through the means of drama. Contemporary dramatists like Girish Karnad, Vijay Tendulkar, Mohan Rakesh, Badal Sircar, Manjula Padmanablian, Mahesh Dattani and others have made significant contribution to the development of Indian English drama. Various issues like gender discrimination, communalism, child (sexual) abuse and homosexuality etc., find an honest and candid delineation in Dattani's plays. He is the first Indian playwright writing in English to be awarded the Sahitya Akademi award. He has an indepth understanding of complex human relations. He expresses himself naturally and clearly. He writes on the burning issues that beset the postindependence Indian society. He has chronicled the social victims and the follies, foibles and prejudices of Indian society. He criticises and exposes the Indian middle class in many of his plays. Western education has a liberating influence on women bringing promise of a new life outside the claustrophobic environment of 'purdah' and other conservative measures. Angelie Multani comments:

> Dattani's themes reflect and comment on the ordinary and everyday conflicts of so many urban people who may be living in transitional periods of history, caught between the firm undertow of tradition and social values and the pull of modernity and globalisation.
>
> (Multani 11)

Dattani depicts the marginalised groups of society. He shows the mean, ugly and unhappy aspects of human beings. He is a spokesperson of all the marginalised people. Going by tradition, women's lives have been organised and manipulated by patriarchy in all ages, all cultures and all countries by establishing values, norms, roles, gender perceptions and idealism that prescribe unequal means, methods and routes to achieve the so called wholeness for women. Dattani often uses the family unit as his locale and narrative enclosure. The family is a vital institution. It is the primary social unit in any community; the individual's opening into the wider social network. As the first site of development, the family provides sustenance to the individual and sets the conditions of growth. Challenged with the individual's desire for independence and growth, the family may be denotatively seen as a closed door or an open door; as a prison or a gateway to freedom. Dattani takes the action out of the streets and brings the tension into the home. The fragmentation of the family, the deceit, discord, and power equations within the family are portrayed with sensitivity and psychological insight.

The play selected for this paper is *Tara*. Which addresses issues like, role of women in public and private domains, female infanticide, mother-daughter relationship and assertion of personal identity. The helplessness of women in Indian society has been depicted in the play. How preference is given to a male child over a female child has been highlighted by Dattani. Whenever the question of choice comes between male and female, it is the male who is chosen. Women also need space to breathe freely and flourish.

Tara also brings to light the bizarre reality of the woman playing second fiddle to man. The viciousness of the grandfather and his mother not only takes away the life of the girl but also ruins the life of the boy who was very much attached to the sister. The fateful leg which was preferred to be given to the boy, could not only make Tara a perfect woman but also save her life as the leg would have been complete success with Tara's body. It was the male oriented choice because of which the leg was given to the boy and became useless after a few days, making Chandan handicapped. Tara represents the girl-child born in any Indian family whether urban or rural. The condition is worsened when the girl is handicapped.

Dattani illustrates the continuous struggle of contemporary urban Indian in familial, social and cultural spheres to create his individual identity. The dramatist's strength lies in his depiction of family tensions, the elusiveness of memories and how dreams and disappointments are passed from one generation to the next. The play proves that each person in a family experiences microcosm differently. Only by synthesizing these disparate views do we grasp the full flavour of events. This paper explores the issues of social constraints, forced submission, and unfulfilled dreams. Kate Millet writes:

> Patriarchy's chief institution is the family. It is both a mirror of and a connection with the larger society; a patriarchal unit within a patriarchal whole. Mediating between the individual and the social structure, the family effects control and conformity where political and other authorities are insufficient. As the fundamental instrument and the foundation unit of patriarchal society the family and its roles are prototypical. Serving as an agent of the larger society, the family not only encourages its own members to adjust and conform, but acts as a unit in the government of the patriarchal state which rules its citizens through its family heads. Even in patriarchal

> societies where they are granted legal citizenship, women tend to be ruled through the family alone and have little or no formal relation to the state.
>
> (Millet 33)

Tara is a picture of the modern society which claims to be liberal and advanced in its thought and action but as regards to children there is still a difference between male and female child. Dattani has just made an effort to highlight one of the atrocities perpetrated on a female, mocking at the hue and cry made for female emancipation and equality with men on all grounds. Tara is victim of patriarchal society. Chandan, the son believes in cooperation and equality but Patel does not share the views and perception of his son's generation. When insisted by father to come to office Chandan asks the company of the sister as well:

> Patel : I am disappointed in you. From now on you are coming to the office with me. I can't see you rotting at home!
>
> Chandan : I don't want to go to the office!
>
> Patel : You will come with me to the office until your college starts.
>
> Chandan : I don't want to go to college! (Fighting his tears.) Not without Tara! If she is going in for surgery, I'll miss a year too!
>
> Patel : You will not. I won't allow it.
>
> Chandan : I will not go to college without Tara! (29-30)

The family is a vital institution. It is the primary social unit in any community; the individual's opening into the wider social network. As the first site of development, the family provides sustenance to the individual and sets the conditions of growth. Challenged with the individual's desire for independence and growth, the family may be denotatively seen as a closed door or an open door; as a prison or a gateway to freedom. Dattani talks of the concerns and perceptions of the new woman and shows how they are not satisfied with the status of a housewife bestowed on them by the male dominated society. He shows how those who stood discrimination in the past want their daughters not to do what they had to do. He sums up the change he discems in the attitude of women of yesteryear and shows how passionate they are about their daughter's independence. Patriarchy as a system supports hierarchy, male-dominance, and egotism, and expects that women will always aggrandise men and support them emotionally. Within the patriarchal social world, women regarded as feminine must take pleasure in being dominated and excluded from decision-making in the public sphere. Dattani, in the play demonstrates the mother's efforts to encourage Tara to take her own decisions. She tells Chandan what she expects women to do these days:

Bharati : It's time Tara decided what she wants to be. Women have to do that as well these days. She must have a career.

Chandan : She can do whatever she wants. Grandfather's trust will leave us both money, isn't it?

Bharati : Yes. But she must have something to do! She can't be—aimless all her life. (26) — It's all right while she is young. It's all very cute and comfortable when she makes witty remarks. But let her grow up. Yes, Chandan—The world will tolerate you. The world will accept you—but not her. (27)

Concepts of masculinity and femininity occupy central position in building of the nation. Patriarchal system in India had ensured power to men and the subordination to women. Thus, women are considered to be essentially passive/emotional. They have being assigned procreative function and home-making. Hence, they are confined to the private or domestic sphere. This pushes them to the periphery, whereas men, who are thought to be naturally active/rational are accorded a prominent role in the public or political sphere. Gender roles are:

> socially and culturally defined prescriptions and beliefs about the behaviour and emotions of men and women.
>
> (Anselmi 195).

Patel	:	I was just thinking—it may he a good idea for you to come to the office with me.
Cnandan	:	What for?
Patel	:	Just to get a feel of it.
Chandan	:	You can take Tara. She 'll make a great business woman.
		Patel refuses to accept what his son says:
Patel (firm)	:	Chandan. I think I must insist that you come.
Chandan	:	We'll both come with you
Patel	:	No! (6)

Men think that there are certain activities, which are meant only for women, and hence if a boy is seen doing a work earmarked for girls, they are ridiculed for doing what they are not supposed to do. Chandan helps his mother knit but his father does not like his son doing what he considers a girl's activity. Chandan represents the modern age man who respects the other sex and feels gratitude for them for all that they do to make their life comfortable and happy. For Patel knitting is a female activity whereas Chandan does not believe in this kind of division.:

Chandan	:	Mummy's knitting and I'm helping her sort out her mistake.
Patel	:	Let Tara do it.
Chandan	:	It's okay.
Patel	:	Give it to her.
Chandan	:	Why?...
Patel	:	Chandan. leave that damn thing alone!
Bharati (frantic)	:	Go! Chandan, just go!
Patel to *Bharati*	:	How dare you do this to him?
Chandan	:	Wait a minute, daddy. She never asked me to do any—
Patel	:	Can't you even look after the children ?
Chandan	:	Look daddy. It's—

Patel : What did you do the whole day, huh? Watch video?

Bharati : I can't think of things for them to do all the time!

Patel : But you can think of turning him into a sissy-teaching him to knit!

Chandan : Daddy, that's unfair. (29)

Dattani has also raised the issue of killing of a girl child. Though the people of this country worship female in the form of the goddess, they don't hesitate or feel guilt pangs in killing the same female form in the womb. All the propagandas of equality between male and female and equal opportunities to women in all the fields are belied. 'Female foeticide' speaks of a whole system gone corrupt. It seems to have become the accepted norm. With the laws coming up against female infanticide, more sophisticated techniques like ultrasound are now sought after. Entire society seems to be involved in conspiracy against women, leading society to elimination of half of its population. Such monstrous practices are becoming more and more rampant in a society that is fast losing its secular, social, and humanistic fabric. Dattani talks of female infanticide and shows how new born girls are killed and how insensitive we have become. Roopa and Tara belonging to two different sections of society differ in their perception as well. Roopa accepts the predicament of girls and tells Tara of what Patels did with their daughters. Tara feels disturbed at this information:

Roopa : Since you insist, I will tell you. It may not be true. But this is what I have heard

The Patels in the old days were unhappy with getting girl babies—you know dowry and things like that-so they used to drown them in milk.(Pause)

Tara : In milk?

Roopa : So when people asked about how the baby died, they could say that she choked while drinking her milk (27)

In the context of India there is particularly the issue of dowry that plays a significant role in respect to gender relations. Dowry, was given as a gift by the bride's family to the husband's family, and was regarded as a daughter's compensation for not inheriting any property due to the nature of Indian inheritance laws. It is certainly a great injustice to the daughter that the inheritance her family makes her believe she receives at her wedding is linked to marriage; which means that she—in contrast to the sons in the family—does not receive any share in case she does not marry or has no place in her parents' home, if divorced. This issue is dealt with in detail in Roy's *God of Small Things*. Dattani also touches this theme. Chandan and his father appear to belong to different worlds. When Chandan is informed of his inheritance by maternal grandfather he immediately shows concern for his sister.

Patel	:	He left you a lot of money.
Chandan	:	And Tara?
Patel	:	Nothing.
Chandan	:	Why?
Patel	:	It was his money. He could do what he wanted with it.(40)

Bharati's father, a politician and would-be Chief Minister of the state is a representative of the Indian society. It is his decision that the leg be transplanted to Chandan, though it would do good to Tara. He further emphasises his preference for male grand child by leaving property to Chandan and excluding Tara from any share. R.D. Laing speaks of the position of mother in a family. He compares a family to a flower with mother at its core and children as its petals. Absence or indifference of mother creates emotional vacuum in the later lives of the children. Nothing is more powerful than the memories created by a child's experiences. The child's memories fashion the adult's life. Tara dies in a shock when she learns that it is her mother who is involved in the conspiracy of her separation from Chandan. Dattani seems to convince the women that they themselves are responsible for their sufferings. It is Bharati's prejudice against daughters that leads to the misery. She suffers with nervous breakdown. Chandan suffers with guilt complex for something he was not even responsible for. Tara loses her life. Had Bharati used her intelligence her family would have been saved from such a disaster. In place of having taken firm decision, she grumbles all her life:

Bharati : I wish your father would pay more attention to Tara.

Chandan : He does. He doesn't like to show his affection.

Bharati : Don't tell me about your father. He is more worried about your career than hers. (26)

Dattani establishes that mother-daughter relationship is ultimately subordinated to the directives of patriarchy. If the parents are educated, the steps taken by them are lamentable. Bharati's father, a rich person plays a major role in the decision on the 'fateful' leg. This decision sours the relationship between Patel and Bharati. With a guilt-laden heart, Bharati tries to compensate the loss of leg with more show of affection and love to Tara. She also tries to expiate by the act of donating kidney to her daughter which was ultimately futile. This incident deeply disturbs Chandan as well. He migrates to London with a new name, as an attempt to create a new identity. He tries to get relieved of this pain that he has carried whole of his life by writing a play:

> *Dan:* Give me a moment and the pain will subside. Then I can function again. [pause, more controlled now] Yes. The material is there. But the craft is yet to come. Like the amazing Dr. Thakkar, I must take something from Tara and give it myself. Make capital of my trauma, my anguish, and make it my tragedy. To masticate them in my mind and spit out the result to the world, in anger. (Slowly, as if in a trance, picks up the typed sheets and starts tearing them as he speaks). My progress so far, I must admit, has been zero .... (379)

Tara never loses her self-esteem. She says, "l am strong. My mother has made me strong." (8) She is a fighter who at times expresses her anger at the outside world. She does not feel let down when people mock at her physical disability. She identifies herself with Beethoven, the musician with a disability who established his greatness in spite of being unable to hear his own creations. The women of early generations were scaled in accordance with their physical charms but the new age women like Tara desire to make place for themselves in the world on the basis of their intelligence. On being ridiculed by Roopa she retorts:

> *Roopa* : How dare you! You one-legged thing!
>
> *Tara* : I'd sooner be one-eyed, one-armed and one-legged than be an imbecile like you. (49)

Tara is wise enough to assess her father's dislike for her. Chandan's attempt to convince her of her father's care brings out her bitterness.

> *Chandan* : You should You should care—for people around You.
>
> *Tara* : How do, you expect me to feel anything for anyone if they don't give me any feeling to begin with? Why is it wrong for me to be without feeling? Why are you asking me to do something that nobody has done for me?
>
> *Chandan* : I don't know. Somehow it is wrong to be so-selfish.
>
> *Tara* : Selfish? Yes. I am. I have the right to be selfish, like everyone else! (51)

Feminism means different things to different people, ranging from a wish to change and challenge the whole existing order of things to the desire to bring about a more balanced and saner equality between the sexes and achieve a respectable individual liberty for women with their natural instincts and characteristics intact. Though equality with all its implications at various levels of society is a major issue, one of the fundamental areas where this equality matters and is desired even by the most conservative standards of feminism is in the area of marriage. The goal of feminism is to eliminate sexist oppression by the patriarchal society.

Feminism as a movement might have originated in the West, but with the deterioration in the status of women in India and the subsequent efforts made during the freedom struggle to pave the way for equal access to education and equal status, some of the issues evoked by the West were bound to be taken up by their Indian counterparts. Dattani explores that tender area of characters which has been neglected for years in India. He encourages the assertion of feminine identity and self-esteem, while promoting social acceptance of a more complete and diverse set of social roles for women. His projection of characters, therefore, marks a new age. His rebel-victims are not the outcome of an eccentric vision but they are indicative of the emergence of this disquieting stance which modern literate stands to project. The Indian woman had to strive to attain recognition for her individuality and acceptance by society, of an existence even beyond her gender-based roles. Through the depiction of the female characters, the text questions the attitude of present day India to women, their position in the society and their rights, challenging thus the limits of their freedom. The society, as it is revealed in the text, is still a traditional one, accepting any changes with great reluctance.

Works Cited

Anselmi, D.L. & Law, A.L. "*Questions of Gender: Perspectives & Paradoxes*." London: McGraw Hill, 1998.

Dattani, Mahesh. *Tara*. New Delhi: Ravi Dayal Publisher. 1995.

Laing, R.D. *The Politics of the Family and Other Essays*. London: Tavistock Publications, 1971.

Millett, Kate. *Sexual Politics*. Chicago: University of Illinois Press, 2000.

Multani, Angelie. *Mahesh Dattani's Plays: Critical Perspectives*. New Delhi: Pencraft International, 2007.

8

Need for Communal Harmony: An Analysis of Mahesh Dattani's *Final Solutions*

— D. Suganya

> If you don't like the way to the world is,
> you change it. You have an obligation to change it.
> You just do it one step at a time.
>
> — *Robertson Davies*

Art and artist cannot transform entirely the social conditions prevalent over night. But the sensitive artists record even the minute changes, occurring in society like a seismograph indicating both social upheavals as well as positive signs of growth.

> Dattani is one of the few Indian playwrights in English and the only one in recent years to have raised important social issues in his plays, which are firmly based in a contemporary, immediately recognisable domestic context.
>
> (Multani 58)

Social issues in general include problems of the society, which also affect the individuals because each and every individual is a part of the society. Most of the individuals do not get involved or they are not interested in the problems, which personally do not affect them. But it is a very dangerous attitude and the Individual may suffer the after effects at least in future.

One of the fiercest political rivalries existing today between India and Pakistan is motivated by religious differences. The Partition of British colonial India into the free nations of India and Pakistan did not solve the problem between the two. Hindus and Muslims are still at loggerheads—through their nations—the focal point of the strife being the disputed territory of Kashmir.

Communal riot is a major problem, which curtails the country's development. Communal harmony is the first and foremost requisition for changing India's position from a developing country into a developed country. The firm belief of India's former President Dr. A.P.J. Abdul Kalam is that India's development lies in the hands of children who will be the future citizens. Brotherly attitude will surely do this. It is the duty of the elders to inculcate this attitude in children and eradicate the problem to develop communal harmony.

Final Solutions is a stage play which deals with communalism, religious fanaticism, and the Hindu-Muslim riot mostly endangered by self-centred politicians. The playwright seems to fling a mild satire on those fanatics who do not understand the true purport of religion. On the second level of meaning the play also, suggests the deep-rooted hatred planted by our forefathers. In 'A Note on the Play' Alyque Padamsee writes:

> The demons of communal hatred are not out on the street... they are lurking inside ourselves. (*FS* 161)

Final Solutions deals sensitively with the event of Partition and the incidents following that and how it has continued for generations in the name of communal riots:

> *Final Solutions* is a very serious and delicate drama on well-worn subject of Partition, the violence it unleashed and its after effects which are still reflected in the communal riots that often arise. Dattani, however, is successful in touching the deep sense of futility which fills the heart of those involved in committing such violence.
>
> (Tyagi 195)

In the play *Final Solutions*, the grandmother Hardika in her young age had seen the consequences of the partition and had developed a deep-rooted hatred in her mind and she did not change that even when she grew up. Hardika and her family had lived in Hussainabad at the time of partition and her father had been killed during the clash between the communities. Her son Ramnik was a liberal-minded person. His wife Aruna had certain indepth religious beliefs. She feels that the people other than her community are untouchables. She is proud of her religion. Smita, Ramnik's daughter the new generation girl, entertains no such discrimination.

The action of the play started when a communal riot rocked the city. Two Muslim boys Bobby and Javed sought refuge in Ramnik's house. Ramnik agreed to safeguard the boys from the angry mob waiting outside to kill them and allowed them to stay in his house for that night. Hardika did not agree with the decision of her son Ramnik and she blamed the boys for what had happened to her family long ago. Javed immediately pointed out the illogical line of thinking and argued:

> You blame us for what happened fifty years ago. Today, if something happens to my sister, can I blame you?
>
> (*FS* 222)

Ramnik was a liberal-minded person. He wanted to be a good son to his mother and a good husband to Aruna, and an understanding father to his daughter Smita, and a good civilised host for the boys who took refuge in his house. Hence, he reasoned with his mother not to blame the boys for the riots but tried to support them:

Ramnik : Don't blame them.

Hardika : You can't understand how I feel.

Ramnik : I can. They are not to blame. (*FS* 223)

In fact, Ramnik did not want Smita to give company to Hardika, for he felt that Hardika would tell unwanted things to Smita because of the bitter memories about the minority people, "I don't want her telling my daughter that those people are all demons!" (*FS* 172). The course of the play unravels the consequences and each character's reaction to such decision.

Ramnik agreed to safeguard the boys and allowed them to stay in his house for that night. Javed asked Ramnik what was the root cause of the problemand Ramnik traced it to the huge Mohalla and the Muslim family who lived there:

> The rathyatra started as it does every year from the Vishnu Mandir a few hours before midnight. It passed Shanti Road, Nehru Gardens, and when it reached Kareem Bagh, the trouble started. Nobody knew how. They say someone threw stones at the idol. Someone else says that it was sabotage. It was very unfortunate that the axle of the chariot broke and it keeled over right there in the Mohalla. The idols were broken. (*FS*193)

Smita, Ramnik's daughter recognised Javed and Bobby. She already knew them. Javed was her friend Tasneem's brother and Bobby, Tasneem's fiancée. But Ramnik doubted that, for when she called Tasneem's father he did not say anything about his son. Only then Javed said, "My father didn't tell you about me, because he didn't know where I was. (Defiantly) I don't live with my parents" (*FS*189).

Ramnik was still unconvinced and asked why he had been there to see his sister if he did not live with the parents. Javed sarcastically replied that not only Hindus, even Muslims loved their sisters and brothers. Smita also revealed that he was expelled from his family because he joined the people who indulged in communal riots in the sensitive places. The author brought the unlawful activities of such boys through his powerful dialogue.

Smita (to Ramnik)	:	They hire him! They hire such people!
Ramnik	:	They who?
Smita	:	Those ... parties! They hire him! That's how he makes a living.
		They bring him and many more to the city to create riots. To ... throw the first stone? (*FS* 195)

Dattani clearly pictures how the youngsters are brainwashed and their minds are poisoned by the fanatic people. Javed explained how he came to the city and how he was connected with the riots. He came to the city in a bus and there were a dozen of people like him, later many people joined them and they spent the afternoon by playing cards and then the van came to pick them up.

The youth who came along with Javed provided him with stones and he hit the mob with stones and more people joined him in the rampage. And then he felt something else in his hand. It was a knife and he moved forward holding the knife tightly. Javed moved towards the chariot pushing the people away and as he went near, he heard the bell ringing and he saw the poojari's frightened face. But at the moment, he got confused and Bobby took advantage of the moment and pulled Javed away. But somebody else picked up the knife and stabbed the poojari. Feeling angry, Ramnik wanted to send him out of his house. Without feeling sorry for what he had done, Javed shouted:

> Ha! You want to throw me to the mob? I'm no different from them! No different, do you hear? I do what they are doing—only on a different street! [...] I was there on that street when the rath yatra came and I did precisely that! (*FS* 204)

Ramnik called him a hired hoodlum, but Bobby said that Javed did not do that for money but he volunteered to do it. But Ramnik thought it made Javed all the more repulsive and what the latter did was unforgivable. He had no idea about what brought a change in Javed's attitude. Even then he requested Bobby to bring him to his shop so that he can offer a job. In support of his friend Bobby narrated the minor incident which turned Javed into such a man:

> [...] We were playing cricket on our street with the younger boys. The post man delivered our neighbour's mail. [...] He was in a hurry and asked Javed to hand the letter over to the owner. Javed took the letter ... and opened the gate.

> Immediately a voice boomed, 'what do you want?' I can still remember Javed holding out the letter and mumbling something, his usual firmness vanishing in a second. 'Leave it on the wall', the voice ordered. Javed backed away, really frightened. We all watched as the man came out with a cloth in his hand. He wiped the letter before picking it up, he then wiped the spot on the wall the letter was lying on and he wiped the gate! (*FS* 200)

The postman, when he came out of the next house, was shocked to see this and he consoled the boys that the man was slightly crazy. The next day, the neighbour was praying and the prayer bell was ringing continuously. Suddenly the neighbour came out screaming furiously on the streets. All the boys peeped out. None could understand a word he was saying. Later Bobby came to know that someone had dropped pieces of meat and bones into his backyard. Bobby guessed who was the culprit. He admitted:

> I didn't speak to Javed for many days after that. I was frightened of him. For months whenever we played cricket and heard the bell, we remembered that incident and we avoided looking at Javed. And for Javed,he was–in his own eyes–no longer the neighbourhood hero.(*FS* 201)

Ramnik asked Bobby how he felt when he heard the prayer bell and he replied that he was as angry as Javed but he didn't throw meat into his neighbour's backyard. Instead, he felt ashamed of being a minority person in the society. He was also pretending he was not a part of his own community. Bobby after that incident felt ashamed of being a minority person in the society. He was also pretending he was not a part of his own community. He even changed his name from Babban to Bobby so that nobody can identify his religion. Ramnik apologised that his own community was also to be blamed for the incident that changed both Javed and Bobby. He offered them some milk to drink and also offered a job for Javed in his shop.

> In *Final Solutions* we see the frenzied, demonic power of blind faith and superstition—the power of prejudice, hatred and resentment dominates the play. (Kanthan 32)

Ramnik gave the boys some milk and it had symbolic significance. He, further, added that when anyone searches for peace it would be hidden in the armpits of the majority.

Like Javed's neighbour who provoked his arrogant character, Aruna, Ramnik's wife also had certain religious beliefs. She had firm faith that the God to whom she prayed everyday protected her house. She did not want her husband to bring trouble on their heads by protecting the boys from the angry mob outside but when Ramnik explained to her about the danger lurking outside for the boys, she developed a soft corner for them and agreed to give protection. But her generosity did not extend to the level of giving water to the boys. She was reluctant to oblige her husband's request. Guessing the conflict in her mind, Bobby defensively said that they did not want water though they were very thirsty. This small incident clearly brought out the religious intolerance and the practice of untouchability, which were deeply ingrained in the minds of people.

> Aruna holds the glasses with her thumbs and index fingers, on the sides which have not been touched by their lips. She takes them away and keeps them separate from other glasses. (*FS* 185)

A little while later, the mob outside dispersed and the situation became calm. After confirming with Ramnik whether it was safe to go outside, Aruna wanted to go out with Smita to collect drinking water from the tap outside. When Javed came forward to help her, Aruna recoiled with horror. Only then, Javed realised the situation. When Smita picked up the small brass pot from the pooja room, and left, Aruna in a tone of confession explained to Javed that she had her customs and beliefs and she had nothing against them. All religions are equal and one but the ways to God are many. She also added that usually they would not allow outsiders to fetch their water for they used to bathe their God with it. It must be pure and uncontaminated. Smita felt that, Aruna's explanation worsened the situation further. She defensively explained that being a Hindu stifled her mother. Though she knew her mother was wrong, she could not openly express her views. Moreover, Aruna was proud of her religion and would not listen to her daughter's advice. Aruna in turn tried to explain how she developed that kind of attitude:

> I have always taken pride in my religion. I never felt my mother was stifling me. I was so happy knowing that I was protected. I grew up listening to stories of our Gods and how they slew the demons to protect the good people of their land. And I was thankful to my mother for showing me the path of truth. I was happy. (*FS* 211)

But Smita finally won Aruna over to her way of thinking and made her agree to the boys' filling up the water. Still Aruna did not want Javed to touch God's vessel. Defying her mother's intention, Smita makes Javed to fill God's vessel.

> *Javed* : Have you filled your God's water?
>
> *Smita* : Oh I forgot. Here, you fill it. (Thrusts the pot to Javed) He recoils and the pot falls down, making an unpleasant noise.
>
> *Javed* : I don't think we should fool around with that.
>
> *Smita* : No, I suppose you are right. That is why I wanted you to fill it. To prove that it is not going to fly off into the heavens with your touch, putting an eternal curse on our family. (*FS* 218)

The next morning the boys were getting ready to move out of Ramnik's house. At that time Aruna who was preparing for the pooja, rang the bell. Javed stiffened and Bobby realised what was happening to him. Trying to clear the prejudice Bobby moved towards the pooja room. Realising his intention, Aruna ordered him to stop but Bobby entered the pooja room and

> [...] suddenly picks up the image of Krishna which is tiny enough to sit in his palm (*FS* 224).

Aruna begged him to put that back. But

> Bobby (extends his hands and shows the image to every one.) See! See! I am touching God. [...] Your God! My flesh is holding Him! Look, Javed! And he does not mind! (*FS* 224).

Bobby tried to put reason into Aruna's thoughts and he showed that God hadn't burnt him into ashes and God didn't cry that he had been contaminated and God rested in his hands and He knew Bobby didn't harm him. He broke Aruna's false beliefs about God and religion. Bobby addresses Aruna thus:

> You can bathe Him day and night, you can splash holy waters on Him but you cannot remove my touch from His form. You cannot remove my smell with sandal paste and attars and fragrant flowers because it belongs to a human being who believes, and tolerates, and respects what other human beings believe. That is the strongest fragrance in the world. (*FS* 225)

In horror, Aruna cried that there was nothing left that is sacred in this world. But Bobby concluded if they understood and believed one another, nothing could be destroyed. He told Hardika if she was willing to forget, he was also willing to tolerate.

> Though Dattani's play is, at least on the surface, about the events that take place one night when two Muslim boys take refuge from a mob in a Hindu household, it is really a remarkable examination of the prejudice and deeply held mistrust which lies just beneath the skin of our liberal, secular attitudes and which has a tendency to surface and surprise us. Dattani takes the action out off the streets and brings the tension into the home. (Benegal 61)

According to Dattani, theatre has always been a mirror for man. Theatre is a reflection of his world of eternal conflicts that plague him, through which he has experienced a gamut of human emotions. He believes that:

> The magic of the theatre is in reconstructing space, time, weight and flow, the essential components of life itself. To me the theatre is the art of representation and not of imitation. A complacent audience is a dead audience. A static play is a dead play (Subramanyam 132).

Theatre is a very complex language created by man. Drama must portray the human condition.

Dattani observes great care in stage directions to explain the stage lay out. He clearly explains the stage set-up for each act in his plays. In this play *Final Solutions*:

> The stage is dominated by a horse shoe- or crescent-shaped ramp, with the ends sloping to stage level. Most of the action of the mob/chorus takes place on the ramp. (*FS*165)

Within the confines, the ramp is a structure suggesting the house of the Gandhis' with just wooden blocks for furniture. However, upstage, perhaps on an elevation, is a detailed kitchen and a pooja room. On another level is a room with a roll top desk and an oil lamp converted to an electric one, suggesting that the period is the late 1940s. There are several instances when Hardika, the grand mother, and Daksha, the young bride, are on this level at the same time, although they are the same person. Lighting is also given the same importance. Hardika should be positioned and lit in such a way that the entire action of the play is seen through her eyes.

The role of chorus in this play is remarkable. Through chorus, Dattani seems to communicate to the audience the present setting of communal passion and disgust. There are five Hindu masks and five Muslim masks. The mob/chorus becomes the chorus when they 'wear' either the Hindu or the Muslim masks.

> Well through this beautiful technique of masking and unmasking the some person, the author seems to speak a lot of things. Religion is one; God is one; but the interpreters are different. (Prasad 211)

Final Solutions is a powerful and disturbing play. It ends with the redemptive power of Bobby whose touching of the idol cauterises the wounds of a society divided by communal and religious violence. The play ends on a note of hope with Ramnik telling Hardika "If you call them, they will come" (Kanthan 33).

The play is really a remarkable examination of the prejudice and deeply held mistrust which lies just beneath the skin of our liberal secular attitudes and which has a tendency to surface and surprise us.

> Dattani takes the action out off the streets and brings the tension into the home. (Benegal 61)

The issue, which Dattani has raised in this play, is not confined to only our land, but it has assumed a universal character.

> It is a confrontation between Arabs and Jews, whites and blacks, Hindus and Muslims, traditional and modern, and above all, between the innocent general people and crafty politicians. (Prasad 209)

A good playwright is merely an observer. Like a sponge Dattani absorbs from everyday life and experiences and responds to the sensitive issues that surround him. He often tackles taboo subjects that are still under wraps in the South Asian society, but does not aim at changing society, only to offer scope for reflection that will give the audience some kind of insight into their own lives. Dattani says:

> I believe in bringing out the complexities of any conflict and discussing the issues surrounding it. Even one person from the audience walks home thinking about the argument I have created on stage, my job is done.
>
> (Ali: www.indiacurrents.com)

He attempts to bring socially relevant subjects out in the open and place arguments around the issue and he does not provide solutions to any particular problem. He awakens the society's consciousness about the various issues of the society in which we live.

Final Solutions deals sensitively with the aftermath of partition, highlighting the gaping religious divide that is still deep-rooted in the minds of many. The playwright stresses on the need for communal harmony and religious tolerance if both the countries are to prosper in future. In this context, Dattani's *Final Solutions* is a great move in a positive direction.

Works Cited

Ali, Firdaus. "Play It Wright, Mahesh" July 20, 2005. U 16 October 2005. <http:// www.indiacurrents.com/news/view_article.html>

Benegal. Vivek. 'Psychological Playgrounds' Rev. of *Final Solutions and Other Plays*. *Indian Review of Books*. 4.1 (Oct-Dec1994): 61.

Dattani, Mahesh. *Final Solutions* in *Collected Plays*. New Delhi: Penguin Books India, 2000. All references cited in this paper are from this book with notation *FS*.

Kanthan, Kasturi. 'The Strongest Fragrance', Rev. of *Final Solutions and Other Plays, The Book Review*. 19.3 (Mar 1995): 32-3.

Multani, Angelie. 'On Mahesh Dattani's Dance Like a Man: The Politics Production and Performance' in *Seagull Theatre Quarterly*. 11 (September 1996): 58-60.

Prasad, Amarnath. 'The Plays of Mahesh Dattani: A Fine Fusion of Feeling and Form', *Indian English Literature*. Vol.V Ed. Basavaraj Naikar. New Delhi: Atlantic Publishers and Distributors, 2005. 202-13.

Subramanyan, Lakshmi. 'A Dialogue with Mahesh Dattani' in *Muffled Voices*. Ed.Lakshmi Subramanyan. New Delhi: Har Anand Publications, 2002.

Tyagi, Alka. Review of Collected Plays of Mahesh Dattani. *Indian Literature*. 44.4 (July- August 2000): 193-5.

http://www.maheshdattani.com

http://www.greatestquotations.com

http://en.wikipedia.org

9

Dattani's Dramatic Technique

—A. Madhavi Latha

Mahesh Dattani's plays are remarkable for the technical craftsmanship. He ensures that the enactment on stage will be effective when detailed stage directions are given. He uses space very skilfully, sometimes as confining and sometimes as widening. He moves from one part of the stage to another from one level of the stage to another, and he lights up different areas of the stage at different times. As he does this, his characters move in time. Age becomes youth, 1990s become 1947 and, past, present and future come together. The complex structure of these plays matches their complex and disturbing thematic quality. Dattani, very often places one character at a higher level so that the play is seen from his review point.

Dattani says that theatre has always been a mirror for man, a reflection of his world, the eternal conflicts that plague him, through which he has experienced whole gamut of human emotions. Man has created a very complex language called theatre, a language that has the ability to redefine the natural concepts of time, space and movement. A language that goes beyond the verbal and beyond the physical. Through his language of theatre he has been able tc see himself for who he is, what he has made of himself and what he aspires to be.

There is a constant danger of disillusionment of the theatre, because we do not see ourselves or our aspirations in the theatre. So, it becomes important to do the kind of theatre that means something to you personally and also to go to the kind of theatre which engages us enough for us to relate to in the way he has spoken about. Only then is there the true synergy between the artist and the audience.

That is why there is the need to look at identities both for the performer and the audience. It is not enough to say we are Indians and we shall see Indian theatre. We have to arrive at the true Indian mess of our theatre.In a plural society such as ours, which is culturally as diverse as the European continent, and a civilisation that is as ancient as the world, it is very difficult to define what is quintessentially Indian. Obviously a more pluralistic approach is required. The conventional way of defining by linguistic and regional divides does not work for creating artistic identities any more, or it probably never has. The spaces that Dattani goes beyond region and language are the most useful. These are more of ideological spaces and the whole purpose of making them is to come closer to our identities rather than create further hostile divisions. We have enough of those in our country.

Dattani roughly describes the three spaces as (1). The traditional, (2). The continual and (3). The radical. None of these spaces are mutually exclusive.

The traditional: According to Dattani we need not go into the traditional aspects of our theatre. There are enough people who are traditionalists who can vouch for the permanence and completeness of our classical theatres and dance forms. In fact, the word 'Natya' is used for both Dance and Drama. We can pride ourselves on our integrated performing art forms which are complete in every sense of the world. A *varnam* in a *Bharathanatyam* concept contains everything that theatre and dance all over the world strive for. It has technique, it has grace, it has power, it has emotions and most definitely it has style. A *rasika* who has the capacity to enjoy this experience is truly a traditional in the best sense of the word.

The continual: A lot of us seek our identities in our roots or traditions whether they are rural or urban, regional or international, or a mixture of all. It may be important to draw from these roots and to create works that are largely inspired from where we come from. To a lot of people their roots are a greater form of identify even if they have moved away from the traditions that they seek inspiration from and yet they need to be true to their times. This state of transition has created many great works in our country. Watching a play by Girish Karnad or Kambar gives us the satisfaction of viewing our past and our roots through a view finder that definitely belongs to the present. It is an important bridge that reminds us of where we come from and where we are today. It is interesting that both Karnad and Kambar have used the same Kannada folk tale to give us two gems *Naga Mandala* and *Siri Sampige*. Both are quite different from one another, yet they share common roots. This is something unique to Kannada theatre.

The radical: While it is absolutely vital to have tradition and continuity, all is not well with that. We do need change. We do need people who are willing to explore and develop new forms and languages. The radical theatre of today is in all likelihood to become the traditional theatre of tomorrow. Some of the most powerful works in theatre today are from radicals like Rabindranath Tagore, Badal Sircar, and Vijay Tendulkar. Tagore was among the first of the twentieth Century dramatists to put the focus on the caste system and gender inequality through his plays. If traditional and continual theatre is linked to our roots, radical theatre is linked to our spirit. It soars like a bird exploring new horizons and offering us vantage points that we didn't know existed. Both form and content have been enriched by radical thinkers in our theatre.

Hence, in order to form our cultural identities we need all the three. Tradition, continuity and change. It is when we accept the need for all three in our theatre that we can truly have a theatre movement that is inextricably linked to the development of cultural, social and individual identities. So, according to Dattani theatre is the representative of life.

Special mention must be made of Dattani's technical craftsmanship Datani has ensured that their enactment on stage will be effective with his stage directions. He uses space very skillfully, some time as confining and some times as widening. He divides the stage into different segments. He moves from one part of the stage to another and one level of the stage to another. He focuses the light at different areas of the stage for proper effect. Past, present and future come together. According to Kasturi Khantan:

> The complex structure of these plays match their complex and disturbing thematic quality. Dattani very often places one character at a higher level so that the play is seen from his viewpoint. Often characters are interchanged. Questions are asked at one point, between two characters are answered by the conversation between two characters in another part of the stage.
>
> (Kasturi Kanthan 32-33)

Dattani's plays would seem very grim indeed, were it not for humour- humour that can be wild, wicked, double–edged or slap-stick. He wields it with such confidence that he is not afraid to paint sober or even tragic moments with a shade of the comic. Then there is suspense, which he handles like a mystery-writer, giving away little tensions, heightening the tension and jabbing you in the gut many times—fond as he is of multiple climaxes.

Dattani blends time and space in his well made plays. He loves traditional art forms, especially *Bharatanatyam*, which is integral to *Dance Like a Man.* His plays fuse the physical and special awareness of the Indian theatre with the textual rigour of western models like Ibsen and Tennessee Williams. It's a potent combination, which shocks and disturbs through its accuracy, and its ability to approach a subject from multiple perspectives. Post-colonial India and multi-cultural expression of the contemporary; they require public spaces in which the mingling of Eastern and Western influences can take place. Through his fusion of forms and influences, Dattani creates such a space. This is in itself a political and social statement of astonishing force says Michel Walling in his *A Note on the Play*:

> Critics have compared his technique to that of Ibsen's, perhaps struck which all his plays unravel to reveal the present peace: be it the guilt of the educated liberal secularist who ghosts of the past. Some dark secret which comes back to torment the most confront again the truth

> that his family fortunes were built in the loot and spoils of engineered riots, or the retired dancer couple who come face to face with human cost of the pursuit of their negligence. One would rather attribute this to Indian story telling traditions as manifest in Kunti's dark secret of Karna's parentage, or the inevitable revelations in countless Hindi films where the hero and the wrong doer must confront the terrible truth of their twin hood it is true how ever that these four plays have a pervading ambience of menace and darkness but ultimately they are life alienating and redemptive despite the cruel twist they deliver.
>
> The four plays show the writer's progressive ease with form as he shifts from a decidedly naturalistic style to experiments with different innovations: playing with the unities of time and space through flashbacks, flash-forwards and working on the physical realities of staging using split-level stages, hidden rooms and other devices like having the same actors playing different characters. The plays are crafted meticu-lously and the dramatic tensions carefully built up and regulated with small giveaway hints dropped from time to time leading up to the climatic revelation which makes it that match more credible. Dattani uses the devices of the 'well made play' but gets away without becoming predictable.
>
> (Vivek. Benegal 61)

Dattani is a theatre practitioner who loves art and not himself in art. Painstakingly, he works with the actors to recreate his text in a form which suited their approach to performance: a sub textual approach characteristic of actors with a Western training. Watching this was an object lesson in openness, responsiveness, and cross-cultural collaboration. To Dattani a play is never really finishes. Plays only really happen in the theatre, as ephemeral events. The apparently permanent printed text is just one approximation to what might occur when the piece is performed.

Dattani has built a substantial oeuvre which can today be viewed and weighed. The main characteristics of the author's method tend to be repeated, with variations, from work to work. He takes great pain in his stage directions to explain the stage lay out expects the observers to fallow him in detail. Dattani presents his themes in a multiple narrative way, moving back and forth across time. He highlights the characters at different levels. Through a technique reminiscent of cinema he builds dramatic tension as it cuts rapidly from one scene to another.

In Dattani's plays, the plot tends to follow a particular pattern. A visitor or a stranger enters into a family with an introduction. Through him a series of events are revealed. Past events are unmasked. Some dark secrets of the family are revealed. Once the action begins to fallow, the interest of the audience is substantial strengthened as a number of lesser revelations lead us to the final theatrical coup.

Each play is something of a theatrical *tour de force* from within which the characters don't always emerge fully. They often have crackling lines of dialogue but there is little ballast to them. It is not character that drives the action; rather, a series of hints and revelations lead us into secrets that the protagonists would prefer to conceal. By the end, they stand exposing, not on what is revealed. The human core is not what it is about; the situational drama is what holds the attention. (Kusum Haider 24-25)

The constantly shifting nature of Dattani's stage space became the starting point for a kaleidoscopic approach to the text. In the play *Dance Like a Man* during the first flashback the actor who plays Jairaj immediately turns in to Amrithlal by simply wrapping the shawl, his most prized possession, around his shoulders. Dattani uses the shawl as a symbol to signify the stature of Amrithlal. Viswas is intrigued by the ornate cupboard, a solid rose wood; every article in the house is antique. He finds a splendid brocade shawl for dowry. That itself indicates its worth. That shawl is a present to Amrithlal from the Mysore maharajah, as an award during Dussehra that is the most prized possession. Whenever he has visitors, he wraps it around. He is the first among the educated elite class to shun western suits and wear kurtas and shawls on formal occasions.

Through Viswas, Dattani expresses the views of Amrithlal and prepares the audience mentally that he is against the wish of his son, Jairaj:

Viswas : What a granddaddy she had! He must have been a terror. No wonder her father is a weirdo. (*Clears his throat and puts on a mock-father voice.)* So, you want to be a dancer. Hah! Hah! Hah! Son, you will never amount to anything in life. Look at me. Look at what I have achieved. Yes. Look. Look. Look *(points to the furniture.)* What's that you say? There's more to life than money? You ungrateful wretch! (396)

Dattani depicts the stature of Amrithlal with his shawl around, through Viswas. Later in the first flashback Jairaj after giving his consent to Lata's marriage with Viswas, Ratna exits to the bed room. He notices the shawl. That is the last memory of his father. He feels happy as he soon will get rid of the shawl by giving it to Viswas as a dowry as he asked for it. When ever he sees the shawl the picture of his father walking about this room disturbs his mind. He wants to be away from those memories.

> Jairaj wears the shawl. He is immediately fixed in a spotlight. The music builds up until suddenly jathis or dance syllables being recited can be heard. The living room now changes into a lovely rose garden. Spotlight picks up a young man with his back to the audience, dancing. He wears dancing bells and a band around his waist. A young woman is sitting in front of him. The characters have all changed. Jairaj becomes the father, Amritlal Parekh.
>
> Viswas becomes Jairaj. Lata is now Ratna. Their ages remain the same as those of the previous characters they played. It is now the 1940's. (413)

Dattani has already given a clue to the audience through Viswas by making him Amritlal with the shawl. When Jairaj wears the shawl and when he is fixed in a spotlight and when the living room changes into a rose garden with young Jairaj and Ratna the audience are taken to the past. This technique of changing characters by simply changing the shawl is a novel idea of Dattani.

The young Jairaj unable to bear with the restrictions of his father any longer and decides to leave the house along with his wife. Young Ratna exits behind him. Then the garden becomes the present day living room. Amritalal becomes the older Jairaj as he removes the shawl. The older Ratn's voice from the bed room picks up from where the young one's trailed off. Older Ratna speaks to older Jairaj as usual.

The second Act again takes the audience to 1940s. In the second flashback the younger Jairaj and Ratna comes back defeated only after two days. Amritlal forgives them and seeks the help of Ratna in helping Jairaj to grow up like a man and he departs. Young Ratna exits. Amritlal picks up the news paper and becomes the older Jairaj again the lights are brightened and the garden changes into the living room, then he calls for Ratna, the older Ratna enters from the kitchen. Young Jairaj and young Ratna comes as Viswas and Lata four of them participate in the joyful conversations of Lata's rave reviews.

Old Ratna breaks down with jealous of her daughter, Lata's development and rave reviews. She then exits into the bedroom along with flute music. Jairaj exits to the kitchen. The living room changes into the garden, bathed in moonlight. After a while, the young Jairaj and Ratna enter from the garden, Ratna is wearing a splendid Bharatanatyam dress. Jairai is evidently drunk. Amritlal is away receiving the acclaim for serving the nation. In this third flashback the death of their infant Shankar is revealed.

> Ratna (screaming). No!

Jairaj rushes up the stairs. Ratna looks up and slowly goes up the stairs as music plays. The lights dim. She exits hurriedly.

> The music contaminates in a scream which comes from the older Ratna. The garden changes to the living room. The music however continues, perhaps muted. The lights remain subdued. The older Ratna comes down the stairs almost in a trance. The older Jairaj enters, and stands in shadows, watching her as she sits down. He moves and

> stands beside her. They are both fixed in a spot light. All senses of time is abandoned now. (446)

Through the dialogues of Jairaj it is revealed that many years have passed and many changes have taken place. The ancient house is demolished and built a posh house. When Jairaj is revealing the changes that have taken place spotlight picks up the younger Jairaj and Ratna in the dance hall. Both of them were in dance costumes and wear dancing bells during Jairaj's speech. They smile a lot and perhaps even laugh. When the younger Jairaj strikes a pose the younger Ratna laughs and hits him playfully. The younger Jairaj and Ratna smile and embrace without any prejudices. After his death Jairaj expresses that they dance perfectly with unison without missing a step or a beat and they laughed at all the mistakes they made in their previous dances. They have come to an understanding Jairaj says, "We were only humans. We lacked the grace. We lacked the brilliance. We lacked the magic to dance like God."(447)

This is the statement of maturity, understanding and realisation. At the other segment the younger couple is ready to dance and salute the audience while the music builds up and the spotlights fade.

In this 'well made play' structure, Dattani bends time and space to suite his will. Through out the play time moves back and forth within the same scene. His ability to create meaningful and moving drama has established him as the leading figure in English theatre today. He is the only Indian playwright with a consistent body of work in English.

> To direct a play is a process of making the word flesh. When the words are Mahesh Dattani's, the flesh is already contained within the word; the written texts are fully realised through the process of performance. Dattani's plays fuse with the physical and spatial awareness of the Indian theatre with the textual rigour of Western models like Ibsen and Tennessee Williams. It's a potent combination, which shocks and disturbs through its accuracy, and its ability to approach a subject from multiple perspective. (Michael Walling 229)

In the play *Bravely Fought the Queen* the set is centered on a slightly abstract inner space, furnished with three white blocks, which represented the Trivedi household and the office. The only naturalistic element in this area was the bar: a glowing blasphemous shrine to alcohol. Around this central area was another world: red and dusty full of torn newspapers, discarded whisky bottles and cigarette packets, the beggar woman's tarpaulin, a wheel chair. This was an India at once alluring and terrifying, both for the bourgeois characters of the play and for its western audience.

This play is the world of Kanhaiya, the sexually alluring young cook and the dark arms of the auto driver who embodies Nitin's sexual guilt; of Alka's liberating dance in the rain; and of Baa the living embodiment of the past with its attendant guilt and shame. Her presence is undercutting the apparent naturalism, and upsetting the fragile fictions, which the characters had created. This is a play about performance; and uses the theatre to demonstrate how, in a world of hypocrisy, acting becomes a way of life. Paradoxically, it is only by the overt performance of the theatre says, Michael Walling in his Note on the play.

In this play past and present exist simultaneously, when Baa speaks from the past and her lines alternate with those spoken by Jiten and Nitin. The dialogues of the characters in one segment are intertwined with the dialogues of the other segment characters. The questions asked by a particular character in one segment will be answered by the other character's conversation. The dialogues are woven with good craftsmanship and with lot of skill. The characters of a particular segment will not give direct answers, but their conversation comes in between the dialogues of another segment and gives apt and reasonable answers to the readers or to the audience.

In Act I entitled, 'The Women', the segmentation of the stage is described in a picturesque way:

> The upstage centre is dominated by a well-stocked bar. On a higher level is the bedroom of Jiten and Niten's mother,

> referred to as Baa. She is bedridden and is visible through the screen wall when it is back-lit. A staircase is visible along with a small landing which leads to both Baa's bedroom and Dolly's bedroom off-stage. Upstage left is a largish window overlooks the front of the house. Next to it is a stereo system –music can be herd. It is a thumri sung by Naina Devi. Downstage left, exit to the kitchen and downstage right is the main door of the house. (233)

Dattani loves traditional art forms of dance and music. In this play, Nayana Devi's thumri has given lot of importance. The mud mask on the face of Dolly and Lalitha's shopping bag containing bonsai plants are of great significance. In this Act Baa rings the bell at crucial movements to distract the attention of the audience from a particular conversation. When Lalitha is explaining about the bonsai plants, how the roots and shoots are cut to make the growth stunted, Baa rings the bell.

In Act II, The Men, the stage gives the idea of Trivedi's business significance.

> The office of the Jiten and Nitin Trivedi. An advertising agency. Pin-ups of campaign in a board. A huge photograph of a sensuous model with the Re Va Tee logo. Two larger desks with executive chairs. A comfortable couch next to Jiten's desk. A small desk belonging to Sridhar, which is over crowed with papers and assorted items. There is also a rather odd-looking bonsai on his table. One doorway leads to the reception area, another to the toilet. The level representing Baa's room remains as in Act I. so does the well-stocked bar. (264)

The character Baa is essential to reveal the past incidents. Even in the second Act when Sridhar is talking about bonsai Baa rings the bell, to intervene the conversation. Sridhar indicates if it is not bounded or shaped correctly the plant becomes grotesque and ugly. It conveys the meaning that if the characters are molded from their childhood then they will grow with perfection unlike the grotesque and ugly bonsai. Indirectly it is indicated that Baa is responsible for the behaviour of her children. The conversation of Lalitha and Baa in the upper stage mixes up with the conversation of Sridhar, Jiten and Nitin in the office:

The telephone rings. Sridhar answers it.

Sridhar : (on the phone). Hello? Yes, he is here. Just a minute. (To Nitin.) It's your wife.

Lalitha : Can I help you?

Nitin : *(on the phone)*. Hello? Ya.

Baa : Where is Praful?

Lalitha : Who? Baa. Dolly, where is your brother?

Lalitha : I'm not Dolly! Dolly will be ...

Baa : You are not Dolly. You are not Lally. Who are you?

Nitin : But where do you think we are going?

Lalitha : Dolly is dressing up. They are going out.

Baa : Those girls go out, go out, go out a-a-all the time to.

Lalitha : I think their husbands wanted them to.

Nitin : *(rudely)*. Hasn't anybody told you?

Baa : Oh! Jitu and Nitin are taking them out?

Nitin : No. Dolly knows.

Baa : My Nitin is afraid of going out in the dark.

Nitin : That's very strange.

Lalitha : Did you need anything?

Nitin : I can't. We are working.

Baa : Ten years old and he is still afraid of the dark. Afraid to sleep in the dark. Afraid of his father—who is as black as night!

Nitin : I think you should keep Baa company. She is lonely. (Hangs up.)

Simultaneously, the spotlight in Baa's area goes off. (272)

In the plays of Dattani the incidents are not sequential. They are simultaneous just how the things or events happen in our real life. Again when the business men are discussing on Re

Ve Tee ad, about taking the money from Praful and about selling their old house, their conversation is intervened with Dolly and Baa, and gives too many memories.

Baa : Wait! What are you doing?

Jiten : Baa isn't going to live longer than a year.

Baa : No, no! Don't hit them! They're only boys! They didn't steal! Nitin, tell him you didn't steal it!

Nitin : I don't want to sell the old house. Ever.

Jiten : One and a half crores. At today's market.

Baa : I gave them the money! Yes, I took it from your purse and gave it to them!

Nitin : That's wher we grew up.

Baa : Why should I not? It is my money!

Nitin : Too many memories.

Jiten : Sentimental fool.

Baa : Mine Every paisa is mine! Mine from my father !

Nitin : It—it belongs to Daksha. Maybe we should do it up and all live there.

Baa : This is my house! My house!

Nitin : We could sell these twin houses.

Jiten : No! I built them. We built them. They are ours!

Baa : Don't shout! Who are you to shout at me?

Jiten : I'll never live in the old house.

Nitin : Why not?

Jiten : Too many memories.

Baa : You hit me? I only speak the truth and you hit me? Go on. Hit me again. The children should see what a demon you are. Aah! Jitu! Nitin Are you watching? See your father! *(jerks her face as of she's been slapped.)* No!

> No! Not on the face! What will the neighbours say? Not on the face. I beg you! Hit me nut not on... aaaah! (*Covers her face weakly as her scream turns silent and the light on her fades out.*) (277-78)

With this conversation the readers or the audience will understand the past memories of Baa and how it is related to the present situation. Baa dwindles between past and the present. Her mind is not fixed to the present. It is wavering between the past and the present. She mixes up the situations. In Act III Free for All! the stage setting is the same as in Act I; mixing up of characters conversation reveals so many family secrets and their characters. The queries of one area are aptly answered by the characters in the other area. This type of drama technique is very interesting. It will make the audience to watch and listen to the stage very attentively. In one situation the conversation of Baa and Nitin mixes up with Dolly and Jiten:

> Dolly : Go on. What are you waiting for? Strangle me
>
> Nitin : It all happened because you denied Daksha was your blood!
>
> Dolly : You should have strangled me then, when Baa told you.
>
> Baa : That was the day I got the letter. Praful was lying!
>
> Dolly : I know! He lied! But what a price to pay!
>
> Nitin : So he lied. But you did far worse!
>
> Baa : No!
>
> Jiten : Baa provoked me. It was her fault!
>
> Baa : I did not want this I did not know....
>
> Dolly : You didn't have to listen to her! She called me a Whore and you believed her?
>
> Baa : I was angry with Praful. (310)

This is a prolonged conversation, where the incidents of fifteen years are recollected and revealed. The cause for Daksha's physical deformity is revealed. This is a play about performance; and uses the theatre to demonstrate how, in a world of hypocrisy, acting becomes the way of life. Paradoxically, it is only by the overt performance of the theatre that such acting can be exposed for what it is. For example, when Dolly reveals the fact that her child was seriously disabled at birth by Jiten's violence she begins to dance as Daksha would dance- disjointedly, wildly, with ever-increasing frenzy, until at last she breaks down in a gut-wrenching grief —by exploiting layer upon layer of performance, of unreality, Dattani allowed his actress a route to emotion in its rawest form: the pain, the anguish in the blood- knot of the family is his constant theme.

Mahesh Dattani frequently takes as his subject the complicated dynamics of the modern urban family. His characters struggle for some kind of freedom and happiness under the weight of tradition, cultural constructions of gender, and repressed desire. Their dramas are played out on multi-level sets where interior and exterior become one, and geographical locations are collapsed.

Tara centres on the emotional separation that grows between two conjoined twins following the discovery that their physical separation was manipulated by their mother and grandfather to favour the boy (Chandan) over the girl (Tara). Tara, a feisty girl who isn't given the opportunities given to her brother (although she may be smarter) eventually wastes away and dies. Chandan escapes to London, changes his name to Dan, and attempts to repress the guilt he feels over his sister's death by living without a personal history. Woven into the play are issues of class and community, and the clash between traditional and modern life styles and values. Just as in any other play the stage is segmented into:

> A multi level set. The lowest level occupies a major portion of the stage. It represents the house of the Patels. It is seen only in memory and may be kept as stark as possible.

> The next level represents the bed-sitter of the older Chandan (referred to as Dan for clarity) in a suburb of London. There is a small bed, and, in the foreground, a small writing table with a typewriter and a sheaf of papers. A part of a wall covered with faded wallpaper can also be seen. This is the only realistic level.
>
> Behind, on a higher level, is a chair in which Dr Thakkar remains seated through out the play. Although he doesn't watch the action of the play, his connection is asserted by his sheer God- like presence.
>
> On the stage level, running along the cyclorama and in an L-shape, downstage right, is the galli outside the Patels' house. Which can be suggested by cross-lighting.
>
> The play starts without any music. A spot picks up Dan at his writing table. He is typing furiously. He stops and removes the sheet from the typewriter. He looks up and speaks to the audience. (323)

The play begins with Dan's monologue. Dan is the older Chandan. He recollects his memories and wants to write Drama in two acts *Twinkle Tara.* A spot on the stage level picks up young Chandan and Tara. Both are limping but on different legs. Patel and Bharati are seen in another area. The same character comes to the stage of Tara and becomes young Chandan.

After the conversation the light spots on Dan who suddenly jerks as if woken from a nightmare. He wants to interview Dr Thakkar under the caption Marvel in the world of Medicine.

> A television show type signature tune fades in whirl the spot fades out. Although Dan is interviewing Dr Thakkar, he remains where he is, in darkness. The tune ends and a spot picks up DrThakkar, seated as if being interviewed in a studio. (330)

In the interview Dr Thakkar gives detailed information about Conjoined twins—developing from one fertilised ovum are invariably of the same sex, and of the surgery. Throughout the play Dr Thakkar will be there and the interview will be continued till the end of the play. Then the spot fades on Dr. Thakkar.

> Spot fades out on Dr Thakkar as we hear the explosive opening of Brahms' First Concerto.
>
> The street area is lit. Tara enters the street. She mimes meeting someone and smiling, starting a conversation. After a while, she slowly lifts the leg of her trousers to reveal her artificial limb. She laughs in an ugly way. Then she says goodbye and enters the living room as the lights cross-fade.
>
> Chandan is lying on his back on the floor, listening to the music and conducting an imaginary orchestra in the heavens. (332)

Music has much influence on Dattani's sense of perspective. Again lights cross fades to Patel on the phone talking to Dr Kapoor. When Bharati wants to reveal the injustice done to her, Patel objects. Patel he himself wants to reveal it his children. Dan's dialogue from his stage intervenes:

> Bharati : I will tell her.
>
> Patel stops.
>
> I will tell them everything.
>
> *Patel goes to her and slaps her. The moment she recovers, Bharati looks at him with some triumph.*
>
> Patel : You wouldn't dare tell them. Not you. Please, don't!
>
> Not yet!
>
> Bharati : Then let me do what I want to do.
>
> Patel : (defeated). You cannot tell them. For their sake, don't! (Looks at her suddenly with determination.) If at all they must know, it will be from me. Not from you.
>
> *Cross-fades to Dan who is busy typing. He stops and reads out his last line.*
>
> Dan : If at all they must know, it will be from me. Not from you.

> *Dan continues to type as the lights cross-fade to the living room. Tara and Chandan are watching a movie. Bharati is knitting. As the movie ends.* (345-346)

The act ends with the sobbing of Bharati, where as Dan unwinds the sheet and reads aloud, the story of 'Twinkle Tara' up to Bharati sobs.

In the second Act the second movement of Brahm's First Concerto starts and light focus on Dan and Thakkar. At the end of the play Dan realises that he achieved nothing. In his vision he sees Tara and himself walk without limping and Tara hugs him once again as they were in the comfortable womb. Dan moves between past and present in the past. He is Chandan, escapes to London and changes his name to Dan. There he attempts to repress the guilt he feels over his sister's death by living without a personal history. Both Vijay Tendulkar in *Ghashiram* and Mahesh Dattani in *Tara* have exciting visual impact on stage, then *Tara* experimented with the form of the 'well made play', breaking the unities of space and time to produce a gentle introspective 'memory play' on stage. According to Kusum Haider:

> The most noted and most grandly presented of these plays is *Final Solutions* which was launched to acclaim by Bombay's Theatre Group. It addresses issues drawn from the 1992 riots in Bombay and is certainly a brave effort to look at matters. We usually prefer to our biased, narrow, some times murderous selves. Yet in many ways this is the least satisfactory of this collection of plays. Here alone does Dattani move away from the dramatic conventions he observes elsewhere into a direct commentary on real events. It is a different kind of theatre, less subtle, more obviously 'dramatic'. It may be a challenging and worthy response to challenging and worthy response to unconscionable events, but it could prove more ephemeral than others as a creation for the theatre. (Kusum Hyder 24-25)

Final Solutions is like Tendulkar's *Ghashiram Kotwal* in technique. Mob/ chorus are there in both the plays. The stage setting has a vital role in the plays of Dattani.

> The play is dominated by a horseshoe- or crescent-shaped ramp, with the ends sloping to stage level. Most of the action of the Mob/Chorus takes place on the ramp. Ideally the Mob/Chorus should remains on stage in a crouched or stylised position throughout the play.
>
> The Mob/Chorus comprises five men and ten masks on sticks.The masks are strewn all over the ramp. The players 'wears' a mask by holding the stick in front of him. At more dynamic moments, he can use it as a weapon in a stylised fashion. There are five Hindu masks and five Muslims masks. The Mob/Chorus becomes the Chorus when they 'wear' either the Hindu or the Muslim masks. But when referred to individually, they remain Chorus 1, Chorus 2, etc. The players of the Mob/chorus do not belong to any religion and ideally should wear black.
>
> Within the confines of the ramp is a structure suggesting the house of the Gandhi with just wooden blocks for furniture. However, upstage, perhaps on an elevation, is a detailed kitchen and a pooja room.
>
> On another level is a room with a roll top desk and as oil lamp converted to as electric one, suggesting that the period is the late 1940sthis belongs to the young Daksha, who is in fact the grandmother, also sometimes seen as a girl of fifteen. There are several instances when Hardika, the grandmother, and Daksha, the young bride, are on this level at the same time, although they are the same person. Hardika should be positioned and lit in such a way that the entire action of the play is seen through her eyes.
>
> When the play opens, Daksha is reading out what she has just written in her diary. Hardika is seated, motionless, on the same level. (165)

The play begins with the young Daksha or Hardika as a young girl. Past and present are fused through the figures of Daksha and Hardika. The lay begins with Daksha reading from her diary. She writes about independence and also about the communal feelings. She gives complete description about Hussainabad incident in which her father was killed by Muslims.

> Daksha slowly closes her diary. Silence. Daksha leaves her diary close to Hardika's feet as a slow low drumbeat is heard. She rises and stands behind Hardika, her back to the audience. Hardika picks up the diary and speaks directly to the audience. (167)

Daksha's diary establishes the history of division- the sense of 'us and them' the link between personal experience and political belief/ social hatred. A communal riot is invoked in the very first scene of the play, a riot in which Daksha's father was killed, a riot which firmly creates for Daksha. According to Angellie Multani:

> The 'them'-history is present throughout the action of the play sometimes repeating itself directly, through statements made by Daksha/Hardika, sometimes indirectly, through situations of violence which have been enacted before, and are too frighteningly familiar. History is also evoked and used by almost every character on stage [Angelie Multani 58-60].

When ever the cross fades to the Mob/Chorus they slowly wear the Hindu or Muslim masks according to the situation. When they are behind the masks they become more frenetic. The lines could be explored for harmony and discord, but only for dramatic effect and not for musicality.

Chorus 1	:	The procession has passed through these lanes. Every year, For forty years!
Chorus 2, 3	:	How dare they?
Chorus 1, 2, 3	:	For forty years our chariot has moved through their mohallas.
Chorus 4, 5	:	Why did they? Why did they today?
Chorus 1	:	How dare they?
Chorus 2, 3	:	They broke our rath. They broke our chariot and felled our gods!

Chorus 1, 2, 3 : This is our land!

How dare they?

Chorus 1 : It is in their blood!

Chorus 2, 3 : It is in their blood to destroy!

Chorus 4 : Why should they?

Chorus 5 : It could have been an accident.

Chorus 2 : The stone that hot our God was no accident!

Chorus 3 : The knife that slit the poojari's stomach was no accident!

Chorus 4, 5 : Why should they? It could have been an accident.

Chorus 4 and 5 continue to question. 'Why should they?' 'Why should they?' 'It could have been an accident', while Chorus 1 mutters, 'No accident, no accident ....' and Chorus 2 and 3 continue, 'The stone that hit our God was no accident, the knife that slit the poojari's stomach was no accident.' Soon they overlap and say it together. Chorus 1, 3 and 3 build their parts to a crescendo. They all finish together on the word 'accident'. (168)

The mob is unruly. They are crying out for blood. At one moment they hold both the Hindu and Muslim masks far away from their bodies as if they have plucked them away. They sway as if in a trance while their humming suggests mob hysteria. So in every incident the chorus explains the situation with their action. They even carry one of the choruses like a dead body being taken for burial. Their heads are covered with prayer caps. They feel very insecure, as they are less in number.

The Hindu chorus feels that they cannot be complacent about their glorious past seeing them safely through. Their bellowing pales in comparison to the whispers of a pseudo-secularist who is in league with the people who brought shame to our land.

Throughout the play the emphasis is on Noor Jehan's music. The lilt of the music is stopped by the mob smashing the records by throwing the stones, when Daksha was young and also when she is old. It symbolises that the melody of life is disturbed by the people with communal feelings and with savage ideas. The same tempo repeats. Nothing has been changed in the mentality of the people. This is an eternal problem with out any solution.

Joy is the essence of life and theatre should exude delight. *Where There's a will* is such a play. It is not only thought-provoking and introspective but also provides an evening of pure entertainment.

This play has philosophical twists. In this play Hasmukh Mehta has control over his family through his money and forgoes an opportunity to improve her relationships. The play *Where There's A Will* is Dattani's first play. Drama technique in this play is different from that of others. In the first act the stage is divided into three spaces.

> The lavish house of Hasmukh Mehta.
>
> There are three spaces: the fancy dining-cum-living room, the room belonging to Hasmukh and Sonal Mehta, and the hideously trendy bedroom of their son, Ajit, and his wife. Preeti.
>
> Ajit is in the living room, talking on the phone. Preeti is drifting in and out of the kitchen, loading the table with food for dinner. She is pregnant. Hasmukh enters through the main door with his walking stick. (455)

Hasmukh narrates the events to the audience in a prolonged speech. In his soliloquies he expresses his anguish about his son Ajit. Ajit is a spend thrift. Mehta wants to save all his money. But unfortunately he dies. After his death Hasmukh rises from his 'body' on the bed. He moves behind the bed and speaks in normal but low voice.

> Hasmukh : I am dead. I can see my own body lying still on the bed; looking peaceful, but dead. I never imagined it would happen so soon. Well, it has. *(To the audience)* Didn't I tell you that if I carried in smoking like that I'd be dead

in no time? I didn't believe it myself. I thought I was joking!

Sonali enters from the kitchen and slowly makes her way up to her bedroom.

There's my wife. Coming up to our bed-room. I can see through the walls. How will she react when she finds out? She will tear her hair and beat her head against the wall! Let's see.

Sonali enters their bedroom. She looks at 'him' lying down.

Sighs.

Sonal : Are you asleep?

Hasmukh : No, I'm dead.

Sonal : Of course, he's asleep. He just has to lie down on the bed and he is dead to the world!

Hasmukh : She has a way of saying things.

Sonal : *(notices the cigarette and stubs it out).* Oh, so you've been smoking; have you? Do you want a second heart attack?

Hasmukh : I just had it, thank you.

Sonal : Who am I talking to? The four walls?

Hasmukh : How right you are.

Sonal lies down on the bed beside 'him'

Don't go to sleep, you silly woman. For I have to wait for Diwali before you find out I'm gone? (476)

When they find out that Hasmukh is dead, he or his ghost grins from ear to ear for the first time. Later throughout the play the ghost of Hasmukh will be moving with other characters and he will be intervening with other conversations.

Mahesh Dattani is always adventurous in his ways of using the theatrical space at his disposal: multiple levels, breaking the bounds of the proscenium, wondrously inventive use of lighting to give height, breath and depth. In *On a Muggy Night in Mumbai*, he reaches new heights.

Although the setting is basically interior with different space—Kamlesh's flat, mainly the living room and the bedroom—there is also the mental space indicated by the stage directions. Then there is not only the skyline of Mumbai beyond, but there is the real world out there, indicated by the niggling presence of the wedding going in at ground level.

The outside world is always pressing in- the heart, the sounds, the people pestering Bunny, the kids who find the photo. Very few dramatists are able to give this sense of a whole society touching the participants in the on-stage drama-it recalls Ibsen at his social best.

It is a play about pattern, how society creates patterns of behaviour and how easy it for individuals to fall victims to the expectations society creates. The characters in this play are stereotypical. They are a carefully balanced with a depth of experience that exceeds traditional expectations. They are brought together in such a way as to bring out the conflicts, repressions and past secrets which are assailing Kamlesh and Ed/Prakash, and the new 'romance' between Ed and Kamlesh's sister Kiran are beautifully counterpoised until the revelation at the climax of the first act that Ed and Prakash are the same person- which always draws a gasp of astonishment from audiences.

This is a refinement and development techniques Dattani has deployed in his earlier play. John McRae in his A Note on the Play says, "his (Dattani's) special theatrical quality is to build tension in a social context, leading to a classic dramatic confrontation which involves not only the characters themselves, but which also confronts the audiences with its own expectations and attitudes." Every act builds a climax of revelations and self- discoveries. The intrusive wedding music becomes the accompaniment to a dance of death indoors- and the audience must go through the classic cathartic emotions if terror and pity as the characters masks fall, their emotions unravel, and their lives disintegrate. The drama technique of Dattani is revealed clearly by the deep study of the stage characters.

> The stage is divided into three acting areas. The first is a small flat, beautifully done up in 'ethnic chic' fashion. A huge poster of Meena Kumari in Pakeezah offers relief to a stark white wall. The windows overlook the Mumbai skyline and act literally as a window to the city with its glittering lights. The flat is too high up for the noise but the partial view of the 'Queen's Necklace' suggests that the flat is located in the up market area of Marine Drive, though not quite Pali Hill. The entire flat is almost too perfect to be real. Yet it speaks a lot of its occupant. Kamlesh, and his attempt at creating a world where he can belong.
>
> The second area, a completely non-realistic set comprising three levels, is black expansive, Characters in this area are immediately suspended in a ' shoonya' where they are forced to confront their inner thoughts.
>
> Below this is Kamlesh's bedroom. The bedroom is realistic, but hidden behind a gauze wall, giving it some mystery and secrecy.
>
> The backdrop of these three acting areas is the Mumbai skyline, engulfing the created world of Kamlesh, the secret private space of the bedroom and the deeper space that belongs to the inner thoughts of the characters. (49-50)

When the lights fade out on the two characters, Kamlesh and the Guard, it fades in on the highest level of the darkened area. The music stops with the entrance of Ed. Ed's love care and concerned are revealed in this act. The beginning of the act two is very important. This is the crucial point of the play. The audience will understand the relationship of Kamlesh and Ed in their first meeting. Dattani's dramatic technique at this juncture is very skillfully woven into the play.

> The characters are in more or less the same positions as at the end of Act I, but now they are in silhouette.
>
> The second level is lit. Ed is sitting on a park bench looking around. He spots someone walking by His eyes follow him. The person walking by, whom we don't see, turns around and walks past Ed again. Ed smiles at him, again following him with his eyes as he walks by. Now the person walks by again and this time Ed gestures to him to sit next to him. The person sits down next to Ed. (80)

Ed speaks to the person who is sitting beside him. In this prolonged conversation he reveals his mental condition to Kamlesh, how he is craving for a male companion. Dattani depicts the agitated mind of a homosexual and how he searches for a stereotype, when he finds Kamlesh in the park he realises that he is the right choice. If he had not found any companion he thought of ending his life by jumping over the balcony out of frustration. Ed speaks by looking at the person closely. The audience cannot see the person who is sitting beside Ed. He converses with him in such away as if the person is responding. When he was talking to him Kamlesh enters and stands behind Ed. Ed continues to address Kamlesh as if he were sitting next to him on the bench. Kamlesh asks him to hold his hand. He wants every one to see how beautiful they are together. Kamlesh asks Ed to close his eyes and imagine that he is standing behind them and watch how they are together. "Ed gets up and stands behind the bench on the other side of where Kamlesh is." They stand and watch themselves supposedly kissing each other with admiration.

Then the light fades into the living room as Kamlesh steps off the platform and joins the people there. Kiran is seen in the bedroom. In another situation Ed enters when Kamlesh and Kiran move to another level of the empty area. Ed continues to address them as before:

Ed : Mind if I dance with your sister? .... Would you care to have this dance with me?

Soft music : 'Begin The Beguine' *or similar. Ed mimes dancing with Kiran*

Kiran *(to Kamlesh)* : I quite like your friend.

Ed : No problem, just follow my feet. Relax...

Kiran : He told me how he met you at Sushma's party.

Ed : There you go. Once you relax, it's a lot easier.

Kiran : And he told me you thought he was gay! Whatever gave you that idea?

Kamlesh moves to the third level.

Ed : I love ballroom dancing. It is very difficult to find the appropriate partner...

Kiran *(laughs)* : I mean, he doesn't look gay.

Kamlesh : *(on the third level, as if to Ed).* Prakash, can I tell my sister about you? (90)

Here the dialogues of Kiran with Kamlesh intervene with the dialogues of Ed with imaginary Kamlesh. Then Kamlesh moves to the third level and converse as if with Prakash or Ed. His imaginary conversation intervenes with real conversation of Ed and Kiran from another level:

Kamlesh : People will know anyway, sooner or later. If you are seen with me.

Kiran : People talk. It is difficult for me. You are a man, I know you have it hard too, but it is easy for you to be... invisible.

Kamlesh : How long shall we continue to hide? We can't hide forever!

Ed *(stops dancing)* : Let them talk. If a man and a woman want to dance together, what's their problem? We will stop after this number. Let them see. *(Begins dancing again.)*

Kamlesh : Let them talk if two men want to love one another, what's the harm?

Kiran : Being divorced doesn't help. Every one seems to know all the details. Or think they do. At that party I felt their stares, as if they were saying, 'That's Kiran. The one whose husband dumped her.' Kamlesh take my advice. Don't let people know about you. You will spend your whole life defending yourself. If I had the choice, I would stay invisible too.

Kamlesh : Are you embarrassed to be seen with me?

Ed : Relax. Don't be so afraid of what people think of you. But if you are really embarrassed, we could stop. *(Continues to dance.)* (90-91)

When Kiran steps on to Ed's level and dances Ed moves to Kamlesh's level and Kamlesh moves to the level where Kiran was earlier.

Kamlesh : Kiran, I want you to be happy. No matter what mummy and daddy may have felt about your divorce, they love you too.

Kiran : Oh I feel a little dizzy. (*Mimes dancing with her head resting on Ed's shoulder.)*

Kamlesh : Of course, I am happy. I may even have some good news to share with you.

Kiran : Please Ed, let's stop. I—I don't feel too well. *(Stops dancing, and sits down on the level Kamlesh is standing on.)*

Ed : Let's not get too emotional. Think for yourself. There is normal future.

Kiran (*mimes accepting a glass of water*) : Oh, thank you! Don't worry about me. God! Everyone's looking.

Kamlesh : Well there is someone special is someone special I am seeing.

Kiran : Where's Kamlesh? Ed, please find Kamlesh.

Kamlesh : He is rather shy. He still has a long way to go in coming to terms, but I am helping him.

Ed : Kamlesh, I can never forget what you did for me. You were there for me when I needed. someone.

Kiran : Kamlesh, will you take me home? I am not happy with the situation.

Kamlesh : And I am going to make it big in Bombay. Life can be so simple and wonderful. (92)

Here the three characters speak from different level. Kiran speaks to Ed, Ed speaks to Kamlesh and Kamlesh speaks to Kiran. They speak from the three levels. This technique is different from that of the conventional plays which are very interesting. Again Kamlesh moves to Ed's level and asks him not to wrench his soul from his body. Lights in the living room come on when Ed enters the living room when Deepali, Bunny and Ranjit are there and asks for Kiran. From the other levels Kiran and Kamlesh shouts for Ed:

> Kiran : Ed! You go by yourself! Really, I am not making a fuss! No, I can't! I can't!
>
> Kamlesh : Prakash! Please!
>
> Kiran *(overlapping Kamlesh's plea).* : Ed, no please......
>
> *Ed looks warily at Deepali, Ranjit and Bunny.*
>
> *Blackout while a wedding band can be heard from the window with hooting and whistling from the crowd.* (94)

Dattani's dramatic technique is unique of its kind. It is beautifully crafted. One actor, moving from one role to another and the incidents shifting from present to past and past to present, marks it as unique. The play travels back and forth between several generations and back and forth.

All these plays of Dattani show a rich variety of theatre form. Our ancient traditional forms offer the urban playwright a lot of technical freedom with the help of music, mime and exotic imagery. All the modernisation and westernisation of the urban life is depicted on the stage. Dattani's stagecraft in the contemporary Indian Drama has highlighted his drama technique. The drama depends on the participation of—author, actors, and audience to accept the operation of theatre and the conventions associated with it. The page is only a raw material for the stage from which the performance is created. Dattani, the writer, actor and director could weave his plays colourfully with all his talent as a craftsman and tries to communicate his ideas through this dynamic medium. With his technical craftsmanship Dattani has become the successful and celebrated dramatist in the contemporary Indian drama in English.

Works Cited

Benegal,Vivek, 'Psychological Plygrounds'. Rev. of *Final Solutions and Other Plays*. *Indian Reviews of Books,* Vol.4, No.1, Oct- Dec 1994.

Haider, Kusum, 'Essentially a Comic Muse'. Rev. of *Tara and Final Solutions. The Book Review,* Vol. 22, No. 3, March 1998.

Kanthan, Kasturi, 'The Strongest Fragrance'. Rev. of *'Final solutions and other Plays*, *The Book Review,* vol.19, No.3, Mar 1995.

Multani, Angelie, 'On Mahesh Dattani's *Dance Like A Man*: The Politics of Production and Performance'. *Seagull Theatre Quarterly,* No.11, September, 1996.

Walling, Michael, 'A Note On the Play', Mahesh Dattani, *Collected Plays.* New Delhi: Penguin Books India, 2000.

10

Factors Influencing the Evolution of Drama in Bengal

—Saumitra Chakravarty

Though drama as an independent literary genre was a rather late arrival in the annals of the history of Bengali literature, its birth had been heralded centuries earlier. Officially, drama and the commercial theatre with its proscenium stage was indebted to Western influence and the largesse of the Western-educated bi-lingual literary elite of Calcutta. But in the mammoth melting pot of the history of Rarhbhumi, part of which later emerged as Bengal, the ingredients of histrionic representation were inherent in its turbulent social vicissitudes. These theatrical ingredients were evident in every aspect of local life and culture—from religious ritualism to the spiritual experience of re-enacting the exploits of gods and saints, from the folk theatre of the rural masses to the poetic duels of the urban elite, from seasonal rites, work songs and wedding rituals to masked dances and processional tableaux.

As Asit Kumar Bandopadhyay notes[1],Western drama had its roots within the church in the Miracle and Morality plays and later acquired secular overtones as the players moved from within the sacrosanct confines of the church to the open marketplace. In Bengali theatre, however, it may be said that religious and secular theatre enjoyed an almost parallel growth and when the former was silenced by foreign invasion and religious fundamentalism, its secular/folk variant kept the banner flying so that their later merger could oversee the development of indigenous theatre among the common people.

In a checkered history of conquest and domination in Bengal, the pursuit and practice of dramatising religious texts, rituals and myths, witnessed several major changes. It was also exposed to various factors which deliberately or inadvertently fostered its growth. These stages in the evolution of the drama of Bengal, saw its passing not only from the religious to the secular, the Classical to the folk and back again, it also saw its emergence from private courtyards, palaces and manor houses of the urbanised rich to the public domain for the benefit of the rural masses. Along the path of its growth, it recorded the myriad influences of religious and cultic groups and the outcome of social events and movements. The Vaishnava cult, the Natha cult, the Sakta and the Shaiva traditions, as well as the Islamic tradition, albeit to a limited extent (since the Islamic conquest of Bengal in the thirteenth century resulted in an official ban on theatrical presentations which were forbidden under the sharia), all left their imprint on the drama of Bengal. This essay will attempt to focus briefly on the factors that spurred the development of Bengali drama, leading to its official flowering on the proscenium stage of the commercial theatre in the nineteenth century as an offshoot of what is called the Bengal Renaissance.

The Influence of Sanskrit

Chronologically speaking, the first of these was the result of the Aryan influence that swept Bengal as a result of the annexation by the Mauryas. As P. Guha Thakurta notes[2], the flourishing trade led to the rise of urban centres, patronising art and culture where classical Sanskrit theatre played a significant role, a role which continued over the centuries. The influence of Haswabardhan, Bhaskaravarman, Yashovarman and Lalitaditya was keenly felt. A noteworthy example of local composition in Sanskrit was an early play called *Lokananda*, a Buddhist grammarian in A.D., sixth century complete with four acts and a prologue, which appears to have enjoyed immense popularity. The influence of Sanskrit on Bengali theatre continued with periodic interruptions throughout its history right upto the nineteenth century when the influence of Western themes and dramaturgy successfully usurped its place. To quote a few examples of this impact at different stages of this history, we have towards the end of the sixteenth century, King Lakshman of Bhulua, who composed two plays *Vikhyata Vijaya* and *Kuvalayashwa Charita* towards the end of the sixteenth century. His son Amara Manikya composed *Vaikuntha Vijaya* and a court poet named Kavi Kartik wrote *Kautuka-ratnakara*.

Once again, even in the heyday of dramatic revival during and after the Bengal Renaissance, the influence of Sanskrit was manifested through the many translations which flooded the theatre. The reason for this will be analysed later in this essay. Significant among these was *The Fatal Ring*, the English version of Kalidasa's *Abhijnana Shakuntalam* staged on the newly established Sans Souci Theatre in Calcutta. Other translations during the time include Krishnamishra's *Prabodhachandrodaya*, Kalidasa's *Ratnavali* etc. Scholars in Bengal composed Sanskrit plays like *Amaramangala* (1913), by Panchanan Tarakaratna, *Nala Damayanti* and *Symantakoddhara* by Kalipada Tarkocharyam. In addition to this, the influence of Sanskrit manifested itself in the elaborate settings, the grand costumes, the dramaturgical devices, the introduction of the Sutradhara.

The use of mythological stories which formed a vast repertoire of potentially tragic or tragic-comic themes, were also directly traceable to the influence of Sanskrit drama. In fact Jogendranath Gupta's *Kirtibilas* (1852), credited with being the first original tragic composition of modern Bengali theatre, exploits this influence in the use of Nandi, Sutradhar and Nati, all of which was also used by Ramnarayan Tarkaratna in his *Kulin-Kulasarvaswa* (1854). Ramnarayan, an orthodox Sanskrit scholar, also translated a number of Sanskrit plays, including *Benisamhara, Abhijnana Shakuntalam*, *Malatimadhava*, which fetched him considerable renown in the literary and theatrical circles of the day. However, his forte lay in his unparalleled dexterity in his satires, *Kulin-kulasarvaswa* and *Navanataka* (1865) also under the influence of Classical literature in which he lashed out against social evils like the kulin system[3] and polygamy which irked the wrath of the kulin Brahmins to an extent that they almost succeeded in putting a stop to the staging of the play.

Even Michael Madhusudan Dutta, the jewel in the crown of the literary scene of the Bengal Renaissance, who was responsible for the emancipation of the theatre of Bengal from the shackles of orthodoxy, initially chose mythological themes in his first two dramatic ventures, *Sharmisha* (1859) and *Amravati* (1860) following the Sanskritic influence. This in brief, is the history of the influence of Sanskrit literature on Bengali theatre. If this history records gaps in its growth, it is mainly due to the adverse impact of the Islamic conquest which put an end to official stage performances.

The Vaishnava Cult and the Influence of Sri Chaitanya

The *Chaitanya Bhagavat* of Vrindavamadasa says, "Ekadina Prabhu balilena sava sthane. Aji nrytya karibana ankera vidhane" (C.B. M, XVIII,6).—One day the Master said to everyone there: Today I shall dance in a sequence of acts.

To the literary community of Bengal, this announcement of Sri Chaitanya Mahaprabhu heralded the true birth of drama in Bengal, or at the very least, its glorious revival after the ban pronounced by the Islamic rulers of Bengal. The text notes that Sri Chaitanya assigned roles to his disciples in the enactment of the exploits of Lord Krishna (Krishna lila) and commanded them to fetch bracelets, bodices, silk sarees and ornaments. Chaitanya himself danced in the role of Lakshmi with costume and this performance in the house of his disciple Chandrasehara, gave great joy to his followers, men and women alike.

Initiated in the early sixteenth century by Sri Chaitanya (1486-1530), Gaudiya Vaishnavism, thus, exerted a major influence on Bengali indigenous theatre through its enactment of the Krishna lilas. In her essay *Caitanya's Performances,* Bozena Sliwczynska notes that "Dancing, singing, reciting or listening to stanzas from favourite works are often mentioned as activities very much enjoyed by the Master (Sri Chaitanya), provoking his moments of ecstasy. Reciting from works of great Vaisnava poets-Jaydeva's *Gitagovinda*, Candidasa and Vidyapati's poems as well as of his pupil Ramananda Ray's drama—pleased him a lot and created a perfect ambience for his euphoric and frensied states. Enacting Krsna-lilas was an important part of the devotional practice of Caitanya and his circle."[4] Sliwcynska goes on to state when the performance at Chandrasekhara's house came to an end, and the disciples were sad at heart, the Master, as the *Chaitanya Bhagavat* notes, became a veritable embodiment of the Jagan Mata (in the forms of Lakshmi and Chandi) that he had portrayed in his performance. He was the Mother and they, the disciples, his sons and he suckled them at his breast. Thus Master and disciples were at one—and drama found the most vibrant exposition of its true purpose—that of involving dramatist, performer and audience in the action of the performance as active participants.

In addition to this, the Vaishnava cult contributed other plays, though mainly in Sanskrit.The plays of Rupa Goswami, Sri Chaitanya's close associate and disciple included *Bidagdha Madhava* (1524), *Lalita Madhava* (1529), *Dankeli Kaumadi* (1549) and a critical work on Sanskrit dramaturgy by Ramananda Ray entitled *Nataka Chandrika Jagannath-vallabha* and *Chaitanyachandrodaya* by Kavikarnapur and *Sangit Madhava* by Govindadasa directly or indirectly spurred the growth of Bengali drama and at least one of them was translated into Bengali and made available to the lay community.

Some of the religious jatras included *Kaliyadamanpala*, *Vidyasundarpala* and its practitioners were Sisuram Adhikari, Paramananda,Sridam, Sudam and Badan Adhikari. Krishnakamal Goswami wrote a number of plays about the divine exploits of Lord Krishna like *Raiunmadini*, *Swapna-*

vilas etc. This influence of the Gaudiya Vaishnava literature had a powerful effect and even Rabindranath Tagore came under the influence of its lyrical and dramatic potential as is evident in his lyrical drama *Bhanusingha Thakurer Padavali.*

Other Religious Influences on the Indigenous Theatre of Bengal

P. Guha Thakurtha claims that a strong evidence of the religious influence on narrative theatre can be traced back to the *charyapada* or *charyagiti*, paeans to the Lord, popular in Bengal from the ninth to the twelfth centuries. All these songs composed by Tantric Buddhist mendicants to propagate their religious doctrines through dance. In the Natha cult[5], oral compositions dealing with the origin of Natha siddhas, the rescue of Minanatha by his disciple Gorakhsanatha from the intoxication of material pleasures and the exploits of Queen Moynamoti were performed for the community for purposes of evangelisation. In these indigenous dimensions of the theatre, the lead narrator (*gayen*) describes an event, himself enacts the various personae associated with it and their actions all in the third person. He sings and dances swinging a whisk (*chamar*) while choral singers (*dohar*) provide vocal and instrumental support using the *mridanga* and *mandira*.

The Islamic conquest silenced the voice of the official theatre of Bengal, to a large extent the significant influence of Sanskrit drama and dramaturgy and the performances in the courts of kings and the courtyards of temples. But even in this uneasy interregnum, drama found expression in its many folk manifestations, which even embraced the lives of Muslim saints and *pirs*. While on the one hand, it led to the decline of the tantric Buddhist and Natha cultic performances, it brought alive Shakta and Shaiva religious performances which added a folk angle to the Puranic myths through the advent of the Mangal Kavyas, (known as 'local epics') which dominated rural life and culture in Bengal from the fifteenth to the eighteenth centuries. These stories, largely folk versions of goddesses like Chandi, Manasa (snake goddess), Lakshmi/Kamala, Shashti (goddess worshipped for begetting children), were part of a tradition intended to revive the flagging faith of the rural populace in a benevolent Hindu deity (preferably female, Mangal/Mangala indicates her benevolent form), who could perform miracles for the welfare of her devotees at a time Islamic rule threatened the life and faith of the people. They basically involved narrative performances of these Kavyas accompanied by vocal and instrumental music. The narrative performance was spread over a period of eight days during a particular season with day and night sequences. It was often accompanied by visual support in the form of scrolls and pots on which local artists painted scenes from the stories of these compositions. The most well known of these Kavyas, the *Chandi Mangal* of Kavikankan Mukundaram Chakraborty provides evidence of this sort of multi-media performance in the signature piece (*bhanita*) where the poet says that he is accompanied by musicians and actors in his vocal recital. Elsewhere he claims that the narrative performance also included '*geet*', 'badya', 'natya' and 'nritya'.

Mangal Kavyas dedicated to Dharmathakur, a folk version of Shiva, had a single performer dancing to the accompaniment of a drum. This custom later mingled into the *gajan* traditon even today performed by the devotees of Shiva on the occasion of Chaitra Sanktranti, on the eve of the Bengali New Year. The tradition of *gajan*[6] and the belief in Dharmathakur led to processional performances through the use of tableaux, music and dance. P. Guha Thakurta narrates how the sandal of Dharmathakur used to be carried during the twelfth century on a golden palanquin with much ceremony and a clown with a painted face (*sang*) accompanied the procession. Even today *sang-jatras* and different forms of masked dances are performed during the *gajan* festivals of Shiva and Dharmathakur. These masked dances, enact the lives of gods and goddesses. The author further notes that the masked dance of the Gambhira festival owes its origin to an shamanist or spirit cult performance of the Koch community.

In spite of the ban on theatre, considered inimical to the Islamic shariya, the Muslims had their own enactments of the lives of their saints during the fifteenth and sixteenth centuries called the *yusuf zulekha*[7]. This introduced the Arabic and Persian influence into Bengali theatre. *Rasulbijay*, *Maktul Hussein*, *Kashemer Ladai*, *Karbala*, *Khizirer Jari*, established parallel to the Hindu enactment of the Puranic myths and enjoyed royal patronage. In one such text, the first mention of puppetry with wooden rods is found. Processional theatre was also practised, accompanied by players wielding bamboo poles and musicians playing on drums and gongs on the day of the full moon of the month of *Magh*.

Secular Indigenous Theatre

The 'jatra', an indigenous form of theatre, popular in Bengal and comparable to the 'tamasha' of Maharashtra, was performed all through the night on open air stages or under a canopy for a predominantly rural audience. Melodramatic themes, loud music, declamatory speeches, dramatic monologues, stylised acting, gaudy colourful costumes, harsh lighting and song and dance sequences to mark scene transitions, are some of the characteristics of the Bengali *jatra*. The musician sit on either side of the stage and it is really meant to be participative theatre. A particular feature of the *jatra* is the appearance of a character called *Bibek* or conscience who plays the role of an ethical commentator on the action and the characters. *Jatra* could be both religious or secular. Some of the religious forms of *jatra* have been discussed in the preceding sections. The secular ones had the potential to be coarse or even erotic and vulgar catering to common rural taste. Asit Kumar Bandopadhyay comments, "Some 'Jatrawallahs', however, catered to the vulgar taste of a section of the audience by making a highly publicised erotic presentation of the story of Vidya-sundar."[8] The *jatra* assimilated into itself all prevalent forms of folk tradition of music, dance and singing including *Jhumur*[9], *Gambhira*[10], *gajan gan*, *panchali*[11] for a comprehensive coverage of the folk paradigm. *Jatras* still remain popular in villages, particularly during festivals and in their urban adaptation, they are sobered down to cater to the urban taste while retaining their folk flavour.

The Western Influence on the Bengali Theatre

The arrival of the British and the spread of Western education brought about a sea change in Bengali drama and the theatre. The establishment of the Serampore Mission near Calcutta in 1800 and the arrival of Sir William Carey spurred the task of translation and the strengthening of the Bengali vernacular through the compilation of grammars and lexicons, all of which gave a much needed fillip to the Bengali vernacular in order to bring it of age in modern times. This task was further facilitated by the establishment of the Baptist Mission Press which printed and popularised the translation activity and grammatical compilations made by missionaries and later their local apprentices. Translation brought exposure to (a) Western literary and philosophical texts (b) Sanskrit texts and treatises (c) Persian and Arabic texts in a medium comprehensible to the common man.

Drama took over a whole new meaning to the Western - educated Calcutta elite. The proscenium stage was established. Gas lighting was introduced. The affluent manor-houses of Calcutta and their intellectual owners, the Tagores, the Sinhas (Kaliprasanna Sinha and his Vidyatsahini Sabha) composed plays, translated extensively from Sanskrit and English and French originals and staged plays in their own courtyards for a select circle of fellow literary connoisseurs. By and by, drama in Bengal began to reach out to a wider audience. Commercial theatres began to open in and around Calcutta—the Chandernagore Theatre (1808), the Chowringee Theatre (1815), the Sans Souci Theatre (1815). The first Bengali play on a Bengali stage was ironically by a Russian, Hersim Lebadeff, who translated *Love is the Best Doctor*, into Bengali. As earlier noted, the first locally composed and original Bengali play was Jogendrananth Gupta's tragedy *Kirti-bilas* (1852). Contemporary Sanskrit scholars translated Sanskrit texts for performance enthused by the Western Orientalists or chose mythological themes for their own compositions.

But it was to the credit of Michael Madhusudan Dutta, a Christain and a Western educated lyricist and dramatist, that Bengali drama finally broke the shackles of orthodoxy and acquired a whole new dimension. Asit Kumar Bandopadhyay notes that Michael Madhusudan "believed that in European dramatic tradition we find 'stern realities of life, lofty passion and heroism of sentiment' while in our Sanskrit plays 'it is all softness, all romance."[12] It was his conviction that 'ours are dramatic poems...." Noting the deficiencies of contemporary drama, he was firmly determined to enforce a change. He introduced the 14 metre blank verse and themes both historical and social. His historical tragedy *Krishnakumari* (1861) and his social satires, *Ekei ki Bole Sabhyata* (1860) and *Buro Saliker Ghadc Ro* (1860) introduced a whole new genre onto the Bengali stage.

The Impact of Drama on Contemporary Society

But Michael Madhusudan shared the honours in this new advent with other luminaries like Dinabandhu Mitra, whose *Nil Darpan* (1860) (translated as *The Indigo-Planters Mirror* by Michael Madhusudan under a pseudonym and published by Rev James Long), brought imprisonment for its publisher owing to the sesitive subject and precipitated a social revolution by bringing to light the British Governments forcible imposition of indigo cultivation on the farmers and the inhuman atrocities perpetrated upon them. The staging of the play was responsible for the flood of international condemnation, the setting up of the Indigo Commission and ultimately of the withdrawal of indigo cultivation.

The spotlight of the age was however firmly focussed on Girish Chandra Ghosh, popularly known as the 'Garrick of Bengal.' But as Asit Kumar Bandopadhyay points out, whereas Garrick was mainly an actor, Girish Ghosh was actor, translator, dramatist, composer and innovator. "It was due to his untiring efforts that Bengali drama became a commercial success. He, for the first time, made acting a fine art and initialed a special style of acting. He could convert an illiterate or a common dancing girl into a fine actress[13] by his training."[14] Ghosh established the National Theatre and the Star Theatre. He experimented with various types of music on stage. His vast repertoire of compositions included lyrical dramas, *Agamani* (1877), *Akalbodhan* (1881), mythological dramas, *Abhimanyubadh* (1881), *Jana* (1894), *Pandavgarh* (1900), historical plays, *Siraj-ud-daullah* (1906), *Mir Kasim* (1906), social plays like '*Praphulla*'(1889), and under the pervading influence of Sri Ramakrishna Paramahansa (whose ardent disciple he became) and the Hindu Revivalist Movement, the great *Bilva-Mangal* (1888). Sri Ramakrishna himself attended some of his performances. He modified the 14 metre blank verse of Michael Madhusudan and made it more suitable for theatrical presentation. It came to be known as 'Gairish-chanda' after him.

Bengali drama had, indeed, come of age. The colossal advent of Rabindranath Tagore steered it onto fresh heights of greatness of social representation, philosophical representation, philosophical insight lyricism, song and dance. Tagore evolved mixed genres like the lyrical dramas enacted through song and dance sequences as in *Bhanusingha Thakurer Padavali* (1884-85)), *Shapmochan*, *Chitrangada*, *Chandalika*, *Balmiki Pratibha* (1881), *Mayar Khela* (1888), which Tagore used to propagate his revolutionary ideas on women's liberation, the evils of the caste system, etc. He wrote humorous plays and social satires like *Chirakumar Sabha* (1926), *Baikunther Khata*, influenced by the Western models of dramatic symbolism as W.B. Yeats, Strindberg, Maeterlinck, Tagore composed *The King of the Dark Chamber* (1910), *The Post Office* (1912), *Raktakarabi* (1925), *Kaler Yatra* (1932), in which we find eloquent poetic symbolism critiquing the doctrine of universal mechanisation, the tyranny of the shackles of the machine over the beauty of Nature and the yearning of the human spirit for freedom, the conquest of industrialisation over agriculture.

The dark events of the twentieth century, the two wars and the genocide that followed, the coming of communism darkened the vision of Tagore as it did that of subsequent dramatists. Many younger dramatists and poets revolted against what they called Tagore's romantic view of the world and they experimented with Western models and dramatic and philosophical movements. The terrible Bengal Famine of 1943 prompted Bijon Bhattacharya's *Nabanna* (1944) and then the launch of the Indian People's Theatre, an anti-Establishment for voices of protest. While commercial theatre suffered a decline in the post-War era despite the tremendous advances in stagecraft and lighting (like that of the almost legendary Tapas Sen), sound effects, the sixties and seventies saw a spurt in parallel theatre and the formation of dramatic groups like Shombhu and Tripti Mitra's *Bohurupee*, Rudraprasad Sengupta's *Nandikar*, Little Theatre Group, the Calcutta Shakespeare society who launched experimental plays or translations or adaptations of European plays of the nineteenth and twentieth centuries to capture the malaise of the twentieth century. There was some fine acting and directorial talent in the likes of Utpal Dutta, Shombhu and Tritpi Mitra and later their daughter, Shaoli, Rudraprasad Sengupta, Ajitesh Bandopadhyay et al. Original compositions of playwrights like Badal Sircar, *Evam Indrajit,(*1963) *Baki Itihas* (1965) *Pagla Ghora* (1967), well known for his Naxalite sympathies and anti-Establishment views and his pursuit of street theatre, courtyard theatre, devoid of the elaborate trappings of conventional stage and the egalitarian 'Third Theatre', Manoj Mitra, *Chakbhanga Madhu* (1972), *Narak Gulzar* (1976), *Banchharamer Bagan* (1977) where he blended humour, satire, fantasy and pathos to convey tales of social injustice and others. However, for all the potential, the technological advances as well as the Bengali's proverbial love of theatre, another renaissance in the annals of theatre in Bengal is not yet imminent. Without assigning blame to television and the cinema as viable and more attractive alternatives, it is time for a day of reckoning.

Notes

1. Asit Kumar Bandopadhyay, *The Complete History of Bengali Literature*, Modern Book Agency, Pvt. Ltd., Calcutta, 1966.
2. P. Guha Thakurta, *The Bengali Drama: Its Origin and Development,* Routledge, 2001.
3. A social custom introduced by King Ballal Sen in Bengal whereby the upper classes had to marry their young daughters, usually by the age of twelve within the same *kul* or clan, resulting in polygamy or vast age differences between the child bride and her often, middle-aged or elderly groom. It continued till well into the nineteenth century.
4. *The Banyan Tree,* Vol I ed by Mariola Offredi, Manohar, New Delhi, 2000.
5. The Nath sampradaya in the Vaisnava sahajiya cult of Bengal survived mainly in north Bengal. Ethnological studies indicate a long tradition of narrative theatre in the Natha cult.
6. A Spring festival in Bengal when followers of Shiva perform the wedding of Shiva to Harakali, fairs and gaily colored tableaux-processions are held.
7. A story in verse written in the Bengali language, also enacted romantic stories like that of Laila Majnu, usually during the time of the Bengali New Year.
8. Asit Kumar Bandopadhyay, *History of Modern Bengali Literature,* Modern Book Agency Pvt. Ltd., Calcutta, 1986, p. 126.
9. A festival closely related to agriculture, performed through dance, song and in some forms, theatre for better crops in the month of Jaistha.
10. A festival of songs and dances in praise of Lord Shiva, often in the form of dialogue between the singers. Today, even contemporary social problems are represented.
11. *Panchalis* are long narrative poems celebrating the glory of a deity.
12. *History of Modern Bengali Literature,* p.132.
13. Binodini Dasi is a fine example of this, she later rose to fame as Nati Binodini, well known for her acting and singing talents. Her personal sacrifices for the cause of the theatre at the request of her teacher and idol, Girish Ghosh, are recorded in her memoirs.
14. *History of Modern Bengali Literature,* p. 146.

Works Cited

Asit Kumar Bandopadhyay, *The Complete History of Bengali Literature*. Calcutta: Modern Book AgencyPvt. Ltd, 1966.

Guha Thakurta,P. *The Bengali Drama: Its Origin and Development*, Routledge, 2001.

Mariola Offredi (ed). *The Banyan Tree*, Vol I ed by, New Delhi : Manohar, 2000.

11

Oriya Theatre: A Playwright from Orissa—Hrusikesh Panda

— Lipipuspa Nayak

Post-independence Oriya proscenium theatre had peaked in the sixties and seventies when mobile stage groups like Annapurna Theatre and Janata Theatre toured across the state to perform plays by noted playwrights of the period. The groups would camp in dorps and small towns for days together, and perform to packed spaces. The tours were immensely popular, and at times were extended on public demand. These plays were traditional well-made plays that drew largely on the theme of social realism; they portrayed characters and situations from the here-and-now to which the audience related instantly. The plots were conventional and revolved round problems of everyday life. Thematic variation in the form of suspense plots and adaptations from scriptures too sustained the popularity and success of these extended shows. The stage groups utilised intricate stagecraft, which included attractive lighting, equipments, costume, make up and trendy music and songs. The action on stage was elaborate and loud that bordered at times on melodrama. Yet the performance by artistes was so powerful that it ensured the attention and participation of the audience, and many of these artistes became icons through Oriya films.

These stage groups occasionally revealed their penchant for novelty and experimentation. There would be shows with only women artistes. A suspense plot would have characters seated among the audience. But these were rare occurrences; the plays largely survived on their realism, both on the thematic and theatrical level. The commercial success of the performances was concurrent with their aesthetic soundness and strength.

During the later half of the seventies, the 'New or Absurd' plays appeared alongside this genre of traditional theatre. This latter class of plays apparently intended to satisfy the intellectual curiosity of the audience, as opposed to the entertaining repertoire of the traditional professional theatre groups. The plays, through the works of a few playwrights, were promptly christened harbinger of the 'New Theatre Movement' by Oriya critics, and this genre of literature has been canonised to a great extent. The plays in real were borrowings of the Absurd Plays of the 50s from the West, and other post-World War experimental trends of the Western theatre. The plays had abstract ideas as plots (for example, psychoanalysis of the sexual obsession of a middle class housewife), which the playwrights 'experimented' through stage techniques that echoed those from the West. Skimpy, one-phrase, disjointed dialogues recurred through the characters cyclically. The action often took place in remote sets (a frequent motif is an inspection bungalow, preferably amid a woods, with a mysterious *chowkidar* at its supervision). The plays wore very few casts, were alien to the Indian (Oriya) ambience and sensibility and were marked by a sense of irrelevance to the surrounding of the audience.

Yet, initially, the newness of the 'movement' held the attention of the intellectuals for sometime. It changed the audience interest and helped playwrights take note of new techniques and themes. Many of these plays were also written for the radio, and in fact, All India Radio contributed greatly to the growth of this theatre movement.

The movement began to lose general audience by nineties, and the audience for these plays began to be limited to people associated with theatre. Some of these plays were too intellectual and unrelated to the reality of the audience. In fact, these plays suited the broadcast mode, and were successes as radio plays, where they responded to the languid intellectualism of the distant and scattered listeners. They definitely failed to hold the collective attention of the audience inside an auditorium. By this time the professional proscenium theatre groups, which continued alongside the new theatre for about a decade, had also declined. The decline cannot be credited solely to the rise of the new theatre movement. The decline of these traditional theatre groups happened over time, alongside the increasing acceptability of Hindi films, a quiet revival of open theatre operas (*jatra*s) and the spatial limitation of proscenium theatre.

As a literary critic I would credit the occurrence of the New Theatre Movement of Oriya literature to a pan-Indian literary process: the import of Western literary trends to Indian literatures at specific turns of history. When in the later twentieth century Western theatre history, stage became largely the domain of the director and its equivalent echoes were heard in theatres across countries, in India, we had the 'New/ Navya plays/ Absurd plays/ Modern experimental plays'—patronising 'intellectualism'. The impact of theatre trends from the West has been an inescapable reality in all the regional literatures of India, and this is true of other literary forms like fiction and poetry. A drift away from Eurocentric norms and towards American trends and theories in literature and criticism for the Indian literary scene is an obvious corollary of this tendency. The New Theatre Movement in Oriya literature therefore authenticates this universal unwritten principle that guides literary practices.

An example from a regional literature will explain the point further. Kannada theatre had its Modernist phase, the *Navya* period, during the mid 60s and early 70s with a tradition of experimental, intellectual plays almost modelled after the post-War Western plays. It is a different issue that at the same time, Kannada stage witnessed plays by Girish Karnad, Chandrasekhara Khambara, and a few others which became popular performances way back in the seventies.

Hayavadana by Girish Karnad was written in 1971. *Hayavadana*, among other theatrical innovations, had a striking feature in its non-realistic/non-naturalistic mode of representation of social relations and interactions that the critics and scholars identified as the turn to 'folk' in Kannada drama. Karnad had company in Chandrasekhara Khambara who wrote two brilliant plays—*Jokumaraswamy* (1972) and *Rishyashringa* (1965). These plays ran parallel to the Modernist Kannada Drama (*Navya*) period, yet belonged to a distinct phase of it. In this phase Kannada drama turned to folk, to rural and regionalised cultural and performance forms, such as Yakshagana, Sannata, etc., and brought them on to urban, metropolitan, pan-Karnataka and even pan-Indian stage. K.Marulasiddappa, a Kannada critic writes: "...At a time when through realist and existentialist type of drama intellectualism had gained more importance and spectators were denied the pleasure of performance, folk touched drama. Modern folk drama, which came into being through the grafting of the old and the new, gave joie-de-vivre to Kannada theatre, which was hitherto a difficult situation." [K.Marulasiddappa, *Adhunika Kannada Nataka*, 2002, p.336.][1]

So the Kannada critic has put the issues in perspective. K. Marulasiddappa is unambiguous in his concern for the *Navya* plays: they promoted intellectualism and in the process denied the spectators 'the pleasure of theatre'. In a way these plays endorsed a decline in audience attendance, taking it as a substitute of intellectualism.

II

It is in this context that I will discuss the plays by Hrusikesh Panda, a frontline writer of eight novels, eight collections of short stories and four plays in Oriya. While the very same observation of Marulasiddapa can be made of the plays of Hrusikesh, our critics are not quite vocal to document this. All his four plays have been staged to packed houses. The infusion of both classical and romantic elements, and other cultural forms into the plots, through the theatre's encounter with tradition, gives these plays a pan-Indian character that has rejuvenated Oriya theatre, particularly amateur theatre. The new ingredients in the plays certainly provided the much needed freshness and pleasure to the audience who were stripped of it with the earlier New plays. And I am sure, there may be many more such plays in the last two decades which would have compelling power on the audience and thrilled them. And yet we wallow in the glory of a dramatic tradition of the 70s and 80s that never really existed for the general audience.

Hrusikesh's plays are titled *Sabdantar* (Another Word), 1995; *1799 or Panchajana Engrej* (1799 or Five Englishmen), 1996; *Brahmarakshas* (*God-demon*, 2007), 1997 and *Vasco-da-Gama* (Vasco-da-Gama), 2000. These plays have been produced in Bhubaneswar, Raurkela, Angul, Berhampur, Jharusuguda, Sambalpur, Paralakhemundi (all these are towns in Orissa), and Allahabad (*Brahmarakshas* was enacted as an entry for the All India Drama Festival in 1999 in Allahabad, where it was adjudged the play with the best script) to packed auditoriums. The plays have been performed repeatedly in Rabindra Mandap, the high-profile performing arts auditorium in the capital city of Bhubansewar over years. They have been performed in festivals of plays. *Brahmarakshas* was published in 1997, and produced first at Townhall, Brahmapur for the sixth Southern Orissa drama Festival in Feb. 1997. They have been staged in open air theatres. Subsequently, the play has been staged in Bhubaneswar for a few more times. In all the productions, the play has been staged to packed houses. It also received awards whenever it was staged as an entry in a competition.

Now why am I giving here all these details about the plays? My concern as a critic is with the goal of theatre that must eventually entertain, and do so enduringly. These plays here bear adequate testimony to this theatrical principle.

Sabdantar is about the abstraction and ambiguity entailed in words. This apparently abstract concept is treated through the poignant story of Brihadhwaja, the king of a tiny kingdom Sindurbahal at a transitional hour of history—when monarchy is on the wane and is getting replaced with present day systems of governance. The recluse in Brihadhwaja can shrug off this eventuality, but his scheming associates nee courtiers, would not let it. They use his figurative status of a king's for realisation of their personal political ambitions, and thereby their material affluence. Brihadhwaja sees through their deceit, but does not have a will to reprimand them as he himself has no desire to swap his role to a present day equivalent of a king. He is also content with the care and love of his maid Basundhara, who in real is his stepsister. During one such mental deliberation on the absurdity of the state of affairs around, in his life's context, he strangely hears a female frog asking him for a kiss. He offers it as the creature insists and the frog turns into a woman, dressed like the mythical heavenly nymphs. She reveals her identity: she is Kumbhika, the dancer at the court of lord Indra. She had been cursed by Indra to descend to earth as a frog while performing on an occasion as her gaze fell on a musician there, and the curse, as it were, was to be annulled only through the kiss of a king. She offers to be a maid-in-waiting to her redeemer, or a court dancer, and Brihaddhwaja does not have a court. She therefore wants to be the queen. Their marriage takes place. The first act ends here.

The second act is enacted eight years later. Brihadhwaja has attained premature senility. He looks self-exiled and stoic. Chakradhara, the scheming hanger-on of the king is now the Chairman of the Panchayat society. The queen, elected a Member of the Legislative Assembly, is in Coastarica as part of the Indian delegation to participate in the World Women's Safety conference. Basundhara, the governess of the king's household is nanny to his children and has not 'ascended' in the ladder as she never nurtured any big ambition and was unconditional in her love for the king. Brihadhwaja misses his wife, with the knowledge that he has lost her to her world of power and limelight; he learns about her busy schedules from newspapers that carries her photographs. He tries to weigh his losses and gains in life, when he hears the voice of another female frog asking for a kiss from him. The frog metamorphoses to a heavenly beauty once he kisses her, and she narrates her tale. She is Kumbhinadi, the sister of Kumbhika and had been spewed a curse by lord Shiva as she had broken his penance at the command of Indra. Kumbhinadi wants to atone for her sister's act and offers the king her love to avenge his hurt. She wants to caress his children, but Basundhara wouldn't allow her as she thinks Kumbhinadi is a witch and may cast an evil eye on them. Kumbhinadi explains: Indra's anger for Kumbhika was jealousy-driven, therefore she carried the attribute of a queen in her transformation to human form after her curse was exorcised. She aspired to become the queen. Kumbhinadi, on her part, was a victim of the rage of Shiva, and her curse churned out of his anger and hubris that banished her to the lowly world of insects, worms, amphibians and reptiles. She has traveled layers of time stretches from her past in the nether worlds to reach her present, and her metamorphosis to the human form is therefore suspect for the onlooker. Kumbhinadi in a protracted monologue at the end of the play demystifies the ambiguity and irony inherent in words as social constructs. She is labeled a witch though her love and concern for the king and his children is absolute, and she has come to avenge her sister's cruelty to her family. She quietly suffers the stigma tagged with her identity. Kumbhika, who uses her wife's status to ascend high up in life, is labeled a queen. It is the people and the society who decide the lexical constructs. Kumbhika comes over as a part of her official program and leaves hurriedly, without meeting her children. She enjoys her world of sycophants and glare of publicity. The cycle of machination in the world of greed and deceit comes a full circle when Chakradhara offers Kumbhinadi a political post. She refuses it, knows that it is the last remaining bait in the ever fragile world of Brihadhwaja that she must evade and redeem him from. She knows that Brihadhwaja is a misfit in the world he inhabits, a ladder that his associates, including his wife, use for ascendance in public and material life. She therefore takes him along to her lesser world of insects and creatures where there would be only sounds, and not words to tie them with 'labels'; they retrogress into the world of the amphibians—a world Kumbhinadi labels as one of 'pure desires'. As they leave the stage the public labels her a 'goddess'; and start singing paeans eulogising her.

1799 or Five *Englishmen* is based on a strong foundation of history, of East India Company in India. In the brief foreword to the play the playwright acknowledges his sources: The Report by Collector William Brown submitted on 15.3.1802; Ganjam District Manual, Madras Presidency (1881) and so on. The play is a critique of the polemical judiciary system, which the British bequeathed to India. Alongside, run subplots of the system of governance of the period, manifest in its manifold incongruities, irony, absurdity and injustice. Set in 1799, when Snodgrass was the collector of Ganjam, a south-coastal district of Orissa, the plot unfolds, in four long scenes, a detailed sequence of social, political, administrative and judicial realities of the period till 1807.

As a matter of fact, the English had started some kind of an administrative establishment in Ganjam around 1768, and the district administrative head was known as a Resident, and not a Collector. The latter designation came into practice in 1794, and the designation of Resident was abolished. The Collector, a direct employee of the East India Company reported to the Madras Presidency.

The play, against this historical backdrop, opens in a forenoon or morning when about a dozen employees of the collectorate—loaders, sentries, constables, office clerks and rent-collecting officials—scamper on the stage as commodities as revenue arrive on ships and boats and are to be stored and entered into record. Merchandise—paddy, fabric, salt, farm produce, gunpowder...—are being carried inside the residence of the collector, which is in real the remnants of a fort. The sentries guard the various exits and entry points, some of which lead to storage rooms and tunnels. The porters bring inside items that come on ships; they also carry goods to the ships for dispatch. The clerks look into papers, and attend to kings and estate owners from feudatory states and lawyers of such people who come to call on the collector. Everyone betrays a very strong sense of fear and subjugation to the collector, Snodgrass, even in his absence on the stage. The creepy activities on the stage are a clear pointer to his brazen show of despotism. The employees appear to have got used to the way the wealth collected as tax and rent and which is to be deposited with the Company, is siphoned to his personal account. Edward Hair, the chief of trade of Ganjam is his accomplice in these sinister designs. Snodgrass's insidious character reiterates itself in the sudden reign of fear among his Indian servants as they learn of his arrival. We learn that greed and larceny are not the only vice Snodgrass substitutes for governance; he is evil; tax defaulters lose their family members and property at his command. He intercepts French and Dutch pirates and soldiers and confiscates their arms. He has a huge palace in Rambha, another nearby town on sea, which he has built with the money for relief measures and shifts the commodities and tax money there, besides spending luxury time. Years ago he had forcibly brought along a temple dancer of a village as compensation towards the unpaid tax of the village, and she—Devadasi—stays in his Ganjam residence as his mistress.

Snodgrass gets his transfer order in a year. Brown joins in as new collector. He is humble, civilised, human; is concerned about how to dispense good governance to the common folk and is a paradox to his predecessor. He comes with two English colleagues, his subordinate officials: Alexander and Skinner. He has been authorised by the Company to enquire into misappropriation of sixteen lakh rupees by Snodgrass. But he is too straight for the trickery and deceit of Snodgrass—no receipts and papers are available for inquiry. Snodgrass sends home his amassed wealth through a French soldier whom he had kept in jail and flees Ganjam in a small boat. Brown starts the enquiry. Quite a number of small kings, tehsildars, zamindars and lawyers of tax-paying kingdoms come to him with complaints that they keep receiving notices for tax default though they have deposited the tax money with the clerks of Snodgrass. Brown gets their statements recorded. Meanwhile a drought hits Ganjam and he remains busy with its management.

The fourth and last scene fast-forwards to 1807. Alexander is the collector now and Skinner, the magistrate—a post newly created by the administration. Brown comes from Madras as the prosecution witness to depose in the trial of the case against Snodgrass. Snodgrass has been sacked by the Company already as he has failed to deposit the tax money with the Company. A few of the former clerks and accountants of Snodgrass, dismissed from service already, are co-accused in the case against him; a few are defence witnesses. A lawyer represents Snodgrass as the latter has fled the place long ago. And at the end, no one is proved guilty, including Snodgrass as there is no evidence. The evidence that Brown had collected towards fraud of about fourteen lakh rupees by Snodgrass (the rest two lakhs he had failed to locate) has been systematically sabotaged following his transfer from Ganjam. The witnesses only remember the irregularities in maintenance of records and receipts, of bribes and frauds during the period, but memory and recollections have no place in a trial, neither is the grasp of the truth that Snodgrass had in real destroyed the district in terms of governance and economy.

The play ends with Brown, sad and withdrawn, who confides to others that he has resigned from his job from Madras Presidency as he considers himself to be unworthy of the service. He further informs that he will not return to Madras and is going back to his home in England. He exits a sad man, with the realisation that he, as an Englishman and a representative of the Company, has his contribution to an unfortunate system of judiciary that acquitted a plunderer for absence of 'proof' of his misdeeds. This system does not arbitrate what is just and what is unjust, it endorses how well you defeat your opponent with logic and eloquence and trickery. This system is bound by polemics, rhetoric, eloquence, logic, craftiness, scholarship and the social and economic status of the accused. He is overtaken by a sense of despondency in the end, as Snodgrass is sacked by his employer not because of his sinister crimes, like absence of governance, taking bribes, troubling innocent men and women, abduction of a woman, being unjust; but he was sacked as he did not pay the Company its tax regularly.

Brahmarakshas (*God-Demon*) builds on a story from *Katha Sarit Sagar* (12:17), by Somadev. A newly married royal couple, the bride a hermit's daughter whom the king meets during a hunting session, spends their first nuptial night under a peepul tree that happens to be the abode of a god-demon. As the god-demon is an ascetic, his dwelling is defiled by the carnal act of the royalty. The king faces the wrath of the god-demon where he asks for the king's life. The king offers a Brahmin youth of seventeen (Pragalva) as a substitute sacrifice, borrowing from tradition, to propitiate the furious god-demon. The demon agrees, with certain appalling conditions, such as, the boy should be volunteering for the sacrifice; the father and mother must usher their son near the demon; the queen must embrace the youth during beheading and collect the spurting blood in a skull-bowl; the king must behead him. The efficient minister arranges for the substitute; he gets a golden chariot studded with gemstones sculpted for the purpose. A summons is circulated, that a youth willing to sacrifice his life for the king will be rewarded the chariot along with a large amount of land. Pragalbha, an erudite, poor youth volunteers and agrees to all the conditions of the minister. He induces his parents into the reality that this one action of his will redeem them and his future generations from penury, and that it is an honour to save the life of the king, so that an entire kingdom is saved. The parents consent to the minister.

Pragalbha comes near the altar of sacrifice where the priest is busy performing the necessary propitiation rituals. Pragalbha impresses everyone with his erudition and disinterest in worldly matters at such tender an age. He refuses to be served intoxicating potion before beheading, which is a normal practice so that the sacrifice is spared the pain of being killed. As the rituals linger, he learns about the inside intrigues of the royal court: the minister aspires for the throne and seeks his help in the matter—as his last wish before the god-demon; the newly married queen, who is a hermit's daughter, falls in love with him, the *kotwal* spies for the king anticipating some rewards each time, the minister has an affair or two in the lane of the gypsies. He is befuddled. The sagacious youth, at the time of beheading, bursts into uncontrollable roaring laughter. His laughter confounds and weakens the fury of the god-demon and he refuses to have him as his food. The youth is saved.

The original story by Somadev ends with this climax. The plot in *Brahmarakshas* moves further; universal and contemporary issues sneak into the thematic fabric and the play becomes a contemporary metaphor. The god-demon asks Pragalbha to explain his strange behaviour, and Pragalbha, in long monologues, deliberates on the hypocrisy of human behaviour that eventually nurtures a world order beyond all limits of cruelty and reason. The king surrenders his reason to his love for life and romance, and wants to go in for a substitute sacrifice—a young subject whom he as the king has sworn to protect. The queen, for whom the king subjects himself to this ghastly injustice, turns out to be cruelly adulterous. The experienced minister is scheming for the throne with help from him, a death-bound youth who is old enough to be his son. The parents, who nurtured him with their own blood, and taught him that righteousness overshadows wealth, voluntarily accept the wealth to hand over their son for sacrifice. The Brahmarakshas is an ascetic; he has the strength of a demon and the righteousness of an ascetic. Yet he agrees to violence and slurp the blood of a young boy. Pragalbha, with his precocious wisdom and sage-like detachment from worldly ties, sees through this incongruence and the all-pervasive injustice, and guffaws uproariously.

Shame overtakes everyone on stage, including Brahmarakshas. But the characters are relaxed as they have been spared the anger and violence of the demon, and prepare to leave. Then, in an apparent volte face, Brahmarakshas warns them to stay on as he wants to pronounce his version of the truth that regulates worldly issues, and the audience is treated to another climax. The story of Brahmarakshas becomes an allegory for the fate of the people at the top. He is an ascetic as he has been banished by Brahma, the creator. Everyone is afraid of him as he has the strength of a demon, and since he has been cursed by Brahma, he is bound by righteousness and truth. He is thus a sad loner in a world of utter insensitivity, a world convoluted between values, rites and rituals. This contrary position is what makes him a god-demon. He has given up the worldly life to become an ascetic, but the world does not let him live alone. The world, in the shape of the colonial king, transgresses into his world of self-banishment, and destroys his abode, peace, abnegation, *sannyas*, and distance from political and economic society. Pragalbha further questions him to justify his action, which would have subjected everyone—the king, queen, his parents—to the path of sin. Brahmarakshas delivers a moving concluding speech, where he sensitises the characters about his position in the creation. With a curse from Brahma he hangs between the heaven and the earth and leads an insufferable life, carrying the burden of sin of others. His action was not one of violence as he had given a week's time for its execution, it was an attempt to educate everyone on the ephemerality of worldly ties and the dwindling distance between the glamour of power and sentimentality.

The central point in the original story is that when a person faces the ultimate injustice, when he has crossed the stages of depression, withdrawal, anger, rebellion, compromise and assimilation, the victim laughs like an insane person. In *Brahmarakshas*, if the statement of the god-demon is taken as the final statement of the play, then, it is about abnegation and resignation of the people at the top, from the worldly matters, because the world will not change much, in terms of values and propriety. Pragalbha had hopes of laughing off the absurdities of the world a few thousand years ago. Brahmarakshas cannot hope to shake up the world with his laughter. If the play is taken as a metaphor of human life, it begins with juvenile excesses, passes on to youth, moves to the intrigues and complexities of adult life, and ends with withdrawal, and *sannyasa* and *vanaprastha*.

Vasco-da-Gama, in five scenes and a prologue and an epilogue, is a narrative of a village Alin Singh (this word from a dialect of a forest community in Orissa in translation means—village of Sago-palm juice), tucked in a remote corner of Orissa. Inhabited by 23 families of a forest community, this sylvan hamlet falls victim to the missionary interest of proselytisation. One fine morning the newspapers, news channels, internet flash the news that a church in this village has been torched and a nun raped. The faceless village acquires an overnight limelight of infamy. Two Delhi-based journalists, supported by a local news reporter reach the village to investigate into the event.

The play begins with a prologue where the journalists—Lovelyn and Arun, accompanied by Charan, a local reporter appear. They have come with the preconceived notion that the Hindu community has torched down the prayer hall of the Christians and is responsible for the rape of a nun, and want to conduct an on-the-spot investigation of the finer nuances of the event. They meet the police official and the accused in the crimes Bhagirathi, who has been arrested by him. They also meet Megha, the nun who has been raped. Lovelyn, particularly excited and triumphant, updates her news studio in Delhi through satellite phone on the developments, till Megha, emaciated and drained out—begins feebly to protest what she terms 'the suicide of a truth'. She reveals that she has been raped by a man called Pilimon, but they dismiss her speech as hallucinations of a rape victim. She appeals to be heard, to relate the truth that is not being reported here. The stage darkens; we wind back in time.

Scene one establishes the village Alin Singh amid its picturesque beauty, supplemented by the simplicity of its inhabitants and their rituals. Buyani, the shaman of the community is entranced to exorcise the evil spirit of a young woman Megha, who is the nun in the prologue. Megha has fever. Two other villagers are present: Jani, Megha's father and the priest of the community and Jaman, a farmer. An elaborate voodoo ritual is performed; Buyani diagnoses that Megha has been possessed by the dead spirit of her brother, who had committed suicide. Buyani invokes the dead brother's spirit and he speaks through her. The audience learns that he had gone to Hyderabad as an indentured laborer with his wife to repay the loan he had taken from Solomon. Solomon stole his wife there, and there was no news of them Megha's brother came back before the scheduled tenure of his indentureship, and was panicky that Solomon might return to ask back his money. And his sister nagged him about his missing wife, and the hurt was too much, and he therefore ended his life by hanging himself.

Bhagirathi, the only educated youth from the village and the son of Jaman, who loves Megha, comes home and witnesses the scene. He monologues that Megha does not take medicine in spite of his repeated instructions, and goes back. Pilimon, the school teacher peeps from a distance at the show. The characters chant a hymn like song to rid the place of the dead spirit.

Bhagirathi was a student of Pilimon and after matriculation, has been employed as an excise inspector. He is a questioning mind and is skeptical about the sermons of Pilimon. Pilimon is a Christian, who in his discussions with Bhagiarthi, dismisses the customs and ceremonies and practices of the community, who are Hindu, as superstitions and wants them to embrace Christianity. He dissuades them to take medicines, provided at the government health centre, and asks them to surrender to the mercy of Jesus Christ. Pilimon also doubles up as the moneylender and encourages the villagers to indulge in their customs and propitiating practices for which they will need money. He takes away their land and its produce as security for the loan he dispenses, and the villagers would not know to calculate the compounding interest of their loan money. He persuades Naik, the village chief to arrange for a buffalo as sacrifice to exorcise the spirit in Megha.

A young Sub-collector Arya and Deputy Superintendent of Police Bijay visit the village. They learn about the naïve villagers and try to help them. They offer to take Megha to the hospital as she suffers from Malaria, and give her medicine. They find out about the irregularities at the school, which Pilimon has converted to a church; he imparts teachings from the Bible there and misappropriates government money towards students' welfare. Pilimon conspires with Naik, the community chief not to let Megha go with two young officers (later we learn that he confiscates the medicine and flings it to water). After the officers leave, Pilimon takes over, and pronounces that the spirit possessing Megha can be exorcised only through a stronger spirit, a Christian spirit—the spirit of Vasco-da-Gama, who has with him a huge arsenal of swords, guns, canons, bombs and missiles. The villagers are puzzled, a brief uncertainty reigns the atmosphere, and then Megha begins to sway—an indication that she is invoking the ghost of Vasco-da-Gama. And the stage, at this point, sheds its realistic oeuvre and enters the realm of fantasy. We suspend our belief willingly, and see Vasco coming out of a coffin from the graveyard of the village. In a mix of the real and the fantastic that borders on neo-realism, he walks on stage, enquires about how India has progressed as he has been sleeping for the last four hundred and seventy-four years, and more importantly, how many families in Alin Singh have been converted to Christianity. He threatens the villagers with his gun, a technique he recalls was highly successful in his times, to embrace Christianity. He christens Megha Mary and commands Pilimon to take her as wife. The villagers are shattered at this sudden encroachment, on their social and cultural foundations, yet are petrified to offer even a teeny-weeny resistance. In fact Jaman, we learn a little later, puts an end to the ignominy by killing himself.

A leaflet circulates with the information of a healing congregation in Alin Singh of about fifty thousand people. The leaflet sings paeans to the miracles of Vasco-da-Gama, the messenger of God, who through his touch would heal people of their disabilities, like blindness, deafness, inability to walk and so on. Arya and Bijay confront Vasco; Arya outwits Vasco in knowledge and counters him on his wrong mission where he is disturbing the social fabric of a country with an ancient and developed civilisation. Arya gets his transfer order following his prohibitory notice on the congregation, on the grounds of law and order problems and inadequate infrastructure. In his last speech—a long, moving monologue—Arya urges Vasco to spare countries like India, where 68,000 castes and 400 languages follow a tolerant principle for a peaceful coexistence. He asks him to stay off his menacing neo-colonialist designs that drain poor countries of their minimal resources. Bijay arrests Vasco as he has violated the Sub-collector's order to cancel the congregation, and in the epilogue we learn that he too had been transferred following this. Mary (Megha) reveals a weird disposition and wants to ensure that the villagers attend the Church services; she wants that Jani, the communist priest, as the custodian of the religious psyche of the community must be baptised and with Pilimon and Vasco subjects him to immersion. Jani dies in the process. Bhagirathi arrives from his work place and knows that his father has died. He is inconsolable and Megha is evasive. Vasco orders Pilimon to report in the police station that Bhagirathi, a Hindu youth has murdered an old man while he was going through the process of baptism. Pilimon demands five thousand rupees from Bhagirathi for a burial, that will spare him the offence of murdering a Christian old man, and offers a loan at a high interest.

The sequence of devastation of the community is so rapid and cruel that Buyani, the shaman, gets back her reason; she acts to banish the spirit of Vasco. And, in a reversal to the chain of events, Megha is rid of her spell and springs back to normalcy and her feminine tenacity. She gathers the characters and gets Pilimon and Vasco tied up. They haul Pilimon to the village and dump Vasco in the school/church. A bullet goes off Vasco's gun and the school/church, stuffed with explosives, bursts into flames. The scene, the last, ends with a choral background chanting of the song that the community members sing to ward off evil spirits, this time for the ghost of Vasco.

In the epilogue, we meet the journalists again. The mood of jubilation and excitement of earlier is now replaced by a sense of loss, and even resignation. Truth lies threadbare before everyone, and the event can no more be straightjacketed—assault on the minority community by the majority. Their investigation into the event has brought on surface the complex dynamics of the issue: poverty and cycle of usury of the illiterate villagers; strategic, despicable moves of the government for instant political gains; exploitation by the missionaries masquerading as charity, and above all, the politics and realities of news reporting. A rape will make a headline, not the non-substantiation of an alleged rape; everyone wants a sensational, politically correct version of a story, outside truth. Bhagirathi was the fiancé of Megha, though they had never made love. In fact she can be said to have been raped by Solomon who forcibly married her. Megha, shattered with her losses (the police inspector appears on stage to inform that Bhagirathi has committed suicide), evokes deliriously how innocent and unsullied Bhagirathi was in his relationship with Megha.

The suicide of Bhagirathi is a new development, in the presence of the journalists in the village, for which they hold themselves responsible. For the clichéd and conceited practice of reporting, catapulted by the ephemeral mass euphoria, one more life has been lost. The journalists leave with a burdened conscience. Megha's heart-rending wail fills up everywhere as she pleads the dead Bhagirathi never to visit 'the village of suicides', and we think the play is drawing to a close. Then suddenly, there is light on the grave of Vasco; in one more abrupt denouement, he rises from there and with his menacing stacks of guffaws declares, he cannot be killed and will appear again and again, and the stage darkens finally.

III

These four plays lie, temporally and in spirit, outside the two broad covering labels of Oriya theatre: traditional proscenium theatre and New Theatre. As a matter of fact, these plays belong to that distinct bulk of Indian theatre, which ran alongside or consequent to the 'new' plays, and brought characters and theatricalities back to focus and galvanised theatre audiences and practitioners alike.

Far away from the pseudo-real-existential format and languid intellectualism of the New plays, these plays host unreal characters and ambiences, settings and presentations—kings, queens, frogs, an exiled demon, a white district magistrate of yore, Vasco-da-Gama, a palace, a fort, a forest, a hamlet of forest dwellers—where human and non-human characters and worlds coexist. In *Sabdantar*, a female frog delivers the final statement of the play. Brahmarakshas, a cursed demon is a protagonist, helplessly carrying the sin of humanity. A collector and district magistrate from the colonial time resigns from his job as he cannot dispense justice to the

Indians. Vasco-da-Gama walks the stage as a real character. And yet the plays succeed in entertaining the audience and have held audience attention among different groups of spectators; the plays are enjoyable even for the audience who cannot be bothered with their complex dramaturgy, symbolism and who may not be conscious of contemporary issues. It does not come as a surprise to me that in a cultural-literary form, there is this virtual turnaround with regard to theme and stage elements and theatrical conventions.

What causes this apparent volte-face to happen within two decades, and that precisely ensures audience participation? For one, novelty in the form of nostalgia, for one's own racial elements reflected in their pan-Indian disposition—the plays take their theatrical elements from Indian civilisation, with its myths and legends and tales, its rites and rituals, folk and classical songs and tribal cultures and Indian history. Again, the plays demand ostensible and high levels of stagecraft as they enact extreme and intricate human emotions on stage: a romantic wedding, a court trial of the colonial period, intrigues of monarchy, explicitly violent actions like beheading and murder, real voodoo rituals of forest communities, and so on.

At a different level, the plays are statements on complex universal realities that rivet round tragic human situations. Brihadhwaja is a lonely man in the world of his scheming associates. He is born into a wrong hour, where values alter and he cannot tailor himself to suit these alterations. He is content with his status of a king without a kingdom, an ordinary man who must crave for a little love and care; his once-royal status would not allow him to express it. He loses his wife to her ambitions. He is saddened over the condition of his children, who are deprived of their mother's care. And yet, he cannot show his tears to the outside world.

The play lifts his personal sense of deprivation and sorrow to the level of the universal, where his story morphs into the story of people at the top, self-exiled and in search of an escape. The play also dissects in details the changing exterior of Indian political systems. Monarchy gives way to current forms of governance, and Brihadhwaja is incapable of coping with the intrigues that is only a natural part of the entire game, and that is why, his associates may not be demonised either. It may be equally argued that Brihadwaja would not have succeeded as a 'model' King.

Brahmarakshas and *Vasco-da-Gama* hold up a very realistic picture of current politics and economy on the global scale—of powerful countries demolishing ancient civilisations and ways of life on false accusations. It chronicles shame, the shame associated with power, to be specific the power of neocolonialism. Brahmarakshas tells the king—the colonial predator: 'When you built your palace, you waste out ten times the timber quality trees you use. Only out of arrogance. You kill birds and animals. You are not just brutally violent. You are blind with arrogance...'

And the play also chronicles the sense of shame and remorse of the powerless observer—the intellectuals, the opinion makers whom Brahmarakshas represents, or the administrator-activist bound by the laws of the government system whom Arya represents. Brahmarakshas admits: 'That you have presented such elaborate arguments for your defense King, I am not surprised at all... I am ashen with the smoke of remorse and repentance. That I did not burn away. I wish I could have been reduced to ashes ...'

At one point, the plays become political allegories against the vast backdrop of neo-colonialism, of issues the post-Colonial countries are tragically handed down. Beside cultural disruption, which includes, most importantly, religion, the most disturbing reality of Post-colonialism is the irrevocable loss of flora and fauna of lands invaded by the colonial mastersIn *Brahmarakshas*, the playwright is unequivocal in his statements for environmental issues, an area of concern labelled Eco-Criticism. Brahmarakshas is the archetypal aborigine who is displaced from his abode by the king, the coloniser. The destruction of wild flora and fauna, and ancient civilisations by the colonialists has been mentioned as a matter of fact. The native god-demon, after offering land, food and company to the royalty ('in the tradition of Indian hospitality'), the colonisers, starves as his food fall victim to the royal whim of hunting games. His woods disappear as the king expands his landmass by felling trees, only to assert his monarchical arrogance. In this limitless stretch of insensitivity and insanity, the fury of the god-demon fails to hold; his wisdom and austerity fail him ironically. He relapses into his tragic aloneness, and reverts, fleetingly, to subaltern savagery and violence. *Vasco-da-Gama* is even more disturbing as it handles the most sensitive contingency of a nation's identity—religion. I must say the playwright has been exceptionally bold in his derisive attack on the neo-colonialist forces responsible for disruption of a peaceful country's sociological equilibrium. Megha, the forest dwelling girl transforms after she is baptised. Of course she is under the spell of the spirit of Vasco, but her demeanor of one-upmanship before her fellow villagers is a very standard behaviour in such situations. She orders that Jani, the community priest, must be baptised as an assurance for the conversion of the entire community. Her perception is also a result of her illiteracy, and lineage where ailments are not cured by medicine, but by occult practices, and machinations of people like Pilimon. But the point is, when people like Arya try to help them they are strategically shifted from their positions. This is the irredeemable tragedy of the post-colonial countries—that their policies and governance is remote-controlled by forces from out side. Any skeptic for Vasco's answer to deputy police superintendent Bijay: "I don't obey petty officers like you; I receive my orders from Bhubaneswar, New Delhi, Europe, America..."

The plays share a few common structural traits. The plays betray a pan-Indian character from their haunting preoccupation with the past, where the playwright travels back in history to retrieve his dramatic material. This retrogression relates to both the thematic and the structural dynamics of the plays. The theatrical elements are taken from Indian civilisation, with its myths and legends, its rites and rituals and its folklore, its tribal culture, village traditions, performing arts techniques and Indian history. Indian classicism and aesthetic theories build into the formal fabrics, alongside folk elements, rural riddles, songs, and ancient Indian cultural and traditional customs. There is variation in the use of these stage ingredients and techniques: *Sabdantar* effects a complete recast of the folk in its journey through a surreal world to one of fantasy. The transformation of cursed nymphs to human forms with touches/kisses from kings/princes testifies to the collective unconscious of our folklore.

The playwright retrieves the performing style of *pala*—a once-powerful musical performing art performed by a group of artistes. The lesser characters in *Sabdantar* speak as a group in sing-song regularity, each conveying only a part of the account in turn and complementing the next speaker. Further, as in a *pala*, the possibility of multiple meanings in the speech of these characters leave ample room for country humour, that can juxtapose a somber situation on stage and provide relief to the audience. At the other end of the spectrum stands *Brahmarakshas* with a conscious, extended superstructure that can be identified, fundamentally, with Indian classicism: the characters speak largely a chaste idiom; a song in the play is based on a Hindustani Classical *raga* (Puriya Dhanashree, not mentioned in English translation); *hastamudras* are ascribed to the characters; a range of *rasa*s (moods of Indian aesthetics) are effected in the characters. As the play proceeds, there is a gradual transition from one *rasa* to another. It begins with *vir rasa* or the mood of valour, when the king's prowess is described at the beginning. This is followed by *shringar rasa* or the mood of love. Brahmarakshas appears in *beevaschha rasa*, the mood of terrible, which glides into *bhaya rasa*, or the mood of fear. And so on.

The moods change seamlessly to joy, laughter, suspicion, intrigue, and ends with withdrawal and resignation of the eponymous hero. There has been very few repetitions of the moods. This gradual and continuous movement from one *rasa* to another is a major strength of the play, which holds the audience attention even if the theme and sub-texts are complex. The play also has a small content of countryside songs and riddles. In *1799...* the Englishmen speak in Oriya. Their accent is not faked, distorted or anglicised, as it happens in Hindi period films portraying such characters. The playwright in his foreword to the play has underscored this point. This saves the audience the irritation of artificial speech. The lesser characters speak as a chorus, in turn, emulating performing art styles of the Orissan countryside. As a contrary convention, the gripping tension of the plot, throughout the length of the play, has been supplemented by background use of *raga*s of Hindustani classical music. Hindustani classical *raga*s have specific hours of the day to be sung, and eventually are indicative of the mood of the singer and the listener. The playwright's use of the *raga*s, a powerful structural variation, sets the mood for the scene, which would have otherwise been narrated monotonously through characters and accentuates the poignancy of the events enacted on stage. In fact music has a very strong presence in all the plays, in forms of both off-scene songs and songs sung and recited by characters. These songs range exhaustively, from riddles and banters to songs based on classical *raga*s. *Vasco-da-Gama* is a straightforward narrative of an unfortunate village. The gravity and immediacy of the subject perhaps does not leave much scope for ostensible theatricalities. The presentation is real and authentic, save for a brief spell of fantasy when the ghost of Vasco is invoked. Nonetheless, there are a few real songs and hymns that the community sings to invoke and exorcise dead and evil spirits.

Why does the playwright, in his creative exercise, revert to the past? The use of myth and legend and old sources is certainly a tool to represent reality at a changing time, the way "literature is derived from ritual and myth—man's original modes of responding to reality" (Leitch, American Literary Criticism, 1988, 120). Beside setting aside the past and the present, the mythic method also enables an artist to fuse antiquity and modernity, and ages and cultures. Through the use of theatrical personae like a king without a kingdom, a district magistrate from the colonial time, Vasco-da-Gama, a civil servant of current time and an accursed demon, the playwright achieves a montage as well as continuation of several timeframes of contingencies. As Eliot puts it in *Tradition and Individual Talent*, "the pastness of the past and its presence are affirmed and life is seen as a continuum guided by a teleological principle".

Protagonists of the plays are larger-than-life heroes; prototypes of a tall man at the top. Conscious of their limitations, they are largely losers at the end—they lose out on their battles. It is not that they cannot fight successfully, it is just that they are born in wrong times, where values have changed and an overpowering sense of absurdity hangs heavy; and they lose the will to fight. Contrarily, their social position and status would not allow it (do they run the risk of looking ludicrous, tall as they are and helpless by the same measure? —my comment)—they choose to withdraw to their aloneness and inanity. A sense of despair, therefore, looms large as the plays end. Even in *Sabdantar*, Brihadhwaja's escape to a world of fantasy can be construed as a relapse into his perpetual sense of inanity that dispenses him an aura of an ordinary, sad man.

The plays, thus, deconstruct in the post-Modernist parlance, the collective dynamics that shape the personae of the protagonists: Brihadhwaja, Brahmarakshas, Brown and Arya. *Brahmarakshas* consequently deconstructs, in terms of Psycho-literary views, why an ascetic becomes a demon. The native god-demon could not aspire to the level of Pragalva's laughter. Pragalva had hopes 3,000 years ago. Before the colonial depredation, his laughter could evoke action, could make the powers-that-be sensitive through sheer laughter. A contemporary god-demon cannot hope to shake up the world through his laughter; he will be dismissed as a mad man. As a contemporary metaphor, few will like to associate the god-demon with politicians. The politicians and government servants are more likely to be associated with the king, the queen and their courtiers. The god-demon is likely to be associated with the intellectuals, the opinion makers, the fourth estate, and the judiciary, over whom the society has no apparent control, and who must control themselves. The god-demon merely withdraws to a self-banishment, which is not possible any more in a forest-less land. But yes, his hurt is human, sufficiently so, so that it sensitises the audience on the ways civilisations behave, and mankind acquires its ultimate fate in the fight between civilisations.

In the process the characters grow tragic in stature, represent the people at the top with their loneliness and lend the plays a haunting dramatic mood and endplayed sadness. Even Pragalva is a shade closer to these characters who willingly surrender to their state of forced inertia. Only, he sagaciously demystifies the ways of the world, even dismisses the incongruencies and silly arrogances of ephemeral achievements of 'powerful' people, perhaps because he is young. Through his long monologues, Pragalva elaborately explicates the most vocal and obvious statement of the play: social justice.

Should I say that the playwright belies an autobiographical trait as he creates these protagonists? A bureaucrat by profession, Hrusikesh always confesses that his literature is a result of his helplessness, and not success, as an administrator. For one, his literature is never borne out of any literary dogma, and is the extension of his life which he actually lives. Yet he maintains a distance and remains non-judgmental and impartial as he creates his characters and events. Brown, a white man atones for the unjust action of Snodgrass, his fellow countryman; in fact he takes the sin of the entire British race on himself when he resigns from his service because, it, according to him, "bequeathed the Indians a flawed judicial system where an accused can be acquitted on lack of proof and witness and walk a freeman with head held high". Arya does not grudge Vasco his feeling of racial supremacy and forgives his ignorance; he is worried about something larger and beyond: violence that only breeds more violence, and leads the perpetrators into an inescapable trap. "Why do hundreds of people in your country commit suicide in the name of religion, Vasco?" he asks. "Why do your people produce mass weapons, sell it to other countries and tempt them into war? Don't you get hit or not sometimes by the same weapons that you produce? Don't your boys in schools shoot down their fellow students without any rhyme or reason? Why do your countries sell soft drinks, mobile phones to poor countries, set up there useless consultancies and drain them of their resources? Try to explain to your people, this is sin.... We don't go to your country to create unrest, why do you come to our country and destroy it?" The playwright also bemoans our sense of colonial subjugation long after our independence. That is why, Pilimon, as the insider-accomplice is portrayed as more vicious than the missionaries—he exploits the illiterate community monetarily, with exorbitant interest rates on loans he lends them. Pilimon represents the Indian who, with a little education, succumbs to a colonial mindset that sees everything about the ex-masters, including religion as superior to his own, and with mercenary incentives carries out the mission on their behalf. The plays, therefore, reflect the sense of hurt the playwright suffers as a universal symptom, which is not parochial.

The plays have multiple climaxes and an extended sense of denouement, enacted through long and solemn speeches by protagonists on eternal universal human predicaments: displacement of the native race; loneliness of people at the top; neocolonial machinations.... And the audience is made to go through the predicament of the protagonists. A monologue is not ordinarily tolerated by the modern audience; but the monologues in these plays have enthralled the audience (I have been among the audience for some productions), probably because of the powerful logic, and the subliminal pathos behind the apparent victory of the victims. It was also on account of the histrionics and dramaturgy of the scenes.

The plays, with significantly lesser number of women casts, are also statements on women, not only in terms of literary theories but from the point of view of social realities. The women in the plays are in the world of men, they are strong and are significant from the point of structure. They carry out defining functions and evolve in the course of the plays. Vasundhara provides the king with the shield against machinations of his courtiers, though she does not have a socially approved relationship with him. Kumbhinadi from the nether world provides the king his ultimate liberation. Devdasi, the lone female cast, is the custodian of Snodgrass's establishment at Ganjam. She is wise, firm in her decision, is conscious to stay off the sins of Snodgrass and is the only Indian in the play who does not subjugate to the white collector. That she used to be a temple dancer lends structural soundness to her demeanour; she is unruffled to the trappings of power, and does not yield to the sin concurrent with it. The playwright leaves a scope for her transcendence after Snodgrass's departure, where she acquires power of prescience and she delivers a crucial dialogue before Brown: "... the injustice that took over this place will cause this government to fall. A deadly plague will befall Ganjam; thousands of its population will perish; your administration will fail to save them." (The population of Ganjam was reduced to 6,000, from 15,000, following a fever in 1815.) Indibaraprabha, a hermit's daughter, ironically regulates the sequence of events in *Brahmarakshas*. Her transformation should delight the feminists, despite the streak of hypocrisy in her. But sin is inherent with governance, and the streak of contrivance should reflect her rise and assimilation in a men's world. Her love for Pragalva should be seen as a statement of objection and rebellion against her enslavement by her husband, even if under the orders of the god-demon. Megha transforms from an emaciated, possessed girl to a tough woman to avenge her father's suicide and her insult. She also salvages her village of the infamy, wrongly attributed by a media obsessed with political correctness and public opinion, as she boldly narrates the truth behind the event.

The smaller number of female roles is not necessarily a reflection on the smaller role of women in society, it is a reality of the economics of theatre. Female actors are to be paid. Male actors do not demand payment and also often help financially. So female actors are generally fewer everywhere. In India, there has been the additional problem of culture barrier. Nothing more should be read into this gender discrepancy, because the women have had full and independent roles.

Many post-New playwrights in Oriya theatre have experimented with theatrical innovations, in the use of the folk, myths and legends from the past and rural and regionalised theatrical practices and techniques. In most cases these theatrical elements and techniques appear tailored, obvious and artificial. In contrast, in the plays discussed here no theatrical ingredient or technique appears superfluous. A *sutradhar* or a chorus, an ostensible presence in many post-New playwrights, operates at a metaphoric height in the plays of Hrusikesh. No single character appears and declares himself to be the *sutradhar*; characters perform the role of a sutradhar or a 'chorus' at a metaphoric level as the plays are neo-realist in nature.

In *Sabdantar*, Chakradhar, the scheming associate of king Bruhaddhwaja may be taken for the *sutradhar*, as he is the harbinger of the shape of things to come, and the play has at least eight characters who with their bantering and limericks and riddles will pass off for the chorus. In *Brahmarakshas*, which transposes contemporary questions in time and space, the audience establishes a link with realism through two characters: Gopalia and the priest. Gopalia, with his country songs and riddles and innocuous curiosity is both the chorus and the *sutradhar*. In the game of governance, between the power-hungry king, a sad and lonely ascetic-demon and a sagacious youth who is indifferent to the worldly issues, he is the only person who stands out as an ordinary citizen. He has no gains or losses in this game, but he is the one who raises the most sensible questions in this surreal world, from "Alas, if only this sudarshan chakra were destroying the sinners" in the beginning to "You smile and keep smiling like lord Krushna in Puri paintings. Why don't you say anything, lord?" to the god-demon towards the end. Further, in a major deviation from the classical dramaturgy, the characters performing the job of the chorus in these plays are not always the 'feelers', with minor roles in the plot, often speaking gibberish. Their status, a point about structure, is synchronous with the function they perform, dispelling any scope for redundancy.

For example, in *1799...* the loaders and porters, who naturally cover-up for the chorus, rhyme about sixty-two varieties of paddy that they carry on their backs everyday; the constables and sentries sing-song thirty-two types of titles that are bestowed by estate-owning landlords to faithful subjects. With this strategy, the audience, in a way, is treated to slices of economic and sociological grandeur of the period. The army of porters and loaders and guards at the residence of collector

Snodgrass shares with the audience important information on the irregularities in the administration. They perform this role till the end of the play, long after Snodgrass is gone, where they salvage information from their memory to aid the new officials.

What sociological motivation drives the playwright when he creates this genre of plays? In the Indian context, these plays as products of post-colonial realities are the playwright's attempts to return to his roots along his quest for a national identity. This is a form of protest as well as revenge on the part of the artist. Return to one's roots, through nostalgic use of historically documented past, myths, racial stories, legends, local performing arts techniques, indigenous aesthetical principles and structures is a post-colonial syndrome, a base of resistance and recovery of self of the writer against the reality of cultural disruption of colonialism. In the post-colonial literary discourses, dramas with Indian elements marked the rise of 'the theatre of the roots'.

The plays are post-colonial in fervor not only because of their dates of creation, but the playwright's preoccupation with a number of issues that concern the post-colonial critics. I will not get into the jargons of the post-colonialist discourse; let me just quote Aime Cesaire to summarily substantiate my argument: "...I am talking about societies drained of their essence, cultures trampled under foot, institutions undermined, lands confiscated, religions smashed, magnificent artistic creations destroyed, extraordinary possibilities wiped out... I am talking about millions of men torn from their gods, their land, their habits, their life—from life, from the dance, from wisdom" (quoted in *The Cambridge Companion to Post-colonial Literary Studies* 8). I am sure of abundant parallels between this scholarly statement and most of the content dialogues in these plays. This is true of plays written in other Indian languages.[1]

These plays by Hrusikesh mark the entry of Oriya Theatre into this sub-world of Indian drama, but this recovery of self is not against the cultural disruption of a particular colonial period (that our critics refer to as post-colonial reality). The plays are dated in the post-colonial times, but transcend to talk of universal issues and neocolonialist patterns that ultimately determine the shapes of civilisations.

Postscript: Though to give a roll of honour in this kind of write-up involves a lot of censure, I will risk it nevertheless. A few dramatists like Radha Binod Nayak, Kunja Ray, Harihar Mishra and Ramesh Prasad Panigrahi can be cited as playwrights who have not been influenced by the New theatre, and have written plays independent of the tradition. These plays are highly entertaining, appealing to audience across classes and do not sacrifice on the intellectual content. Most of these plays, again, are interpolation of myths and legends to issues of current times. The plays build largely on stories and events from past and are statements on current and universal issues of humankind. Mention, in particular, may be made of *Raktanadi* and *Kadambari* (The Blood-bath and Kadambari, the Manna, Radha Binod Nayak); *Kalantara* (Another Eon, Kunja Ray); *Nindita Gajapati* (The Discreditable King of Orissa, Harihar Mishar) and *Jane Mahapurushanka Janma Mrityu Samparkare* (About the birth and death of a Great man, Ramesh Prasad Panigrahi).

Notes

1. I can even remember beyond India—Wole Soyinka, for instance, notes such a move in the context of West Africa: more ad more of the highly developed societies are turning to the so-called 'primitive' forms of drama as representing the significant dramatic forms for contemporary society (1996:346).

Works Cited

Barry, Peter. *Beginning Theory: An Introduction to Literary and Cultural Theory*. Manchester and New York: Manchester UP, 1995.

Crow, Brian and Chris Bansfield. *'Girish Karnad and an Indian Theatre of Roots'* in an *Introduction to Postcolonial Theatre*. New York: CUP, 1996. pp. 136-160.

Day, Martin S. *The Many Meanings of Myth*. Lanham: UP of America, 1984.

Nikhila H. *Forays into Folk: Recasting Womanhood in the Kannada Drama of the 60s and 70s*. Journal of Karnatak Studies. Vol.2, no. 1, Nov. 2004—April.

Panda, Hrusikesh. *Charoti Nataka*. Bhuabneswar: Athena Books, 2008.

Panda, Hrusikesh. *God-Demon*. Tr. Nayak, Lipipuspa, NewDelhi: Sahitya Akademi, 2007.

12

Telugu Theatre: Evolution and Glory

—C.G.K. Murthy

Theatre arts have been providing entertainment round the world with themes centred on the life styles of people of various regions besides helping them discuss their social issues while instilling dynamism among them. It is an undisputed fact that drama promotes social, cultural, political, historical and spiritual awakening among the audience. Since drama flows from life experiences it is the most powerful genre among all forms of literature. Hence, eminent dramatist J.B. Priestly opined that just as life is the bedrock for drama, similarly drama should become the role model for life.

Drama is an artistic expression of the progress of society. Throughout the world theatre developed and expanded through multifarious experiments. So also the Telugu theatre firmed up its foundations from the early days itself. Broadly Telugu theatre has passed through two important stages, viz., from the beginnings of Telugu literature up to 1860, the first stage during which Yakshagana or street plays were performed. From 1860 the second stage started on the model of Sanskrit and English dramas. Here, we are concerned more with this second stage.

In the Telugu-speaking areas, a notable feature of the Telugu theatre, both in writing and staging the drama was that it was mainly the teachers working in colleges and schools, mostly Telugu pundits, who wrote the plays and were leaders and directors of the drama troupes that were staging them.

They adapted the English, mainly Shakespeare's, and Sanskrit dramas into Telugu. Thus play writing started in A.D 1860. but staging the drama started in 1880. There were many phases through which the Telugu theatre traversed since its birth in 1860 to the contemporary period of modern Telugu drama.

During the first period 1860 to 1880 there were four eminent playwrights of Telugu drama among whom Korada Ramachandra Shastri of Machilipatnam, also called Bandar, was the pioneer. He wrote an independent work *Manjaree Madhukariyam* in A.D 1860. which however was printed very late, around 1908. Later Kokkonda Venkataratnam Pantulu translated a Sanskrit work *Narakasura Vijayam* in 1871 and published it the following year. His methodology of transliterating the Sanskrit *Shloka* into Telugu verse and the Sanskrit prose into Telugu prose is still relevant even today. Paravastu Venkata Rangacharyulu transliterated Kalidasa's *Abhijnana Shakuntalam* into Telugu and two Acts of the same were serialised in a weekly. Acharyulu introduced pure Telugu in place of original Sanskrit.

Vavilala Vasudeva Shastri translated and published Shakespeare's *Julius Caesar* into Telugu with the title *Caesar Charitram* (History of Caesar). He also wrote an independent drama *Nandaka Rajya* condemning contemporary internal social squabbles of his days. Vavilala was not only the first to attempt transliteration of English dramas into Telugu but was also an author of independent Telugu dramas. Since he wrote the above two dramas in 'Tetageeti' metre of Telugu verse he was, therefore, the first verse drama writer in Telugu. However, there appears no evidence of staging the dramas of the first four dramatists and hence they remained only as the first Telugu playwrights.

Enacting the Plays

The second stage commencing from 1880 to 1881 can be described as the first Telugu drama enacting phase. In 1880 the Dharwad Drama Company of Maharashtra toured in the Andhra areas and ignited the imagination of people from far and wide in the state. The elite, the poets, connoisseurs of arts and the poor and the wealthy attended their performances with amusement and craze. The Dharwad troupe not only gave their performances with discipline but also attracted the crowds with wonderful stage techniques. Therefore, many consider this phase as the first phase of modern Telugu theatre or the people's theatre. The Dharwad Drama Company spurred the interest of the Telugu people and instilled a sense of dedication and determination towards theatre among them. Thus, the contemporary Telugu theatre we see today has its origins around 130 years ago. As a follow up to the Dharwad Drama Company several theatrical troupes, societies and associations were established in the coastal Andhra areas of Andhra Pradesh. These imbibed the discipline and the norms and regulations of the Dharwad Drama Company. Kandukuru Veeresalingam Pantulu, famous as the Raja Rammohun Roy of the South, established Vidyarthi Nataka Samaj in 1880 in Rajahmundry and got enacted his own writings. In the light and right path of Dharwad, by 1886 several enthusiastic drama associations were established in Vizayanagaram, Visakhapatnam, Kakinada, Rajahmundry, Eluru, Machilipatnam, Vijayawada, Guntur, Tenali, Nellore, Bellary, and at various places. During this phase the playwrights were founders of drama associations, their presidents and were also directors of the dramas.

Veeresalingam's first independent Telugu drama is *Brahma Vivah* and in 1880 itself his Telugu Translations *Ratnavali* from Sanskrit and *Chamatkara Ratnavali*, Telugu adaptation of Shakespear's *Comedy of Errors* were staged in Rajahmundry. He could impart flavor of Telugu culture and tradition to his Telugu version of *Comedy of Errors* and caused myth of a original creation. In Guntur during 1881-85 Kondubhotla Subrahmanya Sastry established the Hindu Nataka Samaj, later called First Company, and got staged *Gayopakhyan*, *Harischandra*, *Yugandhara Vijay, Draupadi Vastrapaharan* etc., in all about 30 dramas which he authored. Unfortunately none of the manuscripts are available now, but it can be said that the stories of the subsequent famous dramas were written by Kondubhotla in those days itself and adapted them for the stage. In 1883 Vaddadi Subbarayudu established the Hindu Naatakojjeevan Samaj in Rajahmundry and not only wrote the *Venee Samhar* and other dramas but also acted in those plays. Veeresalingam's *Abhijnana Shakuntalam* in 1883 and Vaddadi's *Veni Samhar* ruled the Telugu theatre for a long time. During 1882-84 in Machilipatnam Nadella Purushottama Kavi wrote as many as 32 dramas in Hindi as well as Telugu (like *Satya Harischandra*) for the Hindu National Theatrical Society and himself played certain roles in his dramas. Kavi experimented with role-oriented language in his plays and became the first to advocate employing appropriate language for the characters in the plays. Kondubhotla's Nataka Samaj arranged dramas in Rajahmundry and other towns and won acclaim from several quarters. In 1885 Hindu Nataka Samaj was established in Kakinada and Jayanti Bhava Narayana wrote some plays for the Samaj and also acted in them.

All-Round Progress

The third stage of the march of Telugu theatre started from around 1886 and play writing achieved all-round progress during this phase. In 1886 Sarasa Vinodini Sabha was organised under the aegis of Dharmavaram Ramakrishnamacharyulu. He wrote as many as 30 original dramas like *Chitranaliyam* (1887), *Vishada Sarangadhara* (1889) blending Eastern and Western theatrical practices. He played the lead roles in those plays and was acclaimed as the Andhra Nataka Pitamaha (grandfather of Telugu theatre). He was not only a great actor but was also an eminent director. He was the first tragedy playwright in Telugu. Creating the scenes and acts, achieving a unique style and employing both as many songs along with poems were the main characteristics of his writings. In fact, he was the first to introduce songs in Telugu dramas. The attire of the characters, musical songs and melodious poems had a magical effect on the audience. Sarasa Vinodini Sabha toured Andhra, Tamila Nadu and Karnataka areas and acquired utmost eminence. Inspired by their performances enthusiasts like P. Sambandham Mudaliar established Suguna Vilasa Sabha in Madras and became Tamil playwrights and actors and gave many stage performances in several languages.

In 1889 Chilakamarti Lakshminarasimham authored dramas like *Gayopaakhyan* and got them staged under his own supervision through the Hindu Nataka samaj. Tanguturi Prakasam who later became famous as Andhra Kesari and was prime minister of composite Madras state in 1946 and later the first chief minister of Andhra state in 1953 did the female protagonist in those plays. Subsequently, Konda Venkatappaiah Pantulu in Guntur and Kasinathuni Nageswar Rao Pantulu in Machilipatnam also acted in dramas and later became famous in politics. Chilakamarthi's *Gayopaakhyanam* and *Prasanna Yadav* were the most popular dramas of those days. Copies of *Gayopaakhyanam* sold over one lakh by 1940s. In Nellore Vedam Venkataraya Sastri wrote *Naganandam* and got it staged by the Andhra Bhashabhimana Samaj. Sastri supported employing appropriate language for each drama character.

A Memorable Year

The year 1897 is a memorable period in the history of Telugu drama. The Baliwala Theatre toured Telugu areas during that year and the pomp and wireworks used on the stage by the company created a feeling of wonder and awe among the Telugu speaking audience. They convinced the local dramatists and artistes that female roles in the plays should be performed by women only. Another very significant development during 1897 was the first editions of Vedam Venkataraya Sastri's *Prataparudriyam* and Gurajada Appa Rao's *Kanyashulkam* were released. These two plays have become the guiding stars and inspiration for the subsequent historical and, social dramas that emanated from Telugu theatrical horizon. While the credit for using the common man's language goes to Kandukuri Veeresalingam, the ultimate in successfully employing it belongs to Appa Rao.

Gurajada's *Kanyashulkam* is a worthy reiteration of drama kindling social consciousness among the common folk. Even today *Kanyashulkam* occupies the top slot for drama's ability to rekindle social consciousness. *Kanyashulkam* stands out as a comprehensive reflection of the inherent truth about the society. With natural characters, lively dialogues and interplay and conflict among varied mindsets and attitudes it remained even today an intimate guest of the unique aspirations of the Telugus. Dramas which have the ideal of narrating the social problems of the day through intelligent comment remain an intimate part of people's lives. Such dramas lend support for social awakening and attain unsolicited and unparalleled popularity.

Around 1895 Marepalli Ramachandra Sastri and others established Kalabhilasha Nataka Samaj in Visakhapatnam and staged several dramas in which Sastri's *Bilhaneeyam* was among the famous plays. In the same year Vanarasa Govinda Rao established Surabhi Nataka Samaj and staged several dramas which he got written for his troupe. The Surabhi drama troupe had later expanded to over 30 branches and spread throughout Andhra Pradesh. It continues to stage dramas in the rural and semi-urban areas of Andhra Pradesh even today. Surabhi troupes have attained the distinction of adopting theatre as its livelihood and the practice of women playing the role of lady characters in Telugu drama started with them. The success story of the familial vocational touring public theatrical troupes of Surabhi Samaj is worth elucidation.

The Surabhi Story

The world theatre is a great ocean and in the inner recesses of that great ocean there is a unique diamond and that is the Surabhi Nataka Samaj establishment. This system did not exist anywhere in the world till 1895 when the Surabhi Samaj was born in the Rayachoti taluk of Kadapa district in Andhra Pradesh. The Surabhi Samaj and the world famous Kohinoor diamond both had their origin in Andhra Pradesh and these two are the pride of the Telugus.

After the fall of the Marathas in the eighteenth century the soldiers migrated to different parts of the country. Some of them migrated to the Rayalaseema region of Andhra Pradesh before 1850s and they were called Are Marathas cr Arekapulu, and they took up such vocations as agriculture, puppetry, street plays, etc. Since they helped the British rulers to crush the bandits the British government granted them some thousands of acres of dry land in Balakonda and Surabhi villages where they settled. Their Maratha surnames, like Vanaras, Aapet, Aatok, Rekandar, had become Telugu surnames. The Surabhis forgot their Maratha origin and did yeomen service to the Telugu theatre.

The Surabhis were living with puppetry as their livelihood in the nineteenth century and were giving performances in the houses of the rich on solemn occasions like marriages, festivals, etc. In 1895 an enthusiastic puppeteer Vanarasa Govindappa refused to play the puppets at a marriage function as he felt it was an unworthy vocation. Procuring the wedding saris, garlands of beads and jewelry of the marriage party the puppeteers innovated and enacted a play *Keechakavadha* from Mahabharat. The drama was a resounding success and the originator of the idea Vanarasa Govindappa became Vanarasa Govinda Rao. Later the landlord Channa Reddy in whose house the drama was staged helped them to learn acting from a Harikatha artiste Raptati Subbadass. The Surabhi Nataka Samaj was thus formally initiated into the theatre. For the first time Govinga Rao made the ladies of his family, his wife and daughters act in the dramas.

In those days male actors were playing the role of female characters and whenever such problem was posed to Govinda Rao he used to say, "Why don't you make your own ladies act in the drama?" In the troupes of Surabhi Samaj there were women, men; youth, children and all lived in a joint family. Everybody lived on the theatre and acting was their livelihood. During the day time they look after the upkeep of the stage paraphernalia and they all move in a group. They would select some central village in a cluster and would arrange their performances for two or three months. Marriages take place within the families of the troupes and every new born will be initiated into the drama within no time. As the families expanded the number of Surabhi troupes diversified and more troupes were started. Today there are around thirty drama troupes of Surabhi family. The plays they enact today include *Parijatapaharanamu, Kurukshetramu*, *Mayabajar*, *Potuluri Veerabrahmendraswami*, *Sri Krishna Leelalu*, etc. They learnt *keertans* from a famous exponent of harikatha and even today they sing *keertans*. It is no exaggeration to say that Surabhi Samajas are the only familial vocational touring public theatrical troupe in the world even today.

Theatre Forges Ahead

During the last stage of this phase another prominent playwright Kolachalam Srinivasa Rao started writing plays and had authored around thirty dramas. He won acclaim as 'Charitraka Nataka Pithamaha' (Grand Old Man of Historical plays). Bellary Raghavacharyulu shot into fame as a celebrated actor after his performance in Kolachala's *Ramaraju Charitra*. Kolachalam not only researched Vedic literature and wrote several articles but also authored the *History of World Theatre* in English published in 1908. Between 1894 and 1895 Panuganti Lakshmi Narasimharao started writing dramas like *Sukhamanjari Parinaamu* and became president of the Manorama Sabha. With assistance from the Pithapuram Raja in 1900 he started writing plays with *Narmada Purukutsiya* His dramas *Radha Krishna* (1911), *Vipranarayana* (1909), *Kanthabharanamu* (1817) are popular even today. Panuganti was the first to translate the entire *Ramayana* into Telugu and he started his famous literary work *Saakshi* articles in 1913.

Ballari Raghavacharyulu became a very popular actor and an all-round performer during this phase. Born in 1880 in Tadipatri of Anantapur district Raghava was a lawyer by profession, actor by vocation and a social reformer by instinct as he shunned casteism and espoused the cause of the low social status of the *dalits*. He dropped his caste name 'Charyulu' in his name and preferred to be called simply Raghava. A celebrated stage artist he was not only popular in Andhra but also acclaimed outside the state. Rabindranath Tagore was full of praise for his performances on the stage. Raghava visited England, France and Germany in 1927 to study the western theatre and did the roles of Shakespearean protagonists Othello, Macbeth, Hamlet, etc. He met George Bernard Shaw and held discussions with him on the theatre. Shaw was much impressed by his talents and asked him to do the role of Shylock in the *Merchant of Venice*. Upon witnessing Raghava's public performance as Shylock, Shaw remarked that had Raghava been born in the West he would have become another Shakespeare. Raghava, who breathed his last in 1946, had a high vision of Telugu theatre and wanted more social plays to be produced than the mythological plays of his days.

A Furious Pace

The period from 1901 to 1920 can be described as the fourth phase in the annals of Telugu theatre. Play writing went at a furious pace during this period. Among the historical plays those quite prominent were *Rasaputra Vijayaamu* of Ichapurapu Yajnanarayana, *Chandra Gupta* of Umar-Ali-Shah, *Bobbili Yudhamu* of Sripada Krishnamurthy Sastri, and *Ramadas* of Dharmavaram Gopalacharyulu. Sripada Kameswar Rao and Machiraju Durga Sankaramatyudu translated several historical plays from Bengali and other languages. The highest number of mythological dramas was produced during this phase and never so many plays were written in this area. Tirupati Venkata Kavulu wrote mythological dramas which attained a permanent place in Telugu literature. Their *Pandavodyogavijayalu* (1911) carved out a niche in Telugu literature for verses in simple spoken word. Balijepalli Lakshmi Kantham's *Satya Harischandra* (!911) and Sriramula Sachidananda Sastri's *Savitri* are other notable mythologies which are being played successfully even today. Others also wrote mythological plays because they were comparatively easy to produce and some others wrote them keeping in view particular actors.

With the Calcutta resolution of the Congress for Swaraj there was new enthusiasm in the whole country. But most dramatists were afraid of making open their views on freedom. However, some writers were dramatising the old historical and mythological plays and were indirectly promoting patriotism through their plays. Among them *Rasaputra Vijayamu* and *Pandavodyogavijayalu* are worth mentioning. Malladi Achyutaramasastri, Dronamraju Sitaramarao, Kasinathuni Veeramallayaradhyudu, Inapurapu Sundararamaiah, Chakravadhanula Manikyasarma, Vishnubhotla Subrahmanyeswarudu, Somaraju Ramanujarao of *Rangoon Rowdy* and *Dharanikota* fame were some of the well known playwrights.

During this phase several dramas from Sanskrit, Bengali and English were translated into Telugu. Also, farcical dramas, a sort of low level comedies, were written aplenty. Kandukuri Veeresalingam was the first to write farcical dramas in Telugu and later Chilakamarthi and Panuganti joined. Panuganti's *Kanthabharanamu* is the pinnacle of this type of drama. *Vidhileka Vaidyudu* (1911) by Vedam Venkatachalaiah and *Lubdhagresara Chakravarti* (1914) by Setti Lakshmi Narasimham were famous Telugu translations of the farcical. *Vidhileka Vaidyudu* was written in the dialect of Nellore district. During this phase some princes like Raja Vikramadeva Verma, Raja Mantripragada Bhujanga Rao, Raja Kotagiri Venkata Krishna Rao and Raja Meka Venkatadryappa Rao wrote dramas in Telugu.

Poets who can write songs for other's dramas either on the request of the dramatist or drama societies have come into existence during this phase. Among them Papatla Kantaiah was prominent. Dramas having 'Sangeeta' (music) as prefix in its tile like *Sangeeta Savitri*, etc. were also issued. Around 1913 drama competitions started in Telugu Theatre and hero worship started along with that. Commercial drama troupes and associations also were started in this period. Owing to mushrooming poets and drama societies several people were handling the same story and theme. Kalidasa's *Abhijnana Sakuntalam* itself was translated by as many as 30 writers and even in independent dramas repetition of theme was pronounced.

National Dramas

As the freedom movement gained pace from 1920 onwards, there was widespread unrest in the country. In the 1916 Congress meeting in Calcutta it was decided to urge for reorganisation of states on the basis of language. The demand of a separate Andhra state for Telugu-speaking people gathered support. The fifth phase of the Telugu drama commenced from this time and some dramatists vexed with the traditional forms of writing dramas have adopted innovative and experimental ways of writing. This new experimentation went in three ways; novelty of thought, innovation in writing and ease in staging the drama. Damaraju Pundarikasha's *Gandhi Vijayamu* and *Panchala Parabhavamu* were among the successful and popular political dramas while among the early plays on Andhra Movement were *Andhra Maata* by Grandhi Subbaraya Gupta and *Andhra Pataaka* by Dronamraju Sitaramarao.

Social Drama

Problem is the seed of conflict and conflict is the inherent aspect of modern life. Social drama, therefore, adopts the problem as its focal point and confirms the theatre to the aspirations of the people. *Chintamani* (1921) and *Varavikrayam* by Kallakuri Narayana Rao were very popular in social reform. The social drama offered by Gurajada on a wider canvas was effectively utilised by these dramatists. Some writers influenced by romantic poetry concentrated on structural technique. *Kumbha Rana* by Duvvuri Ramireddi, *Nartanasala* by Viswanadha Satyanarayana were literary as well as unique tragic plays. So also *Sabari* by Chinta Dikshitulu is a wonderful play in which prose runs like a lyric.

Around 1900 under the influence of English education there was a revolt against, rejection and even ridicule of religious and social traditions of Hindu society and it had further heightened during this period. Tripuraneni Ramaswami Chowdary is the first in this type of writings against the socio-religious traditions of our ancient society. His writings were *Kurukshetrasangram* (1911), *Sambhukavadha* (1920) and *Khooni* (1935). Muddu Krishna in his *Ashokam* depicted the twentieth century sex philosophers' views on the romance of Sita-Rama and Ravana. To deride the Aryan theories and literature they collected some data from epics and attempted to argue against them.

A notable actor that emerged on the theatrical horizon during this phase was Sthaanam Narasimha Rao. Born in 1902 in Guntur district Rao earned utmost fame for over four decades as an unparalleled actor in donning female roles both in mythological and social plays ranging from Chintamani in the play *Chintamani* to Madhuravani in *Kanyashulkam*. Rao won many laurels for his performances till his death in 1971 and he considered action as deep meditation.

From 1928 onwards it can be said that there was a lull in the Telugu theatre. The commercial theatrical troupes had yielded to the age of contract dramas. Staging the dramas has become a ridiculous affair. But there were some good things also during the period. In 1929 due to the efforts of Vanarasa Govindarao the Andhra Nataka Kala Parishad was formed to infuse dynamism in Telugu theatre. Around that time Bellari Raghavacharyulu returned from his foreign tours and attached much importance to dignified style in stage acting. In 1934 *Natyakala*, a tri-monthly periodical, was launched. With encouragement from Harindranath Chatopadhyay the performance of *Kanchanamala* in Machilipatnam by Veluri Chandrasekaharam has unveiled new trend in Telugu theatre.

Birth of a New Era

The year 1943-44 can be described as beginnings of new era or the sixth phase of Telugu theatre. Under the Chairmanship of K.V. Gopala Swami the Andhra University Experimental Theatre (AUET) was established. AUET conducted drama and playlet competitions in Andhra University to enthuse college students on theatre. AUET brought into limelight many a playwright and stage technicians besides providing a forum for the introduction of new trends and conduct of experiments on stagecraft. On the other hand under the president-ship of M.R. Appa Rao, the Andhra Nataka Kala Parishad (ANKP) had widened its scope and threw open the doors for the progress of modern Telugu drama. ANKP breathed new life into amateur theatre and brought into light celebrated playwrights like Aatreya and Kondamudi Gopalaraya Sarma. It had also started drama and playlet competitions to encourage drama enthusiasts. Added to these Praja Natya Mandali of Dr. G. Raja Rao was launched which subsequently created tremendous political and social awakening in the rural areas. These three institutions worked in three divisions and contributed for the resuscitation of Telugu theatre. Further, in the Telugu speaking areas opportunities have brightened for the upcoming dramatists, for new writings and evolution of new theatre. The following new styles of writings and stage techniques were noticeable: (1) doing away with acts and scenes using fade-in and fade-out; (2) depicting play within play; (3) expressing the mental states of the characters through background singing; (4) making the audience a part of the play; (5) creating only mime situations.

Rise of Social Drama

The search for alternative ways of human survival and existence started with Industrial revolution. As a consequence unexpected situations had taken place in the social life and human relations. This was reflected in literature also and writers round the world had identified that for all social aberrations economic inequalities were the root cause. Economic disparities had also divided the nation into castes and groups paving the way for many a crisis. Writers were much agitated since the very survival of mankind was threatened. This feeling had a profound impact on Telugu dramatists and during this evolutionary phase wonderful experiments had taken place in Telugu theatre. Kondamudi Gopalaraya Sarma wrote an excellent play *Edurita* decrying the caste system, its artificial barriers and the social discord it causes. In the early days of drama competitions of the Parishad, *Edurita* won the award. The play makes it crystal clear how in a system of economic inequalities the brotherhood of humanity and its harmonious life is threatened and how they hinder even the matrimonial bonds. Subsequently Pinisetti wrote *Kulamleni Pilla* which depicted the divisive caste system and its inherent destructive nature. Many more plays of this sort were issued deriding the caste system, economic disparities and other divisive forces.

Aatreya who was a gift of Venkatagiri Amateurs to Telugu theatre was a master of the art and technique of the drama. With his in depth knowledge of human nature he had tread new paths in play writing and staging. Aatreya enriched the Telugu theatre with new content and representative social characters by mingling social theatre art with theory and artistic values and utilities. He had powerfully portrayed the middle class moralities and its struggles amid the powerful forces of economic inequalities in his *N.G.O.*, *Bhayam* and *Viswasanti*. The middle classes, their trials and tribulations in clinging to the stale and pseudo values were portrayed in an unparalleled manner by Aatreya in these plays. These plays brought glory to the Telugu theatre and instilled feelings of the need for establishing an egalitarian society among the audience.

Russian Influence

According to the eminent aesthetician Plekhinov's *Flow of water theory,* a renaissance movement which begins in one country would flow to other countries plagued by similar crises like water flowing to the low lying area. During 1940-55 among the many plays that influenced the Telugu theatre, most portrayed the crisis in the society caused by economic disparities and group rivalries. The flood of Russian dramas inspired these dramatists. The dominance of the feudal landlords, their arrogance, exploitation and heart rending cries of the exploited is the principal theme of these plays. Just as Aatreya was gifted by Venkatagiri Amateurs to Telugu theatre, the Prajanatyamandali introduced Sunkara Satyanarayana and Vasireddy Bhaskara Rao to Telugu theatre. Sunkara-Vasireddi authored *Maa Bhoomi* and *Mundadugu* depicting the plight of farm labourers, their sufferings, the cruelties and indignities inflicted on them, and inhuman exploitation by the landlords and their united and relentless struggles. These plays ignited the flame of revolt among the farmers, the exploited and the working class uniting them into a fighting force. The concept of land to the tiller was focused in a heartening and realistic manner in these plays. In those days, these dramas created a wave of enthusiasm in the rural areas and people used to visit these dramas carrying gunny bags and tripod stools for comfortable seating themselves to witness those dramas. *Maa Bhoomi* and *Mundadugu* are best examples of the opinion of Scribe and Sardo that ordinary life experience, events and language familiar to the people would contribute for the success of a drama. The period 1943-45 was the one during which Telugu theatre was progressing hand in hand with the people on the path of conflict, utility and message orientation. Dedicated and disciplined actors like Dr. Mikkilineni Radhakrishna Murty, Koduri Achaiah, Karnati Lakshmi Narasaiah, Perumanllu, Ramakoti were the sheet anchor of Prajanatyamandali in those days. The Little Theatre of Kopparapu Subbarao also lent its supporting hand to amateur theatre in those days.

As mentioned above, in Telugu drama the themes of the struggle of the exploited against the feudal landlords was due to Russian influence and Tolstoy, Gorky, Chekov, etc. inspired the Telugu writers to record the pitiable life of the exploited. Gorky declared that the word 'man' mesmerised him and for that exploited man he would expose the naked truths. For the Telugu dramatists who raised the banner of revolt against social inequalities Gorky's writings became the center of inspiration and support. *Paaleru* and *Kooliraju* by Boyi Bhimanna, *Tirugubatu* and *Kooli* by Kodali Gopal Rao, *Yadha Praja Tatha Raja* by Korrapati and *Annapoorna* by K.V. Ramana Reddi were presented during this wave. Anisetti's

Maavooru and Aatreya's *Parivartana* also belong to this revolutionary type. Telugu drama until this period progressed according to Tennis Werland's definition that the objective of social drama should be to mirror contemporary reality.

Family Problems to the Fore

In post independent India, Telugu theatre discussed several contemporary issues and came to the fore with divergent faces. The common man was affected more by the family problems than the societal problems. The family life for the middle class became a bed of thorns aggravated by social evils and economic disparities and no wonder playwrights gave much priority to family problems. Dr. Korrapati Gangadhara Rao, Bhamidipati Radhakrishna, Kodali Gopala Rao and others wrote several plays on these issues. During this period Aatreya's *Addekompa (NGO)* is the front runner. *Nijaroopalu* of Korrapati, *Aatmeeyulu* of Pinisetti Srirammurthy, *Naalugillachavidi* of Ravi Kondala Rao, *Velluva* of Ramaswami, Yandamuri's *Raghupati Raghava Rajaram,* Raghava's *Kanakapushyaragam*, R.V. Chalam's *Maatatappaku*, Jandhyala's *Sandhyaragamlo Sankharavam*, A. Adivishnu's *Bomma Borusu*, Gollapudi's *Okachettu rendu poolu*, K.S.T. Sai's *Mahaneeyulu*, Bellamkonda's *Punarjanma*, Narasaraju's *Veelunaama*, P.V. Ramana's *Devatalettinapadaga,* Bhamidipati's *Keerti Seshulu*, etc. all had projected the contradictions of human attitude from different angles. American theatre was the inspiration for this sort of plays centered on household problems. British theatre suggested the conflict of personalities for our Telugu theatre. Certain dramas expressing the internal human conflict were also written. *Galimedalu* by Anisetti, *Idi Naatakam Kaadu* by R.V. Chalam and *Dear Audience Sincerely Yours* by Isukapalli Rama Mohana Rao among others searched the internal nature of human beings and attempted to review man's diverse mindsets. The domineering attitude of the landlords in the rural areas and the caste rivalries were the themes of Pinisetti's *Pallepaduchu*, *Kulamlenipilla* and *Annachellelu* in which the writer effectively depicted the rural scenario. Kodali Gopala

Rao wrote many dramas portraying the impoverished rural life and the debased human psyche.

Give and Take

While eminent stage artiste K. Venkateswarrao staged dramas like *Aakasa Ramanna*, *Dongaveeradu*, etc. D.V. Narasaraju, Bellamkonda Ramadasu and Prakhya Srirammurty translated Telugu plays like *Naatakam*, *Veelunaama, Aakasa Ramanna*, *Kalaratri* and *Phani* and introduced them to the people abroad. This sort of give and take is quite common in the world of theatre round the world. As already mentioned, in the early days of Telugu theatre Vavilala Vasudeva Sastry translated the *Julius Caesar* into Telugu. Gurajada Sriramamurty translated the *Merchant of Venice* into Telugu with the title *Venice Vanijya Natakam*. More than two centuries ago William Jones translated Kalidasa's unique drama *Abhijnana Shankutala* into English and introduced Indian theatre to the outside world. Well known German dramatist Goethe danced with ecstasy upon reading the play *Abhijnana Shankutala*. Telugu playwrights like Gollapudi Maruti Rao, Korrapati Gangadhar Rao, Yandamuri Veerendranath and Isukapalli Rammohan Rao introduced world famous playwrights like Bernard Shaw, Ibsen, Eugene O'Neil, Galsworthy, Tolstoy, Chekov, Gorky, Steinbeck, Osborne to the Telugu theatre. It is evident that there was influence of English theatre in *Vishada Sarangadhara* of 'Andhra Nataka Pitamaha' Dharmavaram Ramakrishna-macharyulu. It is quite common when a literary experiment becomes popular in one language and country it will have its impact on other languages and countries also as demonstrated by 'Flow of water theory'. The Greek tragedy had influenced the Italian writer Seneca while several English authors attempted to write dramas on the line of Seneca. Bernard Shaw made no bones of this when he said that he followed the way of Mollier. Lord Byron influenced Alexander Pushkin to a large extent. Many Russian dramas are being staged in the US. So also the Chinese and the Japanese drama troupes stage their performances in the West like Paris, London, etc. Historically

Kautilya's *Arthashastra* mentions that many drama troupes used to participate in the drama competitions that were conducted in India. Since cultural relations are established between the nations like this, a celebrated critic said 'Art is international'. To bring coordination and promote cooperation among different theatres in the world the UNESCO passed a resolution on 27 March 1962 and ever since 27 March is being observed as the World Theatre Day which is being observed in India including Andhra Pradesh.

Craze for Experimentation

From 1965 a typical feature is noticeable in scripting Telugu plays and staging them. An admixture of a multitude of theories and experiments entered the Telugu theatre, turned the nature of the drama into an ugly creature and made the message incomprehensible. Starting with N.R. Nandi's famous *Maro Mohanjodaro* the attractive experiment on the stage became a guiding principle to the playwrights and directors. But one should not forget that in *Maro Mohanjodaro* the contemporary community thinking, group rivalries and a variety of inherent human conflict were portrayed in a powerful manner. The play was not unveiled only due to the attraction of new experimentation but the theme had won the patronage and liking of the overall public at large. No experiment or phenomenon will descend from heaven all of a sudden. It passes through several traditions, conflicting with them, while crossing through the past values. Such experiment should not be casual or a passing phase but should be a value addition to the past values and should enthrall the people. In drama this experimental view requires more competence as it provides new ideas and new insights to the audience who are the principal dimension for the drama. One should not forget that the medium which awakens and provides personal experience to the audience is the drama. All this is to emphasize that the theories and experiments inserted into the drama should not be peripheral and militate against the objective of the theatre.

Commencing with the melodrama state to the depiction of actual realities in the Telugu drama this experimentation had assumed different forms. The effects of a horde of theories like Realism, Naturalism, Surrealism, Existentialism, Expressionism, Absurdist, Theatricalist, Mayor Hold experiment, etc. held their sway and ruled the Telugu drama. Expressing the ideas and ideals simmering in the mind in an artificial manner with emotion and pomp is melodrama. Plays like *Chintamani* and *Rangoon Rowdy* of those days come under this category. With an over anxiety to present a natural idea from a natural view point the playwrights had ignored the entire theme of the story. What they were communicating was the ideal and objective of the past playwrights. To the present day playwrights how the content is staged in a manner captivating the audience has become the ideal. Consequently, plays with themes which can comment on the direction and comprehensiveness of life have become scarce. The playwrights lacked the skill and patience to universally express the different life experiences. Plays which partially touch some aspects of life with experimentation have mushroomed in which the inherent principle and narration of story were hard to decipher. A review of some of the plays of this 1965 period is worth mentioning.

Isukapalli RamamohanaRao's *Dear Audience Sincerely Yours* primarily discusses the love and affection between man and woman, mutual trust and the traditional male chauvinism. The experimental technique was adopted in which the situations in the personal drama appear incoherent, illogical and absurd which even the author agrees and appeals in the very beginning of the play through a character "Please link them up". The writer tells the audience face to face his life experiences and pours out the burning lava of his inner self and the writer is also a character in the play. In the end the audience learn the reality that the leading lady character Susheela did not commit suicide but was murdered and it is the husband who is the murderer and also the playwright. The play focuses on the dual role inherent in man and mirrors the dual nature of man suffering with inhuman traits. At the end of the play there were lots of lengthy and involved dialogues in English by Suhasini, another lady character. The writer leaves it to our comprehension whether dialogues made in English would add justice to the utterances or whether the character would get emotion only through dialogues uttered in English.

Though the subject selected by Rao is not representative of the comprehensive social awakening there is novelty in the selection of the experimentation. But it is important to ponder whether the audience is prepared for such experimentation. A drama which cannot arouse the inner feelings of the audience and contribute to the density of their etiquette cannot attain permanence in the society. In *Dear Audience Sincerely Yours* though the life and experience is local the technique and experimentation is western. Hence, however mature is the western experiment we cannot consider that it would attain a comprehensive personality in the Telugu speaking areas. From this viewpoint the play *Dear Audience Sincerely Yours* had brought in modernity and diversification in playwriting because it gave more preference to experimentation and technical values but it could not win the approval of the audience as the content was not in tune with the times. It was confined only to the surroundings of theatre societies and dramc competitions.

Rao's another drama was *O Boothu Natakam* in which the lady protagonist Varalakshmi was the daughter of a father whose mother eloped with somebody. Though a prisoner of the debilitating middle class traditions and moralities she surprises everybody by turning the traditionally natural feminist slavishness into a burning flame of uprising and feminist voice. About the two male characters, Vittal who tried to arouse sexual feelings in her and Das who loses his passion just with a mere embrace, Varalakshmi says: "These two rascals want me to fall on their feet. I can survive on my own without the nominal wedding knot they tie round my neck". Her ferocious words are an indication of the changing modern social thought about the institution of marriage which demands equality of the sexes. The writer wonderfully projected Varalakshmi as representative of modern woman and communicated that man and woman are the two equal powerful forces of the modern society. At the end of the play the protagonist Varalakshmi utters very poignant and piercing dialogues in English indicating the revolutionary fervor in the womanhood at large which was traditionally a puppet of man's unchallenged power and domination.

The question is whether with the experimentation in this play the playwright's intended message will have any effect on the audience? We have to wait and see whether such of these dramas which depict a partial problem in a heartrending manner, ignoring contemporary principal issues, can attain last long. Here, the playwright is definitely a powerful dramatist. Had the writer selected a theme which aims at the community dynamics, the experiment would have been holistic and complete. Avinesco in his work "Notes and Counter Notes" says that whatever change takes place in the theatre, it should not overshoot the comprehension of the audience.

Another playwright with pen name 'Margashirsha' presented a play *Pasupubottu Perantaniki* portraying the plight of young women being sacrificed at the altar of dowry. The play was in trilug technique and the playwright made one of the characters declare in the beginning that he would be a seed of the psychological revolution of the hapless victims of the dowry social evil. The play won several awards in the drama competitions of various parishads. Though the problem was old the technique and experimentation was novel and different. The playwright appeals for the eradication of dowry social evil as a mass representative of the community and creates awakening in the audience. However, the technique used in the play may at times cause confusion in the minds of the audience. The play should be full of dynamism and not full of techniques as there is a danger of the principal theme washed off by the flood of techniques employed. Bernard Shaw rightly stated that the theatre should exist for the play and not the play for the theatre. The technique chosen by the playwright should promote the interest of the drama, its standard and play writing. Most of the plays that were written during the late eighties and nineties were experiment oriented and hence could win the patronage of the public.

Contemporary Playwrights

The contemporary playwrights are displaying novelty in shape, nature and presentation of the drama. They are portraying diverse human attitudes in a representative and creative manner. During the last decade of the last century several plays depicting the pitiable state of the life of the downtrodden in the present system of corruption, injustice and exploitation were written with the objective of promoting community feelings, cohabiting and humanitarian considerations. Among them *Um Aha* by Anand Hridayaraj in which the playwright declared his intention in the objective of the play as under:

> Even Marx or Gandhi cannot set right the system where the political parties fight with each other for gaining power. Political parties which are unable to provide proper understanding of the system are responsible for the sorry state of affairs in this country.

The play presents the country as a family and the family members represent those occupying the seats of power. The characters and the situations created by the playwright were inspirational, natural and convey the playwright's sincere concern for ushering in an ideal system. Just as the plays *Maabhoomi* and *Mundadugu* had created a movement for awakening among the people the play *Um aha* also takes us towards an equally strong and powerful social movement.

The Telugu theatre entered modernity with N.R. Nandi's *Maro Mohenjodaro* and it had reached the stage of further maturity and diversity with plays like *Nissabdam* and *Rudraveena* of Yandamuri Veerendranath, *Trijaakiyama-darshanam* by Abburi Gopalakrishna, *Um aha* of Anand Hridayraj, *Sahara* by Patibandla Ananda Rao, *Paluke*

Bangaramaa and *Rajasuya Yaagam* by Daadi Veerabhadra Rao, and *Puli Malli Vastundaa* by Srisailamurty. We find much diversity in their performance on the stage though they appear to be common place replete with individual problems, familial life experiences, man-woman relationships and selfish politics. In Daadi Veerabhadra Rao's *Rajasuyayagam* the playwright has admirably presented the judicial system through the character of Vedavati. Sankaramanchi Parthasarathy wrote the play *Prasannaku Premato*, a full comedy but it mirrors woman's identity, individuality and her existence.

In *Halav* Jaladanki Sudhakar portrays a father who could not suffer his terrorist son working against the interests of the country and performs *halav*. An agricultural labourer Naraiah embraces death just for the sake of ten thousand rupees in Valluri Siva Prasad's *Srimukha Vyaghram*. Though the Telugu theatre is emerging with so much of variety and diversity it is a matter of pity that it is confined only to the precincts of the drama associations and their competitions. Theatre will receive the patronage of the people only when it moves in accordance with the aspirations of the people. Even through the universities are spending a decent sum for promoting the drama there is nothing to feel proud of with the state of affairs of their theatre arts departments. The main reason is they are ignoring the traditional Indian theatre and blindly imitating the western theatre.

In the early days of drama competitions of the Parishad, *Edurita* of Kondamudi Gopalaraya Sarma won the award. Acharya Aatreya well-known for his portrayal of human natures in his *N.G.O.* had treaded new paths in play writing and staging. In depicting human natures in the rural backdrop Sunkara Satyanarayana and Vasireddi Bhaskarrao are prominent dramatists. Staging their *Mundadugu* and *Maabhumi* the Praja Natya Mandali kicked up a revolution in the state. Narla Venkateswar Rao depicted the rural aspirations and problems in his plays especially *Kothagadda*. Among those who took up play writing through the radio Devulapalli Krishna Sastri is the most celebrated.

Radio Plays

The dramas that cater only to the hearing faculty of the audience are radio plays. Earlier such dramas were called closet dramas or literary plays and Senica dramas of Latin were of this type. It is very difficult to impress with the radio because only the sound is the relation between the actors and the listeners which involves acting only through the word of mouth. In this process the mike plays an important role and in radio plays mike should be used with utmost care and prudence. A mountain of action and stage effects has to be achieved through a molehill of play on the radio. In India the listener's drama started only with the radio and so it is very young in the country.

Once there was a heated argument between a radio playwright and a stage playwright on a public platform about the supremacy of their formats. A celebrated dramatist was presiding over the meeting. After hearing arguments from both sides the president of the function declared, "Now I follow the difference between these two types of dramas. Whatever it may be, I feel radio play is superior to the theatre play." The radio playwright felt very proud and put on an I-told-you-so face. But the president added, "Because if we visit a theatre play, out of modesty we cannot post haste remove ourselves when the performance is at its worst. But if the radio play is dull and drab we can simply switch off the set". This highlights how the radio drama is literally at the mercy of the listener.

Though listener's plays were comparatively of recent origin several writers achieved skill and mastery in that. The first Telugu radio play broadcast was *Anarkali* by Muddu Krishna. Devulapalli Krishna Sastri wrote songs for the play and was also the lead character, Salim. Gora Sastri is the most celebrated radio playwright. His plays were published in volumes with titles *Aasa Kharidu Ana* , *Komma Sampangi* and *Gora Sastri Natikalu, Kaalaateeta Vyaktulu*, *Loha Gantalu* and *Komma Sampangi* were highly appreciated by the listeners. Subtle humour, light satire, study of human mind and portrayal of the mechanised modern life has made them unique among Telugu radio plays.

Kodavaganti Kutumbarao's plays like *Bharya Roopavati*, *Korakarani Koyya*, etc. were experimental type of radio plays. Kapila Kasipati was past master in experimentation and organisation of the radio play. Vinjamumuri Sivaramarao wrote a thousand radio plays while Nagabhushanam, Krishna Murthy and Giduthuri Suryam won awards in several radio competitions. *Mantri Timmarusu* radio play written by Dr. P.S.R. Appa Rao was broadcast on January 26, 1948. Munimanikyam Narasimha Rao and Nanduri Subba Rao wrote a good many humorous radio plays, Amarendra won acclaim for translating Rabindranath Tagore's writings for radio.

The roll call of Telugu Radio playwritights is much lengthy; to mention a few; Devulapalli Krishna Sastri, Jalasutram Rukminadha Sastri, Sri Sri, Padmaraju, Aarudra, Anisetti, Pinisetti, Rajaikantarao, Karunasri, Boyi Bhimanna, Hitasri, Prayaga, Janamanchi Ramakrishna, Dasarathi, Dr. C. Narayana Reddi, Sri Vatsava, Butchibabu, Gollapudi Maruti Rao, Kondamudi Sri Ramachandra Murthy, Puranam Subrahmny Sarma, Kommuri Venugopalarao, N.R. Nandi, Pothukuchi Sambasvarao, Nanduri Vithal, D. Venkataramaiah, Turaga Krishna Mohan Rao, Balivada Kanta Rao, Panyala Ranganatha Rao, Somanchi Yajnanna Sastri, Lata, Ravi Kondala Rao,Prakhya Srirama Murthy and others enriched this literary format.

All India Radio has been contributing to the growth of the radio plays by organising radio play week celebrations. Popular Plays like *Malapalli*, *Varavikrayam*, *Rajasekhara Charita*, *Kanthabharanam*, etc. were rewritten in radio play format and broadcast over AIR. Akashavani had also broadcast the literary works of eminent men of letters which were re–written in the radio format by Jnanpith award recipient late Viswanatha Satyanarayana. Even lyrical plays were broadcast as radio plays. It is possible to impart knowledge to the illiterate through these plays. Therefore, the government is utilising it as a propaganda tool to publicise its developmental policies and programmes through. With the massive expansion of Doordarshan the telecasts of radio plays supported by actors and supporting artistes has considerably increased. Radio plays are still broadcast by All India Radio though it is not certain about the real impact on its listeners.

Telugu theatre has a glorious history spanning over 130 years and till date more than 2,000 dramas and over 4,000 playlets have been written. More than one thousand writers have enriched this field with their creative imagination and dedication.

However, today the Telugu theatre is moving at a painfully snail's pace with stereotypic age old tendencies, lacking the luster of modernity. Even though the impact of globalisation was felt on the theatre there is utter lack of modernity in its approach and hence continuing in its old traditions. Compared to other states and languages there is lack of staging modern plays in Telugu theatre. Dramas which can usher in social change are few and far between and the wonderful stagecraft is crying for patronage. While in the neighbouring Southern states theatre is blooming with modernity, the Telugu theatre is still in the shackled to old traditions. Except in the state capital there is no trace of staging modern dramas in the districts. In Hyderabad the Janapadam Nataka Repertoire is staging modern Telugu dramas and other plays at the national level. Even though Telugu poetry, art and painting have attained international stature, Telugu theatre is moving at an excruciatingly slow pace. Though there are actors with a high level of talent, the theatre is suffering its death pangs. Patronage for theatre is drying out and staging plays that appeal to the people is not happening which might be the main reason for the decline of Telugu theatre. The situation demands government's intervention to encourage Telugu theatre and restore its pristine glory.

Suggestions

Only when the playwright makes the societal conditions as the sheet anchor of his plays, then only can drama inspire and awaken the people. This involves the writer taking into consideration the contemporary societal situations along with literary considerations. Though the writer utilises western experiments and theories, he must have the competence to adapt them to the living conditions of his society. Experiments and theories should not be introduced in the drama only for the sake of experimentation. They should integrate with the drama and should promote the interests of the play. The subject should be such that a theory may comment on the total human life and not the partial life of man. Every writer must have the common sense, understanding and clear view of what he is conveying, with what purpose, who he is addressing, and in what form. Telugu-speaking people from the beginning immensely liked music and verse and playwrights and directors have to discuss and examine how to introduce them in the dramas. There cannot be progress with mere reality and naturalism. India is a cradle of cultures and from time immemorial song and dance have a pride of place in the theatre. Even in modern times we must remember that the eminent dramatist B.V. Karant built up his plays *Pied Piper*, *Kailasam*, etc. on music only. To restore the past glory to the Telugu theatre the playwrights, directors, actors and technicians and all others connected with the theatre must come together and think of available ways and means.

Works Cited

B.Ramaraju and P. Vasudeva Sastri (ed.). *Vijnana Sarswam—Telugu Sanskriti*—Vo. II, Hyderabad: Vijnana Sarswa Kendram, Telugu University, 1988.

Chaatla Sriramulu. 'Rangasthalam', *Telugu Vaani*, World Telugu Conference Commemoration Volume, Hyderabad, 1975.

Gollapudi Maruti Rao: 'Radio Naatika', *Andhra Pradesh*, Telugu monthly of Government of Andhra Pradesh, Hyderabad, April 1994.

Hanumat Sastry. J. 'Bellary Raghavacharyulu'. *Andhra Jyoti,* Hyderabad, 17th April 2010.

Mikkilineni Radha Krishna Murthy. *Nata Ratnalu*, 1989.

_______,'Modern Telugu Theatre—Then and Now'. Hyderabad : *Andhra Pradesh,* April 1994

N.C. Jain. *Asides—Themes in contemporary Indian theatre.* New Delhi: National School of Drama, 2003.

P.V. Ramana.'Tegulu Pattina Telugu Natakam'. *Vaarta,* Hyderabad, 27th March 1997

_______,'Andhra Nataka Rangamlo Pauranika Charitraka Naatakalu'. Hyderabad: *Andhra Pradesh*, April 1994.

Paturi Srirama Sastri. 'Surabhi Naataka Samajalu'. *Telugu Vaani*, World Telugu Conference Commemoration Volume, Hyderabad, 1975.

_______, *Mahati*. Hyderabad: Yuvabharati, 1973.

13

Unanswered Question: An Overview of Tamil Drama

— K.S. Anish Kumar

Introduction

Drama, primarily a performing art, has been used as a medium of expression and a tool for social transformation. Music and dance are also stage arts which accompanied many dramas and remain as contributory factors for the successful performance of the play.

Critics and writers all over the world often re-iterate the idea that a successful play should be dear to the hearts of the readers and to the audience. History of world drama reminds the availability of plays that are written, taking into consideration readers rather than audience. Byron's *Manfred* and P.B. Shelley's *Prometheus Unbound,* etc. are outstanding examples.

Apart from the scripts and the playwrights (who convert the articulate story into an art to perform), actors—the role players, play a vital role in the successful history of a play, for they not only enact but live the roles on the stage. They also bridge the gap between the audience and the playwright and also sometimes become icons of certain characters as Shivaji Ganesan of Tamil, the unforgettable cine-star of Tamil Nadu.

The history of Indian Drama dates back to the episodes of *Rigveda* and the elements of theory of drama that are available in Bharatha's *Natyashastra*, *Ramayana* and *Mahabharata* and a few folk stories still dominate the stages of Indian drama.

In south India, especially in Tamil Nadu most of the religious festivals are celebrated with dramas as their main content. *Meenakshi Tirukalyanam* (The marriage of Meenakshi) and *Prakalathan* have been staged in and around Tamil Nadu repeatedly. If churches are the cradles of English drama, temples are the cradles of Tamil drama. This motivates the readers to go through the history of Tamil drama. It stands as an evidence of cultural and political history of Tamils and it reminds the present pathetic condition of Tamil drama too. Tamil drama has been the least researched area of Tamil literature. The present situation makes the reader or researcher ask repeatedly the unanswered question, "Can the performing art be resurrected from its present position?"

Tamil Drama: Its Genesis

From the ancient time onwards the Tamils have been known for their interest in the dramatic art and the well known texts like *Tolkappiam*, *Silapathikaram,* etc. stand as evidence for the outstanding knowledge of Tamils about drama. They were also aware of the inevitable kinship between dance and drama, the twin popular performing arts, and it is remarkable that drama has always been blended with dance and most of the dramas were performed by adopting dance as a medium. It is often felt that due to lack of historic sense they have forgotten to compile the scripts. Dr.M. Varadharajan in his book *History of Tamil Literature* rightly reminds, "Bards who collected and compiled poems were least worried about collecting dramatic texts".

Inscriptions reveal that after the Sangam age dramas were staged in temples especially during festival times and rulers like Pallavas and Cholas gave due importance to dramatic performances. During the seventeenth and eighteenth centuries books namely *Pallu* and *Kuravangi* remain as evidences for the structure of Tamil Drama. To Dr. K. Meenaksi Sundaram these texts are just fragments and not dramas in the real sense, for these texts only include dramatic elements.

The Western influence has paved the way for the reformation in the dramatic tradition in India which in turn inspired the Tamil drama artists too. Sankara Das Swamikal was the pioneer of Tamil Drama and was a versatile genius in script writing, direction and action. He himself had directed and staged many plays through his company known as "Swami's Boys company". Along with him Pammal Sampanda Mudaliyar, Suriya Narayana Sastri and others flourished as great playwrights. Their plays failed to present patriotism though they had written playsduring the time when it was at its peak, says Dr. M. Ramaswamy, a well known professor of drama and performing artist. It is pertinent to note that plays were also written and staged against British role by Baskaradas ,including dramatists like S.S. Vishwanathan, K.P. Sundarambal, K.P. Janaki, S.A. Kittappa and K.P. Kamatchi. Most of them were imprisoned by the British for their fierce remarks on the tyranny of the British Government. In 1867 Kasi Vishvanatha Mudhaliyar wrote the first social drama, namely, *Dambatchari Vilas* and this drama underlined another dimension of Tamil Drama and details about stage history of this play is not easily available.

In the 1950s and 1960s Tamil drama has undergone a drastic change in its perception and presentation due to the influence of Tamil Dravidian movements founded by Periyar, who is rightly called the father of Tamil race. The plays of this era followed the social reformist ideologies of Periyar, who attacked the domination of Brahminism, and superstitious beliefs etc. The main content of plays of Annadurai (the chief Minister of Tamil Nadu), M.R. Radha, M. Karunanidhi, the present Chief Minister of Tamil Nadu, the great poet Bharathidasan's *Erarnyian* or *Enaiyatra Veeran* (*Eranyan* or Unparallel Hero) put forth the self-respect ideology of Periyar and also criticised the puranas and religious texts for their stand on upholding the hierarchical power structure.

Venkat Swaminathan, a notable critic in his article on "The Present Tamil Dramatic Environment" opines that "the plays of the Dravidian movements are manifestoes of their own ideology and he condemns them for their representation problems of the people as secondary" (128). It is remarkable that a serious researcher would not easily underestimate their contribution to Tamil Drama and art of writing which instilled the feelings of people to stand against the social evils of Tamil Nadu. In fact, they added a new dimension to the Tamil Drama through their scripts and dialogues which attracted the attention of the audience of the time. They were the first people to liberate the Tamil drama from the clutches of the *Puranas* and through their writings they earned ardent fans throughout Tamil Nadu. The impact of their writings contributed not only to the society but also to them in turn; a few of them became politicians and two of them became chief ministers namely Annadurai and M. Karunanidhi.

Dramatists of the present era concentrate more on the daily problems in domestic and political realms and they started presenting them symbolically, extending the experiment to the dramatic art also. Experimental dramas of Tamil lack wide public appreciation as their presentation and perceptions are beyond the comprehension of the audience. In the history of Tamil drama one cannot exclude the role of verse play and experimental dramas, for these two major divisions remain as the bridge between the past and the present.

Verse Dramas in Tamil

As Raymond Williams opines, "The verse play produced the theatre, but the prose play was produced by the theatre."

In the Tamil Scenario also the contribution of verse play remained as a starting points but the most forgotten area in Tamil drama today is verse drama. The sudden transformation that occurred over the years affected the survival of it. It is worthy to note that the most celebrated, widely read and staged drama *Manonmaniam* is written in verse form. In fact, *Manonmaniam* is an adopted version of Lytton Prabhu's *The Secret Way*; P.V. Chinnapa, a notable actor enacted the role of the hero of the play several times. Prof. Sundaram Pillai is the author of this play of love and politics. The play is named after the heroine Manonmani, the daughter of the Pandiya king Sevakan. His Minister, Kudilan an evil spirited man, who creates a situation where, the Chera king and Chola king will die in a battle. His primary aim is to become the king of the land. He also tries to arrange marriage between his son and

Manonmani and to him this in the only source to become a king but Manonmani has fallen in love with the Chera king, Purusothaman in dream. The dramatist creates suspense and in the end the evil doer get offended as the heroine Manonmani marries Purusothaman. The dream lovers union is the symbolic representation union of the two Tamil kings Chera and Pandiya.

The grand success of this play has prompted many writers to write verse dramas but most of them were not successful is their attempts for A.N.Perumal's *Pani Mozhi* (Language of Snow) and Palani's *Anicha Adi* lack originality. Among the exemptions Sundar Rajan's *Venkaiyin Venkan* (Tiger's Son) may be considered a successful play.

Issac Arumai Rajan, a writer-critic has become a successful playwright soon after the publication of his verse play *Mullai Madam* (*Forest Palace*) which was included is the syllabi of two major universities of Tamil Nadu. The author himself criticises in his article entitled "Tamil Kavithai Nadakam" (Verse dramas in Tamil) that his dramas, namely, *Venkaikal* (Tigers) and *Parai* (Rock) can be cited as successful plays rather than *Mullai Madam* and *Neduman Anchi* for these plays lack originality.

Apart from Issac Arumai Rajan's contributions the well known play *Manonmaniam* stays back as an icon in the history of Tamil drama for it satisfies both the needs of the audience and readers.It is pathetic to note that verse dramas in Tamil are nearing an end as the readers and audience are less worried about the survival of verse dramas due to the influence of mass media.

Experimental Dramas in Tamil

The Tamil dramatic environment has undergone phenomenal change in the midst of the twentieth century in which the playwrights have started writing with a new out look and perception. The consequence of this process has brought in a new trend in Tamil Drama, that is the Experimental Dramas.

Writers like Indira Parthasarathy, Jayanthan, Muthusamy, Cho.Ramasamy, Gnanasekaran, etc. have contributed much to the growth and development of experimental dramas for instance Indira Parthasarathi's *Porvai Porthia Udalkal* (Clothed Bodies) deals with the exposition of inner weakness where the heroine Vasanthi tries to take revenge on her mother who sells her body. She also adopts the same ill-legal action but rather openly and forcibly than her mother. This play prevents how body becomes the capital for survival and a source of revenge.

In Jayanthan's play, *Ninaikkapadum* (It will be remembered) a cine-actress Prabha hesitates to use sexy dress and hence she was substituted by Deva Devagi and the latter becomes popular. Soon after this event Prabha has decided to adjust to the requirement of the industry but her trial ends in pregnancy and she was asked to abort if she wants to continue in the profession. Oppressive sense of guilt makes her a mentally depressed person. The play clearly brings out the harsh reality and unexpected contradictions of life and this play stands as a satire on the film industry of Tamil Nadu.

Cho. Ramaswamy, notable actor and political journalist in his play *Yarrukum Vetkamillai* (Nobody is ashamed) presents the operation of power, and portrays who has power over whom and criticises the crucial and mean behaviour of politicians.

Gnanasekaran, a well known director who directed the film *Bharathi* and *Periyar,* deals with the causes of hungry through his play *Pasi* (Hunger). Through this play he criticises the society which lacks humanity but celebrates caste discrimination.

N. Muthuswamy's *Narkalikarar*, as the title suggests the play is a political satire, which symbolises the monstrous activities of the politically motivated people but it also stresses that one should use his voting right as a weapon for social change.

It is worthy to note that experimental plays call for social transformation through its vivid and symbolic representations. It takes up the language of people as it is. It sometimes uses English as a medium of expression when the playwright feels that English will communicate better than vernacular for instance in the play *Porvai Porthia Udalkal*, Indira

Parthasarathy's female hero uses English words when she encounters her customer.

> Don't behave like an emotional Pimb
> I thought .... Just another girl
> What a woman?
> All men are cowards

Her words are the evidence of the resultant emotions of her own trapped situation and her victimised condition leads to generalisation of exceptions.

Tamil experimental dramas are the outcome of sheer necessity but their reach and survival has to be examined for, most of the time they only attract the attention of very few people. The reasons are Tamil audience generally become pray to emotions and they expect a cinematic influence from a drama. The contributory factor for the lack audience in its symbolic obscure nature.

Dalit Drama

K.A. Gunasekaran, one of the remarkable critics of Tamil Dalit environment who enriched the dalit phase in dramatic art, argues that the playwright should go back to the folk dance, songs, etc. and to him, "Stage is not only a stage. Contrary to it, it is a place for performing arts, events, history and social problems". He believes dalit drama will emerge from folk drama. He also insists that dalit drama will become a tool for protest against those who dominate and he also believes that true dalit drama will evolve only from dalits. In fact, his view point is laudable and the audience has to wait for long time to reach his expectations.

Dr. M. Ramaswamy classifies the Tamil dramatic performances of the present time in to three major categories:

a) Dramatic art that evolves out uf the traditional approach which gives more importance to music, dance and dialogue rather than written texts.
b) Dramatic art that strictly follows written scripts ignoring music and dance.

c) Dramas that are written for the elite audience with a global outlook.

It is interesting in to note that most of the dramas that exist in Tamil fall under the second category which attracted wide audience as it adopted a common language which could be easily understood by the audience. The first and the last categories long for enough audience because the farmer users the rustic language (Highly dialectical in nature) and the later uses highly refined and scholarly language. Apart from this all the categories segregate themselves separate groups, neither the government nor the universities try to facilitate the efforts of playwrights for the benefit of the audience. In his article Venkat Swaminathan rightly observes:

> Each and every group has its own restricted audience. If the financial support is extended by the institutions or universities the new drama will flourish (130).

The harsh reality is that the future of Tamil drama is at stake. The unanswered question is: "Will it survive?" Tamil drama has a rich tradition but has failed miserably to create rich audience. Issac Arumai Rajan, a notable writer-critic, once opined, "Universities should come forward to include drama in their syllabi and this would in turn create an interest among the readers, especially among youngsters".

Some critics are of the view that government has to take necessary steps for the development of Tamil drama and they complain that the governments both central and state failed to address the needs of dramatists and they still feel that the government along with the educational institution can save Tamil drama from the present static and saturated state.

In an discussion conducted on future of Tamil Drama by *Theeranathi* (one of the leading literary magazines in Tamil) Veli. Rangarajan, recorded his views:

> The present education controls the imaginative power of kids rather than increasing it. To make the society healthy, drama should be included in the syllabus. To show to sit and stand teachers should get training from plays. A best teacher should be a performing artist. (43)

The compelling sordid reality is that the atmosphere of Tamil Nadu is not all conducive for the growth and development of drama because of the following reasons.

a) Cinema and mass media have completely taken over the place of drama and dramatic clubs are closed due to the non-availability of audience.

b) Screening cinemas are cheaper than staging plays. Hence, in temples and sabhas people started opting for cinemas.

c) Educational institutions and cultural academics neglected dramas and started staging dances of their own well wishers/protégé.

d) Lack of adequate books on drama and its development for the students led them to forget the genre itself.

e) Most of the dramas which lack explicit portrayal and criticism of life (drama can be used as a tool to criticise life) have created a big vacuum.

It is the duty of the dramatists to create a congenial atmosphere by becoming a cohesive unit to voice their problems to the authorities and it is their fundamental responsibility to attract the audience by creating appropriately alluring scripts dealing with the present major concerns. Playwrights should also go beyond the influence of the visual media by writing scripts that are readable which they can be staged too, a dire need of the day!

Notes

1. *Tolkappiam*, a remarkable grammatical text in verse which is often treated as the document of Tamil Culture and Tradition.
2. *Silapathikaram* (History of Anklet), a celebrated Tamil text, deals with the events and conflicts centered on anklet of the protagonist Kannagi.

Works Cited

Arumairajan, Issac. *Kavithai Nadakam* (Verse Drama). Puthukavithai Poonga (Poetry Special) (18-20), April–July, 2006.

Crompton–Rickett, Arthur, *A History of English Literature*. New Delhi: UBS Publishers Distributors Ltd, 1995.

Ramaswamy, M, K.Murugesan, J.P.Govindasamy (eds.), *Irupatam Nuttrantu Tamil Nadakankal* (Twentieth Century Tamil Dramas) Chennai: International Institute of Tamil Studies, 1999.

Ramaswamy, M. *Tamil Nadakam 'Netru Indru Nalai'* (Tamil Drama: Past, Present and Future). Tanjavur: Ruthra Pathipakam, 2002.

Saminathan, Venkat. *Inraiya Nadaka Muyarchikal* (Dramatic Trails of Today). Chennai: Tamizhi, 2004.

_______, *Tamil Naveena Nadakam* (Modern Drama in Tamil) Chennai: International Institute of Tamil Studies, 1999.

Theeranathi (A Literary Journal from Kumudam Groups), September 2002.

Varatharajan, M. *Tamil Ilakkiya Varalaru*—(History of Tamil Literature) New Delhi: Sahitya Akademi, 2001.

14

Hundred Years of Malayalam Drama

— Santhan Haridas

Although drama took birth 25,00 years ago in ancient Greece, Kerala has a history of drama dating back to only 100 years. Records and reference materials describing history of Malayalam drama are quite few. For that reason the names of several great dramatists are missing from the history of drama.

The modern stage in Kerala took shape by presenting translations of Sanskrit dramas as well as Malayalam dramas which were written in the style of Sanskrit dramas, such dramas gave importance to rendition of 'shlokas' in musical format. They followed the stage-presentation of Tamil dramas of that time. The musical drama-movement was initiated in Malayalam in tune with Tamil dramas of that time. Carnatic music concerts in its full form replaced the rendition of slokas used in Sanskrit dramas. The Malayalam drama stage imitated the sets of Tamil musical dramas, colourful costumes of the actors and instrumentalists. But at the same time, this format of presentation of Tamil dramas, apart from music, were borrowed from Parsi dramas of Maharashtra.

Keralavarma Valiyakoyi Thampuran translated *Sakunthalam* entitled *Abhijnana Sakunthalam* wherein he had admitted that his transalation was in a tough language. *Mariamma Natakam* (by P.K Kocheeppan Tharakan), *Chandrika* (by Kodungalloor Kunjikttan Thampuran) & *Ebrayakutty* (by Kandathil Varghese Mappila) were original Malayalam dramas based on the current social issues. *Chakkichankaram* by Munshi Ramakurup and *Dussparsam* by Seevolli were popular satirical dramas.

Sadarama, a drama by K.C. Kesavan Pillai in 1903, written in tune with Tamil drama *Sadarama,* holds a prestigious position among musical dramas of Kerala. It had earned the respect of Malayalees and it soon became very popular as it was enacted in many stages. Another drama that had attached attention of the profile at that time *Sangeetha Naishadham* was published in 1931; 33,800 copies of it had been sold out till then—a fact, that makes the modern dramatist really envious! Another genius who was in the calibre of such playwrights was Chakrapani Warrier. During that period drama-compositions and the related stage- presentations were flourishing in North Kerala. Kuttamath, Vidwan P. Kesavan Nair, Rasikasiromani Kcman Nair were the leaders who were totally invilved in vitalising the stage. Here mention must also be made of the so-called 'Vellari dramas'.

During that period translation of English dramas into Malayalam was also progressing. The main focus was on the Shakespearean dramas. The aim of those translators was not at all a stage presentation. Although the principal requirements of a drama are the dramatist, stage and the spectators, the dramatists of that period concentrated on their dramas only as a literary form.

Almarattom (Impersonation), a drama written by Kalloor Oommen Philippose in 1866, which some historians describe as the first drama in Malayalam was, in fact, the translation of the Shakespearean drama, *Comedy of Errors*. In 1897, Divan Bahadur A. Govinda Pillai translated *King Lear* into Malayalam and it was staged in VJT Hall, Trivandrum; the famous novelist C.V. Raman Pillai was one of the actors in that. From the period of the debut of the *Sakunthalam*, the dramas and drama troupes were known after famous actors. These actors were singers also. Renowned names of such actors are Thiruvattar Narayana Pillai, 'Kuilnadam' (Cuckoo voiced) Velukkutty Nair, Bubleswaran, Kutteeswaran, Thevalakkara Kunju Pillai, Attingal Narayana Pillai etc. In the next generation the leading actors were Oachira Velukkutty, Anarkali Vasudev, Sebastian Kunju Kunju Bhagavathar, Akbar Sankara Pillai, Vaikam Vasudevan Nair, Augustine Joseph etc.

Among the many drama troupes that sprang up in the country the following names are noteworthy: Thanjavor Balasangham, Kottakkal PSV Natya Sangham, Kadakkavoor Sahrudaya Nandini Sabha.

An inevitable factor of those dramas was a buffoon whose chief function in the drama was merely to make the audience laugh; he was least connected with the plot of the drama.Those days major drama troupes used to hire extra-ordinary comedians for their stage presentations. In 1930 Swami Brahma Vratan converted the poem *Karuna* (Mercy) of Kumaranasan into a drama form; for its stage presentation the chief actors were the famous Sebastian Kunju Kunju Bhagavathar and Oachira Velukkutty. Having been credit with a large number of performances, this drama marked the turning point in the course of music dramas. Inspired by this drama, artist P.J. Cheriyan formed a new drama troupe called 'Royal Cinema and Dramatic Company', which presented popular dramas, like *Njanasundari* and *Parudeesa Nashtam* (Paradise Lost) both written by V.S. Andrews. Later on in 1934, P.J. Cherian started another drama group also called 'Njarakkal Sanmarga Vilasini Sabha'.

The prowess of the music drama forms lasted some more time on the Malayalam stage. Then the turning point came into effect in the history of the Malayalam music drama with the presentation of *Yachaki* (Begger maid) by Vaikkom Vasudevan Nair and Thankam Vasudevan Nair through the Oachira Parabrahmodayam Nataka Samithi. Parallel to this development, there emerged the drama form called *Chavttu Natakam* (Kickdance). All though it followed the Western plots and mode of the presentation, it was successful in maintaining its own identity by incorporating Keralite dance forms. *Karal Mann* was an excellent example of this very fact. It was formulated with the aim in that particular euphoria generated; however this performing art did not take deep roots due to lack of enough encouragement. But later on, with the introduction of novel experiments attempts have been made to revive it.

Towards the end of nineteenth century, novelist C.V. Raman Pillai wrote two farces entitled *Chandramughi Vilasam* and *Mattavilasom*. C.V can be considered the pioneer of the modern prose-dramas; he touched upon the current topics and lives for his plot of the farces. His subsequent farces numbering around nine include *Kuruppilla Kalari* (1909) (The Masterless Martial Centre). E.V. Krishna Pillai, M.G Kesava Pillai, N.P. Chellappan Nair, etc. were the veterans of farce who followed the C.V line. E.V's *Kalla pramanam* (Faulse document), *B.A. Mayavi* (B.A. Juggler) were famous farces. N.P. Chellappan Nair's *Sasidharan B.A*, *Minnal Pranayam* (Lightning Love-affair), *Vikadayogi* (The Fake Asetic) also became very popular.

The 1930's witnessed the emergence of historic dramas. There was stage presentations of novels by C.V. Raman Pillai and Chanthu Menon. Chanthu Menon was the author of the Novel *Indulekha*. Other important historic dramatisations of that period include *Kerala Putran* (Son of Kerala, 1931) by Ambadi Narayana Poduval, *Veluthampi Dalava* (1932), *Kalvariyile Kalpapadpam* (The Holy Tree of Calvary, 1936) of Kainikkari Padmanabha Pillai, *Karnan* (1934) by Nair, *Meher Manikyam* (1937) by N.P. Chellappan Nair, *Harischandran* (1931) by Kainikkara Kumara Pillai.

The period 1930-1940 witnessed new visions in the Malayalam drama field. Both the dramatist and social reformers felt that drama should not be aimed at mere merriment; instead, it should be a medium that prompts the spectators to think, to effect social change by discarding and fighting against the evil customs and practices of society.

In 1930 V.T. Bhattathirippad published a drama entitled *Adukkalayil Ninnu Arangathekku* (From Kitchen to the Stages) which caused much turbulence in the Orthodox Namboodiri community. Kelappan who wrote its preface stated: that very drama was, in effect an atom bomb. In the same year was MRB's drama *Marakkudakkullile Mahanarakam* (The Fiery Hell Inside a screening Umbrella). (In those days the Namboodiri women used to cover themselves in particular with an umbrella.) Then came Premji's *Rhitumati* (The Girl of Puberty) which was a drama with perfect craftsmanship. K.D. Damodaran in 1937 wrote an epoch-making, political drama *Pattabhakki* (Arrears of Lease). It was meant to be staged at ponnani in a farmers convention. The drama discussed economic disparity which was the root cause of social inequality.

In the 1930's the Malayalam drama field was blessed with the translated versions of modern European dramas. A. Balakrishnan Pillai and A.K. Gopala Pillai jointly translated lbson's drama *Ghost* (Prethangal) into Malayalam. At the same time Nalappattu Narayana Menon translated a drama of Norwegian dramatist Materlink, which was titled *Sapatnyam*.

In 1932 under the auspices of Kerala Kalamandalam, there was a competition of dramas written in modern style. Further in 1939 Mekkola Parameswaran Pillai wrote a standard book *Natakadarsanam* depcting the essential characteristics of drama. Of all the translations it was Ibson who influenced the Malayalee dramatists most. N.Krishna Pilla wrote *Bhagnabhavanam* in 1942 (Broken Homes) with the inspiration from Ibsen. The famous and talented actor P.K. Vikraman Nair was the motive force behind it. Although this drama was well organised, it failed to effect a successful performance. N. Krishna Pillai's other dramas, namely, *Kanyaka* (Virgin 1944), *Balabalam* (Trial of strength, 1945), *Anuranjanam* (Compromise 1950), *Mudakkumudal* (Capital Investment, 1953), *Azhimukhathekku* (To the Estuary, 1955) were instrumental in instilling a sense of drama- awareness among literate Malayalee community. Even then neither the commercial nor the entertaining drama troops accorded recognition due to Krishna Pillai's dramas. In 1943 Vaikkom Mohammad Basheer wrote a drama called *Kathabeejam* (Plot of Story), In 1944, Pulimana Parameswaran Pillai write *Samathwavadi* (Socialist) which was the first Malayalam expressionist drama. Pulimana's untimely death was a great blow to the dynamism of Malayalam drama. C.J. Thomas's drama *Avan Meendum Varunnu* (He Comes Again) was a landmark in the history of drama.

1949 witnessed the publication of the important dramas: Edassery Govindan Nair's *Koottukrishi* (Collective Farming) and M. Govindan's *Nee Manushyane Kollaruthu* (You Shouldn't Kill Man). Thus 1945 was a decade of sudden leap as far as

Malayalam drama was concerned. It was in 1945 that Thikkurissi Sukumaran Nair entered the arena of professional drama with his drama *Sthree* (Women). This amazingly revolutionised the whole stage-presentation. The whole set-up of music drama was altered. The singing hero was replaced by a non-singing hero. The place of harmonist on the stage was transferred to the green room. The actor-cum-dramatist Thikkurissi emphasised the importance of dialogue and acting in a drama. And this massive change was whole-heartedly welcomed by the viewing public. Much of the effective dialogues in his dramas were often repeated by the masses. In 1943 Kalanilayam Krishnan Nair renamed his Anandodaya Sangeetha Natana Sabha as Kalanilayam and introduced new dramas.

The decade beginning with 1950 represented a revival of Malayalam-drama and its literature mainly due to the influence of IPTA. Owing to its cultural scheme, the communist movement, in Kerala founded drama troupe called KPAC. They staged their first drama *Ente Makananu Sari* (It is my son who is right) in 1952. It was written by Thoppil Bhasi under the pen name 'Soman'. The drama witnessed unprecedented success: hence it had to be staged during day times also through out Kerala. After that they came up with the highly acclaimed drama *Ningalenne Communist Aakki* (You Make Me a Communist). In the annals of Malayalam drama this drama will stand out forever. But craft-wise the most secure drama of Bhasi is *Surveykallu* (The Survey Stone). His other major dramas are *Mudiyanaya Puthran* (The Prodigal Son), *Mooladhanam* (Capital), *Aswametham* (The Imperial Horse-Sacrifice), *Sarasayya* (The Bed of Arrows), *Koottukudumbam* (Joint Family) etc. N.N. Pillai, the master of histrionics, came up with his first drama *Manushyan* (Man) in 1953. Dramatist T.N. Gopinathan Nair, C.N. Sreekantan Nair, K. Surendran, Jagathy N. K Achari were associated with Trivandrum amateur drama stage. P.J. Antony was in Kochi and wrote dramas for Ernakulam Prathibha Arts Club. He also acted in and directed his dramas. That decade was rich with geniuses like Ponkunnam Varkky, Cherukad, Eroor Vasudev, S. L. Puram

Sadanandan, E.L. Jose, Omchery, K.T. Mohammed, Nagavally etc. Later on, in 1954-55 two dramas by C.J Thomas, '*1128- il crime 27* (1954) and *Aa Manushyan Nee Thanne* (1955) (You Yourself is That Man) became highly praiseworthy. Through Malabar Central Kala Samithi Anniversaries many new dramatists appeared on the drama scene: Theekkotiyan, Uroob, Cherukad, K.T. Mohammad, Mohammad Yousef—all won accolades.

The 1960's unprecedented growth of the drama stage and its literature presented a thrilling surprise. Apart from KPAC (*Aswamedham* was staged during this period), Olassa Viswakerala Kalasamiti, Kollam Kalidasa Kala Kendram, Kayamkulam Peoples Theatre Changanasery Geetha Arts Club, Kerala Theatres (Kottayam), Kalanilayam Theatres were the professional and drama troupes. Vaikkom Chandrasekharan Nair, K.T. Mohammed, P.J. Antony, Jagathy N.K. Achary, N.N. Pillai, Kaladi Gopinath were the active professional dramatists. Among them N.N. Pillai stands out as he paved his own path as a dramatist and director. His outstanding experimental dramas were *Iswaran Arastil* (God under Arrest) *Njan Swargathil* (Me in the Heaven), etc.

Also this was the decade in which Amateur drama troupes were successful enough to make effective ripples. G. Sankara Pillai's experimental dramas like *Pay Pidicha Lokam* (The Mad World), *Bandhi,* (The Hostage), *Raksha Purushan* (The Saviour), *Kazhukanmar* (The Vultures), *Abhayardhikal* (The Refugees), admittedly, vitalised the amateur drama filled. Kanchanasita of C.N. Sreekantan Nair Stands out as a brilliant drama in the whole history of Malayalam Drama. The P.K. Vikraman Nair Trophy (Kerala) drama competition that was started during the date 1960's needs special mention because this was able to present umpteen dramatist actors and actresses. In this connection, the names of dramatists to be remembered are: Sreerangam Vikraman Nair, G. Gopalakrishnan, P.R. Chandran, K.S. Namboodiri, etc.

In the very same decade witnessed major dramas of N.P. Chellappan Nair, C.L. Jose, Kadavoor G Chandran Pillai, T. N. Gopinathan Nair, Paravoor George, P.V. Kuriakose, etc. Two dramas—*Dweep* (The island) and *Nayattu* (The Hunting)—written by C. Radhakrishnan were distinguished in their composition, even then, these did not attract attention of drama critics.

Also it was in the 60's that literary workshops aimed at improvement of drama presentation, acting, etc., were organised on a large scale. The year1967 marked that beginning. In the sasthakotta workshop the main organisors belonged to various cultural and artistic groups. They were: M. Govindan, C.N. Sreekantan Nair, G. Aravindan, Ayyappa Panickar, Prof. G. Sankara Pillai, S. Ramanujam, M.V. Devan, P.K. Venkuttan Nair. Later on such workshops were conducted at Aluwa, Koothattukulam and Dhanuvachapuram. Discussion on the various aspects of presentation of drama, rehearsal of drama- staging were carried out in such workshops. This was the occasion which convinced the drama- workers that drama is an art that is to be practiced. In fact, the commercial group of drama- workers looked down upon these drama workshops. But as irony or fate would have it, some of those commercial groups had to conduct such workshops during the seventies.

By the end of 1960's these sprang up a lot of amateur drama societies in various parts of Kerala. For example, Navarang Kottayam (led by C.N. Sreekantan Nair and G Aravindan) Suvarnarekha, Trivandrum (organised by P.K. Venukuttana Nair) Upasana, Trivandrum (started by Karamana Janardhanan Nair) etc.

The 1970's mark the golden decade of Malayalam drama. Across the length and breadth of the country there emerged umpteen Fine Arts Societies. They staged monthly dramas and thereby strengthened the Malayalam Commercial drama. In Kozhikkode K.T Mohammad wrote and presented various dramas such as *Srushti, Sthithi, Samharam*, *Sakshatkaram*, (creation, state, distruction, realisation), etc. These opened a novel experience to the average drama goers who were fed up with pure realistic dramas presented to them till then. Further it was in the 70's that the scenario of one act malayalam play matured itself trmendously. Thoughout the country spectators got a renewed awareness about one-act plays. These dealt with extremely fresh mode of presentation. A lot of new dramatists also shone like anything during that period. But till now, many of the dramas presented thus could not be got printed and circulated! Another milestone was the first All India Drama Festival held in 1977 at Ernakulam under the auspices of the Kerala and Central Sangeetha Nataka Acadamies. This really inspired a lot of enthusiasts who thereafter were actively involved in the field of amateur dramas. Thus, the state government started in 1978 onwards a Kerala based professional drama competition every year. It remains to be assessed whether and when such competitions really help the development of Malayalam drama. The relevant changes can be effected only if competitions are conducted without discrimination of professionalism and amateurism.

A quite significant turning point of the 70's was the starting of the school drama in the Calicut University. What its director G. Sankara Pillai had envisaged was this: The main aim of the curriculum is to offer a professional standard in all technical and non-technical areas of drama- presentation after a student completes three years of education here. It was in the 70's that C.N. Sreekantan Nair published his *Saketh* and *Lanka Lakshmi* which were part of his trilogy.

In 1967, in the first drama workshops held at sasthamkotta M. Govindan presented as a point of discussion the following :

> Have we got a drama- stage which we call our own? Is it not necessary? That must have close relation with our traditional forms of performing arts.

Later on at Koothattukulam workshop, C.N.Sreekantan Nair presented a thesis in the symposium; there he highlighted the concept of 'Traditional Theatre'. His drama *Kali* directed by G. Aravindan had deliberate sparks of this concept. But it was a failure on the stage. Afterwards, Narayana Panicker's *Avanavan Kadamba* (directed by G.Aravindan) and *Daivathar* could accomplish the idea of 'traditional theatre' (which must combine the components of the folkloric and classical arts of kerala and shape a new mode of presentation) But this concept received a lot of incisive criticism from drama critics and spectators alike. One criticism went like this:

> The nomenclature of 'traditional theatre' is widely spoken about: but it is not yet felt that such a movement has come into being and developed. Actors with heavy make-up with tender palm- leaf, areca nut swathe to cover nakedness, a mask on the face, dialogue –delivering in a sing-song style which is worse than a chakyar or a penthacost believers 'talking in tongues'. They frisk and gallop on the stage under a bright light! Even if all the concerned people and the dramatist's family- members attested that it is traditional theatre, it won't be so! The viewers must certify to that effect!

But even after 25 years, Kavalam Narayana Panicker's traditional theatre has won world-wide appreciation from both the critics and the viewers.

The Malayalam drama theatre which was very active during the first half of the 1980's, became thoroughly exhausted in the later half. This state of affairs affected the professional group more than the amateur one. The presence and influence of the vision made the drama viewership considerably reduced. Even the youngsters were moving away from drama. The functioning of the fine arts societies came to a standstill. By 1990's professional troupes started depending on the stages of festivals of churches and temples.

Thus, the drama—theatre was not at all active during the 1990's. The amateur troupes themselves were participating only in the drama competitions conducted by the Sangeetha Nataka Academy. Even in these bleak circumstances, there are certain amateur drama societies that are dedicated to impart permanent training, rehearsals and drama-presentations. Among them mention must be made of 'Lokadharmi' of Thrippunithura, 'Abhinaya' of Trivandrum, 'Theatre Eye' of Thrichur, 'Rasika' of Trivandrum, etc. Apart from the reduced number of spectators, the factor that drags them back is the financial problems. The established dramatists of that period are R. Narendra Prasad, Vayala Vasudevan Pillai, P. Balachandran, Madhu Master, Baby, Joy Mathew, Ramesh

Varma, etc. Speaking about directors, the names popping up are Chandradasan, Prem Prasad, Rajan Narippatta etc. Kaladharan, Raghuthaman, Ajayan (late), Sreelatha, Shaji, Chandran are well known contemporary actors. Central Sangeetha Nataka Academy awarded the best actor award to Kaladharan in 2006. All though he was a professional actor he joined Narayana Panickar's amateur group called Thiruvarang (now *sopanam*) in 1975. After that he started his own amateur drama troupe called Rasika in Trivandrum. In 1995 he joined Footsbarn Theatre of France. Now he is active in the drama scenario of Kerala.

The children's theatre in Malayalam started functioning in 1970 with the establishment of Rangaprabhath at Venjaramoodu by Prof. G. Sankara Pillai. Rangachethana started in Thrichur in 1980, Surya Children's Theatre in Ernakulam are two children's drama theatres which regularly present children's dramas. The number of dramas written for children is on the increase. A lot of new dramatists are entering this field. The motivating force for the expansion of children's theatre is the annual state youth festival. The renowned books in Malayalam language on writing of dramas are many. In this category, *Uyarunna Yavanika* (The Rising Curtain) by C.J. Thomas, *Nataka Darpanam* (The Mirror of Drama) and *Curtain* by N.N.Pillai, *Naveena Nataka Darsanam* (New Drama—Vision) by Mekkolla Parameswaran Pillai, *Nataka Pravesika* (Introduction to Drama) by Brothers A.D. Harisarma and R.C. Sarma, *Nadaka Roopacharcha* (Discussion on Drama-forms) by Kattumadam Narayan, *Nadakathilekku oru nadapatha* (A Footpath to Drama) by A.P.P. Namboothiri, *Nadakeeyam* (Dramatics) by Kainikkara, *Renga Pravesam* (Entry on to the Stage) by Vaikkom Chandra Sekharan Nair, *Renga Avatharanam* (Stage Presentation) of Kerala Bhasha Institute are worthy of mention. *Nadakadarpanam* and *Rengavatharanam* are outstanding books as they dwell at length on the major concerns and characteristics of drama.

Although the Malayalam drama-theatre is only hundred years old its qualitative significance qualifies for an outstanding position in the history of Indian theatre. It is earnestly dedicated to impart permanent training, rehearsals and drama-presentations. Thus, Malayalam theatre is flourishing in spite of several distractions. Deeprooted regard of the people for their language and theatre surely has sustained the theatre movement in Kerala.

Works Cited

Abraham, T.M. 'Malayala Nadakavum Nadaka vedhiyum' in *Samakalika Malayalam Weekly*, 2000.

Annaiahgowda, H.H. [ed].*Theatre and Drama in Kerala-Indian Drama Today.* Mysore: Mysore University Press,1974.

Bhasi, Madavoor. *Malayala Nadaka Charithram, Malayala Nadaka Sarvaswom.* Thiruvanantapuram: Chanthanya, 1990.

Naryanan, Kattumadam. *Malayala Nataka Prasthanam.* Thrissur: Kearala Sahitya Akademi. 1996.

Nadaka Saahithya Charitam-Malayalam--Bharatheeya Saahithya Charithram,Vol.1. Thrissur: Sahitya Akademi, 1982.

Pillai, N.N. *Curtain.* Kottayam: D.C.Books.

______, *Nadaka Darpanam.* Kottayam: D.C.Books.

Radhakrishnan, N (ed.). *Selected Essays of G. Sankara Pillai.* New Delhi: New Age International Pub. 1997.

Sankarapillai, G. *Malayala Nataka Sahithya Chraithram.* Thrissur: Kerala Sahitya Akademi. 1984.

______, *Karutha Daivathethedi.* Kochi. DC Books.

15

Kannada Theatre–Evolution and Development

— N. Shanta Naik

Theatre developed to its maximum extent in Karnataka. Its origin can be traced way back to A.D. tenth century *Mittravinda Govinda* of Alasingarya was written in seventeenth century. This is the first play written in Kannada language. The Theme–dance, the Folk drama, the 'Yakshaganas', 'Sannata', 'Doddata', Srikirishnnaparijatha. 'Yasagara', 'Gandaligarata', etc., were the entertaining media that dominated in the past. There is no definite evidence to prove when exactly the Kannada theatre was established in the past.

The writers of regional theatres in Indian languages have definitely done injustice to Kannada theatre. Mulk Raj Anand, who introduced the Indian Theatre to Western Readers (Mulk Raj Anand, *The Indian Theatre*) does not mention the Kannada theatres, though he discusses the Telugu, Marathi, Bengali, Hindi, Parsi and Gujarathi theatres. H.N Dasgupta, who collected and presented valuable material on the Indian stage deals at length with Bengali theatre and drama in five volumes (Hemendranath Guptha, *The Indian Stage*).

Basically Kannada theatre emerged from the folk form. In the era of Monarchy a group of people were performing their duties as secret agents as well as drama players. But we do not have any evidence to prove this fact. In order to obtain at least an approximate assessment of Karnnada theatre from the point of view of an academic study, it would be desirable to learn that the territory has been divided into three main parts. These divisions were known as:

a) Bombay Karnataka—(North Karnataka)

b) Madras Karnataka—(South Karnataka)

c) Old Mysore Karnataka

Though these divisions are too limited to cover the entire Kannada-speaking areas, they could be approved for the study of origin and the growth of the Kannada theatre. It is mostly under these divisions that drama flourished with their distinct and almost ındependent features.

a) *Influence of Bombay Karnataka:* Marathi theatre was very rich in those days. The company theatre was the only entertaining media. The company used to go from one village to another village, city to city and had their camps; they were happy with what ever money they got from the people as well as the landlords of the village. There was no steady income. Hence, the Marathi Company occasionally crossed its border to visit Karnataka. Artists like Dhuttargi, Gudigeri etc., were influenced by this Marathi company and started their own companies in Karnataka.

b) *Influence of Madras:* We do not have any written evidence regarding the influence of Tamil plays on Karnataka.

But, Royal Theatre's contribution is much in the field of theatre activities in Old Mysore State. Before one discusses the real theatre in Karnataka it is important to talk about its history. Karnataka has a bountiful flow of literature. Kannada classics, from the time of Kavirajamarga of Nrupatunga of A.D. ninth century indicate from time to time the existence of an active theatre in the Kannada-speaking land, and what is more, they indicate also, a growth of the theatre in two branches: one at the court under royal patronage and the second flourishing among the common people, mostly in the countryside. Occasionally their literary indications get the support of epigraphical evidences and the two together act as the main source of evidence for building up the history of Kannada theatre.

The Court Theatre

Going backwards to reconstruct the history of Karnataka theatre, especially of the court theatre, it is noted that the earliest available written play belongs to the phase of A.D. seventeenth century. It is *Mitravinda Govinda* (AD 1680) written by Narassingaraya; court poet under the patrongage of King Chikka Devaraja of Mysore (1672–1704). He was a nephew of Tirumalaraya a friend and minister of the king. *Mitravinda Govinda* is an adaptation of the Sanskrit play *Ratnavali* of Harsha. *Mitravinda* written in old Kannada with frequent Kannada Padya and Akshara, Gana, Vritta suggests that the language was pretty well adapted for dramatic expression. If it was the very first play ever attempted in Kannada, the dramatic technique and language would not have given an impression of self-development. The inference that there may have been earlier Kannada plays is supported by a verse in *Shabdanushasana* (1604) of Bhattakalanka, which mentioned the existence of the works of *Kavya*, *Nataka*, *Alankara* and *Kalashastra* in Kannada. This statement of Bhattakalanka supports the inference that there must have been some plays and also other dramatic literature in Kannada earlier than the seventeenth century.

The Concept of Nataka Shale

A number of references both literary and epigraphical, are found from time to time to the 'Nataka Shale', possibly a decorated hall specially constructed for performances of Nataka. *Keladinripavijaya* (1763) of Linganna mentions one such was constructed by King Venkatappa Nayaka of Keladi (1582-1629). In his palace at Ikkeri a 'Nataka Shale' was established fully furnished with highly skilled architectural patterns. There was a similar 'Natyshale' which had been built, almost at the same time in the Mysore Palace, as mentioned by Govinda Vaidya, author of *Kantirava Narasaraja Vijaya* (1648). The earliest tangible evidence to the existence of the 'Nataka Shale' is provided by the Mugud inscription, a stone slab standing to this day at the village Mugud close to Dharwar, which records the construction of a 'Nataka Shale' by Shriman

Mahasamanta Martandayya. The inscription is dated AD 1045. These references to 'Nataka Shale' indicate a flourishing theatrical activity in Karnataka from A.D tenth century. But the question arises here is what kind of theatrical performance were taking place.

The Concept of Nataka (Play)

Govinda Vaidya, a renowned playwright of tenth century gives a description of Nataka as, it is a theme–dance, a *natya*, or at the best a *natya-nataka*. As Bendre puts it: "But not *nataka* (drama) in the sense the word is understood today". Ratnakara Siddha, also used words like 'Nataka Shale', 'Poorva Nataka Sandhi', 'Uttara Nataka Sandhi' and 'Nataka' in his work, but actually his descriptions of the gorgeous performances suggest that they were essentially dramatic–dances like the *Dikkannika Natya* and *Jalakannika Natya* performed by *ganikas* or maidan dancers. There is a reference one can find in *Basava Purana* (*Basava Purana*, LIX 27). There are similar references we find in the ancient works: 'sutradhara'—later which was popular in drama is used in *Bharatesa Vaibhava*—gives more emphasis to art and science of natya and was the conductor of the performance. Muliya Thimmappayya—identified him with the *Bhagawata* of Kannada *Bayalata*" (Muliya Timmappayya, Pancha Kajjaya 45). K.G. Kundangar, another theatre activist, puts in a correct way, that the performance is identified itself with the *Kathakali* of Kerala more than with the *Bayalata* of Karnataka (Kundanagar. L.G. *Kannada Sahityadalli Nritya Kalegalu, Parishat Patrike,* Vol. XXIV. 3. 242). Probably, *Bayalta* is a performance performed in an open space. It was just an entertaining means for the villagers in those days. *Bayalata* carries similar features of Kerala's *Kathakali.*

The word *nataka* in Kannada suggests that a theme dance devoid of the spoken word: a definite definition to this art form theatre or drama is provided by Abhinava Mangaraja, author of the lexical work in verse, *Abhinavabhidana* (1378): "The performance would be called a nataka when nritya was performed in the method of 'hastanga' and 'drstigati'. (Abhinavabhidana of Mangaraya (ed.), Mariyappa Bhat, 1952. 25).

Earliest Prose Plays

There was no prose play in existence in ancient Karnataka. Bhatta Kalanka Deva of early seventeenth century makes a mention of existence of prose plays. The history of Vijayanagara dynasty provides some evidence of possibility of the existence of Kannada plays. The great writer B.A. Saletore writes:

> *Gangadasa*, *Pratapavilasam* of Gangadhara mentions that an actor of the court of Vijayanagara on hearing that prince Gangadhasa was in need of a proper person to stage the new drama...proposed to go to the court of that ruler. The farce in two acts entitled *Dhurta Samagama Prahasana* of Joytireeshwara Kavi Vebaracharya must also have been staged in Vijayanagara during the reign of Saluva Narasimharaya (1478). The theatrical world had considerably benefited by *Kaladeepika* of Saluva Gopa Tippa Bhoopala. (Saletore. B.A. *Social and Political Life in the Vijayanagar Empire*. 397)

Even there these theatre activities were held in the court of provisional courts of provinces under the control of Vijayanagara Kings. There was a theatre built by Sankanna Nayaka of Ikkeri.

Influence of Sanskrit on Kannada Plays

Sanskrit was the rich and scholarly language. The earliest writers were all Brahmins and they felt that they could survive through the language of Sanskrit. Even there was a trend that Sanskrit is the divine language spoken by the gods and Goddesses and all heavenly agencies. So it was the only language through which a scholar could express new ideas. Hence, writing in Kannada was thought to be an inferior act. The old Kannada plays were the translations of Sanskrit plays. As Nrupatunga (A.D.9) has rightly pointed out, Sanskrit seems to have been accepted as model to copy. Sanskrit literature has given predominance to its drama and eminent playwrights like Bhasa and Kalidasa must have contributed more to drama. Keshiraja an acclaimed grammarian translated from Sanskrit *Subadrahavana* and *Kirtate*. Nagavarma—II (AD 1145) wrote

Kavyavalokana, which is influenced by Kalidasa's *Vikramorvasiyam*. His other works were Harsha's *Nagananda* and Bhavabooti's *Malatimadhava*. The great poets of the tenth century. Pampa, Ponna and Rama also contributed much to the theatre.

Rama, the third of the great trio, made mention of a 'Nataka Vidhi' in his *Ajita Purana*. He also bought essentially dramatic characters in his *Sahasa Bheema Vijaya* like Kanchuki and Vidushaka. Durgasimha in his Kannada *Panchatantra* (1145) mentioned that the queens Mahadevi and Roopadevi played the roles of Sita and Rama for self entertainment. This patronage continue up to the middle ages. It is helpful to know that the different kinds of theatre emerged in Kannada speaking land in the past.

The Folk Theatre

The court theatre produced Kannada version of Sanskrit plays, it was meant for the entertainment of the privileged elite. The common man perhaps had not access to the court theatre, as some times, queens and kings played roles there in. This explains the development of the folk stage independent of the court theatre which was at best open to the classes not the masses. The court, as a patron of the folk theatre, invited representative folk troupes to stage shows for the benefit of its own privileged audiences. As it was mentioned by Govinda Vaidya, *Dashavatarada Nataka* and *Tarkunda Nataka* were performed by the folk theatre troupe in the court of Vijayanagara rulers (T.S. Sarma, *Jayakarnataka,* Cheruvu Belagal Inscription of Karnool Taluq AD 1514., 1-4) and also evidences of gifts of lands to rural actors are in support of this inference.

Influence of Yakshagana

Yakshagana, the picturesque performance of folk theatre, flourished in the eighteenth and nineteenth centuries. The life and literacy compositions of Pasti Subba (1760 to 1820), a great composer and exponent of Yakshagana, deserve a word of acclamation. He was the pioneer in the field of Yakshagana and the chiselled features of his compositions indicate that Yakshagana was popular in nineteenth century.

Other Folk Theatres of Karnataka

The other folk theatres are *Srikrishnaparijat* which was practiced in and around Bagalkot, Bijapur and Bidar. A group of people who play the role of Hanumanta, Bheema, Arjuna, Rama, etc., from the great epics are called 'Yasagara' or 'Bahrupees'. They just have make up with the dress and go from one house to another house and sing a song from epics to get some money. That's all they aspired to get. Gondalingas are basically singers, who narrate the stories of the King Chitrasheka and Somasheka. *Sannata* is also a folk play performed in Karnataka. The professional theatre had been very much influenced by the dramatic patronage extended to the folk theatre and Yakshagana

The Modern Theatre

The concept of modern theatre emerged with the professional theatre. The theatre run by professional artists is known as the modern theatre and commercial theatre. The idea of professional is recent in India, largely due to the Western influence. The tradition in ancient India was that the actor was always something else by profession and was usually an agriculturist; perhaps, acting on the folk stage some times or was a learned pundit in the court of rulers. The modern theatre of India is young when compared with the professional theatre in other countries.

The National Theatre was established in 1872 in India. It was the first regular theatre in which actors received salary and tickets were sold to the public; it was started in Calcutta. In the other end Bombay did not owe much to the European influence. Parsis, the most intelligent minority in India, brought with them Persian artistic traditions and developed them in India. In a sense they are the pioneers of the modern theatre in Bombay, both in amateur and professional fields, though Bombay also had, as early as in 1770, a play house where a number of English plays were produced. With all these developments in India, Karnataka had to wait for 30 years for the birth of its professional stage.

The year 1856 is memorable in the annals of the western Indian stage, for that marked the birth of the Marathi drama at the hands of Vishnupanth Bhave, one of the gifted clerks of the chief of Sangli who started a professional troup, and named it as Saglikar Sangita Nataka Manadali which began to tour Maharashtra and Karnataka. This company influenced greatly the success of professional theatre in North Karnataka. Marathi professional plays became the rage over the whole of North Karnataka. Kannada audiences crowded to see Marathi plays, often without even understanding their language. It looked as though, in the onrush of the Marathi stage, Kannada drama had been forgotten. The thinkers of Kannada theatre realised that, they have to bring back the glory of Kannada theatre, with the result that in 1870 Sakkari Balachaya, populary known as Shantakavi, wrote against Marathi plays and raised his voice against it. This frustration resulted in starting a company in Gadag in 1877. Karnataka Nataka Company and Veeranarayana Prasadike Kartapura Nataka Mandali were established. It was inspired by Shantakavi. Others who were inspired by this company were Umachgi Lachappa Nayaka, Gudi Raghavendra Charya, Konnur Jeevu Balappa and Kunni Immanna put on boards the play *Usha Harana*—written and directed by Shantha Kavi. Owing to this Shantha Kavi is considered as the pioneer of professional stage in Karnataka. The company moved towards Mysore and Andhra in 1876–77 in search of new audiences. Similarly other troupes too emerged in Karnataka. Dharwad, Ranebennur, Hirekerur, Lakshmeshwar, Hubli, Kalghatagi, Navalgund Nargund, Halasigi Badami, Rabakavi, witnessed establishment of many drama companies in Karnataka.

Kannada Theatre in Twentieth Century

The end of the nineteenth century marked the closing of a significant chapter in the story of the theatre of North Karnataka. The new era produced some of the best troupes and artists and also number of stage worthy plays.

One of the impressive professional troupes was Mahalakshmi Prasadita Nataka Mandali of Venkoba Rao. This company was started in 1903. In the meantime another troupe was started at Bailhongal in Belgaum district. Konnurkar Kadasiddheswara Sangeeta Nataka Mandali had the credit of introducing women artists to the stage. Later on, an actor who carried out a brilliant career for himself as a proprietor was Vaman Rao Master. He was a renowned artist and musician working with Sirhatti Venkab Rao. In 1913, he started his own troupe Vishvagunadarsa Nataka Mandali. He tried his hands in new experiments in the production as well as translation. Another great quality of Vaman Rao Master was spotting talent and encouraging them through providing them an opportunity. The most prominent names we can quote here are Gangubai Guledgudda. Mallikarjun Mansur, GururaoDeshpande, BasavarajMansur, Keshavabhatta Modi and Ranebennur Nallappa.

The other troupes which came to limelight were, Jayakarnataka Nataka Mandali of K. Sitaram Shastri of Sirisi, Vishwa Ranjana Nataka Company of Siddharamappa Handignur, Sri Krishna Nataka Company of Gangubai Guledgud, Sri. Rameshwara Natya Samsthe of Muddu Veeracharya, Basavaraj Mansur and Gohar Karnataki started Vani Vilasa Company, Engi Balappa's Ala Vaibhava Natya Sangha, Sharada Sangeeta Nataka Mandali of Basavaraj Hosamani Kumareswara Sangeeta Nataka Mandali of Gangadharashstri Chitarigi, Lalita Kalodhava Mandali of Kandgal Hanumant Rao, etc., were the professional troupes which dominated the entire Karnataka stage in pre-independence era. In 1880, Chamarajendra Wodeyar of Mysore started a palace company and the first play which was staged at the palace was *Prahalada*. The then Dewan of Mysore, C. Rangacharlu, witnessed the performance. The court poets like Basavappa Shastri Sosale, Ayyasastri, Jayarayachara had contributed immensely to the growth of royal theatre.

Another well-known company which emerged on Kannada soil was Gubbi Channabasaveshwara Krupaposita Nataka Sangha. It was established in 1884 by Gubbi Chendanna, Abdul

Aziz Saheb and Sahukar Neelakantappa. This company made its name in surrounding areas of Tumkur.

The Downfall of Company Theatres

After independence the Indian scenario has completely changed. Modernisation and advent of cinema were the main reasons for the set back to the company theatre. As days passed the taste of people also changed. The concept of ancient text and translations made them change their tastes. The amateur stage diverted the attention of the educated section. The professional stage of the epics, Purana's and other story-based plays were outdated; hence the audience expected change should come on the stage also. In order to attract and sustain the attention of the audience company drama's started employing vulgar dialogues with double meaning.

Sensible audience started searching for a new venue to be opened for all their entertainment. Amateur theatre was supported by the great artists, writers, producers, directors and university professors. As a result the new techniques were introduced. Western theatre and techniques had an enormous influence on amateur theatre. Traditional stage crafts, costumes, make-up gradually changed. The social plays which were performed in rural theatre had a setback. The evening 10 pm to morning 5 am system was gone. The plays meant to edify like *Hemareddy Mallamma, Satya Harishchandra*, *Lavakusha* and others failed to create impact on the traditional audience.

Cinema attracted people, theatre goers gradually decreased. There were several reasons. Nobody had time sit whole day—or night. Within three hours they were getting what they wanted in a cinema theatre. Cinema which takes us to the world of imagination which is unreal. And, brainwash the viewers and persuade them to accept the colourful cinema world rather than the real world. There are the main factors to reject the professional theatre in Karnataka. The concept of drama had totally changed, when it comes to the amateur theatre. B.V. Karanth, Chandrashekar Kambar, Girish Karnad.

Basavalingaiah, Janardhan, Prasanna, K.V. Subbanna Prof. Lingadevaru Halemane, Akshara K.V. may others contributed much to the amateur theatre.

Bandaya movement which is known as protest movement gave a new shape to the stage. They started journey towards the village to create awareness among the people who are sleeping in the slumber of generations. Narguda village had been vandalised by the police and fire was opened killing a few farmers which enraged them to take the law into their hands. They killed a police sub-inspector and a constable. This heroic act was due to the impact of the theatre. The song which became the theme song latter is:

> From where do you come ?
> Where you are going?
> We emerged from the midst of the earth.
> Again where you are moving?
> We tell you that we are going back to
> Midst of the people.

Theatre changed its concept and started a new ideology of street play which goes closer to the people and talk about the problems of common man in common language.

Later Dalita literary movement was started by Prof. Siddalingaih, Sri Mudnakud Chinnaswamy, Dr. N. Shantha Naik, Shiraga Halli—who wrote socially relevant plays worth mentioning a word of commendation. Maskeri M.K. Nayak, one of the promising playwrights, emerged with his powerful plays on the galaxy of Kannada theatre.

Thus, Kannada theatre is vibrant, relevant and patronised well. Girish Karnad, Mahesh Dattani and others have contributed in their own unique fashion, not forgetting the handsome service rendered by H.S. Shiva Prakash and others.

Works Cited

Anand, Mulk Raj. *The Indian Theatre*, London. Dennis Dobson, 1950.

Bhat, Mariyappa (ed). *Abhinavabhidana of Mangaraya*, 1952.

Choudary, S.D. *Glimpses of Indian Poetics*, Sahitya Akademi, New Delhi, 2002.

Deshpande, G.P. *Modern Indian Drama*, Sahiya Akademi, 2000.

Kundanagar, K.G. 'Development of Kannada Drama', *Journal of the Bombay Branch of Royal Asiatic Society*. VI.

Rangacharya, Adya. *Natyashastra,* NewDelhi, 2003.

Salestore, B.A. *Social and Political Life in Vijayanagara Empire,* 2 vols.

Sarma, T.S. *Jayakarnataka,* Cheruvu Belagal Inscription of Karnool Taluq AD 1514.

16

The Emergence and Development of Gujarati Theatre up to 1920: A Bird's-eye View

— Keyur Parekh

In the Sanskrit poetics, it is said: "*Kavyeh idam kavyam*" (Thaker Bharatkumar, 1). It means that any creation of a poet or writer is known as *Kavyam*—poetry. So even the Sanskrit prose writers are also known as poets. It is even said: "*Kavyeshu Natakam Ramyam*" (Thaker Bharatkumar 1). It also suggests that even the form of drama can also be considered as poetry. It is of two types (1) *Shravyakavya* (2) *Drishayakavya*. The work of art which can be heard only is known as *Shravyakavya*. The forms like poetry, novel, short story, essay, biography, etc. are incorporated in the *Shravyakavya* while the work of art which can be heard and seen, provides audio-visual effect, is known as *Drishayakavya*. The drama form is put into this category. One can see the play being performed or enacted, having both audio-visual effect. It gives pleasure to the people of all age groups. The impact of the play is more than that of any other form of literature. As the drama is performed in front of the audience, so its vividness makes a great difference as compared to the *Shravyakavya*. Therefore, the Greek and Shakespearean tragedies created a great impact on the mind of the theoreticians as well as the common audience.

The word *Natya* is derived from *Nat* which has become famous in terms of acting. It reflects different states of mind through the medium of acting. The feelings and emotions of the character are imitated in the drama. Since it is audio-visual, it is also popularly known as *Rupak*. At the same time, even the actor performing the role of a different character is also known as *Rupak*.

So far as the origin and development of Sanskrit drama is concerned, there is no consensus. Both Indian and Western scholars have formed different opinions about the Sanskrit drama. Only a few opinions are convincing.

Bharat Muni offers an interesting story for the origin of the drama. He says that one day Aatreya Muni along with other sages came to Bharat Muni and asked about the origin of drama. In answer to this question, Bharat Muni told him this story. According to him, at the time of Manu, in Treta Yuga when the Universe became erratic, Indra and other gods went to Brahma. Brahma, through his supernatural power, called the four *Vedas*. He took *Pathya* (prose) from *The Rig Veda*, *Geet* (Song) from *The Sama Veda*, *Abhinay* (acting) from *The Yajur Veda* and *Rasa* (essence) from *The Atharva Veda* and created *The Pancham Veda*. Lord Vishnu gave *Vritti* (the four basic tendencies), Lord Shiva gave *Tandava* (a dance form) and Goddess Parvati gave *Lasya* (a dance form) dance. Vishvakarma prepared a stage for avoiding harassment from the devils. The first two dramas were performed were *Tripurdah* and *Samudra Manthan*. In both these plays, the role of women is played by male actors. Bharat Muni brought this art from *Devalok* (Heaven) to *Mrityulok* (Earth.) It is a general tendency to relate any fact to the religious scriptures. So, this story also carries some religious connotations. It clearly suggests that in order to find the root of the drama, we have to go to the precious *Vedas*. That is why: Prof. Maxmullar describes the *Vedas* as the emerging place for the drama.

After some introduction of the emergence and development of drama from the Sanskrit Poetics, it is interesting to know about the drama written and performed in Gujarat. In the Middle Ages, in Gujarat, the very popular form of drama was known as *Bhavai*. As *Jatra* in Bengal and Orissa, *Ramlila* in Bihar and U.P., *Song* in Punjab, *Yakshagana* in Karnataka, *Ramlila* in Gokul and Mathura, *Dashavatar* in Maharashtra, *Kathakali* in Malabar, in Gujarat *Bhavai* has played a major role in shaping the interest of the people. R. Jayshankar explained the term 'Bhavai' as the portrayal of life. This form is related to even the worship of Goddess Bhagavati and is performed by the players in front of the Goddess during Navratri celebrations—the longest festival of Gujarat. The people who are engaged in this drama form are known as *Targada*, because of their ancestor Asait Thakar who belonged to the *Targada* caste. He wrote 360 plays and he himself had performed them with his sons and adopted it as a profession. His three sons were sarcastically known as *Tran Gharwala*. So they are known as *Targada*. Asait Thakar contributed his genius in fourteenth century. So, this form of drama is older than fourteenth century, but it is still relevant in the twenty-first century in India. This form fails into oral tradition of literature. So, it does not have any script. It varies from performer to performer according to the competence of the performer concerned. Hence, today's written script is not authentic. These forms of drama are normally based on religious or ancient themes such as Rama-Laxman, Krishna-Gopi, Shankar-Parvati, etc.; historical themes such as Jasma-Odhan, Viko Sisidiyo and social themes like husband-wife, mismatch of marriage, life, etc.

Prof. Anantray Rawal states that *Bhavai* is usually played in open ground, surrounded by the village people when they are at ease after their dinner. It begins in the night and is performed till early morning. It is not a long single story but a bunch of small anecdotes of different kinds. Every anecdote is known as *Vesh*. After blowing the trumpet, the first *Vesh* is inevitably of Lord Ganesha. In one night, around six *Vesh* are performed. Every *Vesh* begins with a song and then the player himself or herself comes by singing and dancing. Music, dance, disguise and imitation are the basic ingredients. in *Bhavai*, *Hasya Rasa* and *Shringar Rasa* are mainly reflected in this type of drama. It talks about almost all castes and sub-castes along with all their eccentricities and behaviour by humour, satire, etc. The language of this form differs according to the *Vesh*. If the protagonist is a Muslim chap, it is Gujarati-Hindi mixed language, for Rajasthani, it is Mewadi-Marwadi, etc. In the present age, the form of *Bhavai* has disappeared from the minds of young people. It is regularly performed in Ambaji and in the small villages. One must thank the *Targada* community for sustaining such a brilliant art, and also to provide the great actors to the Gurjar Theatre.

As folk literature is oral, the other one is written. But the literature which is to be performed must be improvised. The conflict presented in the modern plays is rarely found in oral tradition. Certain historical plays like *Jasma Odhan* and *Ranakdevi-Rakhengar* are more acceptable and performed more in *Bhavai* than in theatres. Most of the dialogues used to be in poetry form and the movement of the players used to be in line with their dialogue delivery. Then the system of using curtains was introduced which was due to the Western influence. But *Bhavai* used to be performed in the public only because of its oral tradition, and is still so. At the same time, a lot of instruments are used. The character enters immediately after the introduction. The audience is never annoyed with the minimum use of vulgarisation in the language. The role of women used to be performed by males. All strata of the society used to come to enjoy this form of dramatic presentation. The *Bhavai* of *Barot* community used to be less vulgar than the *Bhavai* played by *Targada* community. *Bhavai* was normally played in the temple of Goddess Amba and Goddess Bahuchar. It was a great medium to praise these two goddesses. It is also a fact that to satisfy even the entertainment part of the specific audience, *Bhavai* was performed. But in the nineteenth century, the people shifted from *Bhavai* to the disciplined play. So the Gujarati plays did not come from *Bhavai* but they were borrowed from the West.

Gujarati play is the result of the comprehensive thinking of the age. In the Middle Age, we didn't have any sign of oral or written Gujarati drama. The plays of Premanand are actually found in the later part of nineteenth century and the beginning of twentieth century. Gujarati drama emerged and developed after 1840-50. During this period, the plays were performed in Ahmedabad and Mumbai. The first Gujarati theatre was built in 1842. Before that the British and the Italian groups used to come to perform the plays. Generally, they performed Shakespearean plays. The britishers also built up the British theatre. During this time, Gujarati plays were performed under the influence of the British plays, but they were simply scattered experiments only.

From 1850 to 1860, the Parsis contributed immensely to the Gujarati theatre. They used to perform their plays in Surat and Mumbai, and the element of farce was at the centre. Many foreign groups were also coming to Gujarat and there took place a healthy competition. This provided a conducive environment for the development of Gujarati theatre. The printing press was established, so the plays were available in the book form in great numbers. Many translations were available. It was real renaissance of the Gujarati theatre.

According to the history of Gujarati drama *Gulab* was the first play published in 1862 by Nagindas Tuljadas who was the first graduate in Gujarat. Though the play was based on the English model, it had a great influence on *Shakuntalam*. Simultaneously, like a Greek drama, there was a prologue and even the use of chorus. The language of the play is completely rustic, in typical Surati dialect, leaning towards insulting and vulgar language. In spite of being the first attempt by the author, it is worthy of its form.

The popular name for cultivating the Gujarati drama and theatre was of Ranchhodbhai Udayram. Annoyed from the vulgarity of the language in the performance of *Bhavai*, he wrote about fourteen plays to for the Gujarati theatre. The theme of his plays generally was social and ancient. His reformist approach is explicitly reflected in his plays. *Lalitadukhdarshak* and *Jaykumarivijay* are his popular plays. His praiseworthy play is *Jay Kumar no Jay* which was performed in 1862 but published in 1864. It discusses the contemporary problems of the dramatists, such as women's education, love marriage, etc. It is written in a very lucid and disciplined language but at times it looks very blunt.

Lalitadukhdarshak (1866) was the first tragic play. It was based on Greek and English plays and was completely different from the Sanskrit drama. It was staged for the first time in 1866. The play begins directly without any prologue. The characters are drawn in the right spirit and the language is also used in accordance with the stature of the character. The treatment is melodramatic. His other well-known plays are *Banasurvadh, Nal-Damayanti, Harishchandra,* etc. He was also influenced by Ranchhoddas's reformist approach. So, at times, his plays also seem to be a bit didactic. Hence, the Gujarati dramas, both performed and written, were, in a primitive stage, inclined towards the social reform.

During this period, Narmad wrote a few dramas. He is the exponent of the modern Gujarati literature. Owing to his subjective and serious nature, he is not impressive in this form of literature. Influenced by *Bhavai* and Sanskrit plays, he wrote plays like *Ram-Janki Darshan*, *Balkrushna Darshan*, *Krushnakumari* and *Draupadi Darshan.* These plays are full of flaws in respect to theme, dialogue, characterisation, etc.

In Gujarati drama, Dalpatram is one of the major writers. He did not have any knowledge of English language. He was not even familiar with the Western literature. Even then, due to the friendship of Kinlock Forbs, he wrote a play named *Lakshmi*, based on the Greek character Plutus. It is a satirical play, showing the injustice and unequal distribution of money in society. There is also an influence of *Bhavai* on the character of Bhilda. The presentation is very humourous but at times it becomes uncivilised. Though the structure seems to be Western, it is a lucid translation in Gujarati. Another play of

Dalpatram is *Mithyabhiman*, which is better structured than the previous one. It was most successful in terms of dramatic presentation. The character of Jivram Bhatt became very popular gaving credit to Dalapatram as a recognised Gujarati dramatist.

Navalram Lakshmiram Pandya goes one step ahead. He gave two plays. His first was *Bhatt nu Bhopadu* on Molier's *The Mock Doctor*, whereas the second play *Veermati* is based on *Rasmala*; a historical play. After *Mithyabhiman, Bhatt nu Bhopadu* is another poewrful comedy. *Veermati* is the best play of the age. By portraying Siddhraj, Hemchandra, Navalram established a new trend.

In the same period, Savitanarayana wrote *Rajbhakti-Vidanban*, Harilal Dhruv wrote *Aryotkarsh* and Amrut Keshav Nayak wrote *Bharatdurdasha*. All these plays are based on patriotism. During the same time, we have plays based on the lives of Narsinh, Meera, Sudama, Prahlad, Surdas, etc. Thus, the plays on different subjects were written and performed. They were social, historical, ancient and religious plays. But most of them were artistically inadequate. *Pratap Natak* (1883) is the best example of it.

The play *Kanta* by Manibhai Nabhubhai Dwivedi is a great milestone. The playwright has fictionalised history. The story circles around the theft of a necklace. The psychological presentation of the character of Tarla is amazing. Dr. Dhirubhai Thakar notes that Manilal has given full flow of his poetry in the play so that it seems that poetry is in competition with the play itself. But it was not successful in a grand way. For the theatre, he has written *Nrusinhavatar*. In this play, the literary element is less than the theatrical element. Also, he has translated *Maltimadhav* and *Uttar Ramcharit*.

The renowned poet Kant has offered two dramas of patriotic feeling in *Guru Govindsinh* and *Romanswaraj*. The action of the play is very slow but the spirited dialogue, impressive characterisation and befitting poetry for performance make the play more effective.

During this phase, *Bhrantisanhar* by Krushnarao Divetiya, *Devadevi* by Bhimrao Divetiya, *Sangit Kadambari* by Durganath Dave, *Bejan ane Manijed* by K.Kushro Kabraji, *Analray ane Lalba* by Manishankar Pandit were written, published and even performed.

After having been inspired by *Kanta* of Manilal, Sir Ramanbhai wrote *Rai no Parvat*. It was based on both Sanskrit and Shakespearean dramas. He used the protogonist Lalji Maniar as a ploy to show his value-based and reformist approach. The play discusses issues like moral values, child marriage, old people's marriage, widow's marriage, etc. The last two acts reflect the reformist nature of the playwright. The characterisation and theatrical elements are quite impressive. This play owns a great publicity as compared to the preceding plays. It is the representative of the contemporary age.

In the field of Gujarati theatre, poet Nanhalal is one of the major dramatists. But his plays seem more or less to be the same. Though, his plays are emotionally strong, the variety in theme and characterisation is not found. His plays are completely different from Sanskrit as well as Shakespearean plays. His characters are treated like puppets in the hands of the playwright. His plays have less dramatic elements but the anecdotes, melodious songs, thought-provoking language and the poetic diction make the plays more receiptive. His creative career is credited with plays like *Indukumar, Jaya Jayant, Kalpanatha, Rajarshi Bharat, Shahanshah Akbarshah, Sanghmitra, Jahangir Nurjahan, Shri Harshdev* which are historical plays. *Punya Katha* and *Vishwagita* are philosophical plays and *Premkunj* and *Gopika* are based on rural life.

Balvantray Thakor is another important dramatist of the time. His two plays *Ugati Juwani* and *Soviet Navjuwani* are very popular. The congruity between incident, character and emotion are finely presented in his plays. They are known as social criticism of his time.

The new trend in Gujarati drama is perceptible in the plays of Batubhai Umarvadiya. His two collections, *Matsyagandha ane Bija Natako* and *Maladevi ane Bija Natako,* now known as *Batubhai na Natako,* are influenced by the style of Henrik Isben. The striking similarity is the chief characteristic of his plays. Influenced by the Western drama, the female characters of his plays are more powerful and brighter than the male characters. Interesting and emotional dialogues make the dramas more appealing. Lomharshini adopts a different theme. He is the first dramatist who introduced the one-act play in the history of Gujarati drama.

Kanaiyalal Maneklal Munshi is one of the most popular dramatists. He wrote twenty plays. Some of them are based on ancient themes and some are social plays. His plays such as *Kakani Shashi, Chhiye Tej Thik, Snehsambhram, Dr. Madhurika, Wahre Me Wah, Dhruvswaminidevi, Bhrahmacharyashram* etc. are very touching. His social plays are humourous and at times satiric. These plays reflect the follies and faults of the society. In *Kakani Shashi* the dramatist portrays a modern woman with a sense of liberation. An element of sex is portrayed in *Chhiye Tej Thik* which is quite humourous. His plays based on ancient themes are quite serious. But a touch of modernity can be found in such plays also. His plays are quite vivid and many experiments are done on Gujarati theatre. He is also a great novelist of his time.

Ramanlal Vasantlal Desai is another renowned dramatist of his time. He wrote beautiful three-act plays like *Anjani, Saiyukta* and *Shakti Hriday.* They are very famous for their performance value. Many stage shows of *Shakti Hriday* are performed. He has reduced a gap between the drama and the Gujarati theatre. In his dramas, one finds humour, pathos as well as the aesthetic beauty. There is also a literariness, songs, emotions and humour. All his plays are very much disciplined.

Chandravadan Mehta voluntarily worked for Gujarati theatre. Since he was the actor himself, he contributed immensely in the field of Gujarati theatre by offering subject matters and styles. He also wrote plays for children like *Santakukdi* and *Ramakda ni Dukan.* His social plays like

Nagabawa, Aag Gadi, Mena-Popat, Shikhrini, Panjara Pole, his historical plays like *Sonavatakadi, Dharagurjari, Param Maheshwar,* etc. and his ancient plays like *Sita, Shakuntala,* his radio play *Rangbhandar*, the character play inspired by Narmad, like *Mungi Stri, Dedka ni Panchsheri* and even his poetic plays such as *Atralupta Saraswati* and *Viswamitri* exhibit the versatile personality of the dramatist. Both prose and poetry as well as imagination and reality are incorporated in his plays. The dialogues are used in such a way that the characters who diliver them seem to be very lively. *Aag Gadi* is the best example of it. His contribution is really invaluable to the Gujarati theatre.

Like Batubhai, Pranjivan Pathak was also highly influenced by the Henrik Ibsen. *Ajanta* (1924) was written under the influence of Ibsen. This play is very thought-provoking. The play is full of confrontations but the speech of the king is full of pathos and didactic. The diction is expressive and poetic. So, it becomes quite appealing. The play tends to be more on a pychological level than the physical one. Though very compact the play comments on issues like life, death, love, beauty, the process of ruling the country, etc. in a very aunthetic way. The plays of Yashvant Pandya, namely, *Padada Pachhad, Madan Mandir, Ghar Divadi* are noteworthy for its strikingness of language and intellectual thought pattern.

One of the trio, Krushnalal Shridharani, wrote many plays such as *Valdo* and historical plays like *Padmini, Zabak-Jyot, Dunsku, Pida Palash* and *Mor na Inda etc. Pida Palash* and *Mor na Inda* were written under the influence of Rabindranath Tagore. Just like him, Indulal Gandhi wrote many one-act plays. Umashankar Joshi, Jayantilal Dalal and chunilal Madiya also wrote many one-act plays, especially for performance. The one-act plays of Umashankar Joshi discuss the deep philosophy of life while the plays of Jayantilal Dalal are famous for the witty dialogues and effective stage performances.

Dhansukhlal Mehta is a great playwright who served the Gujarati theatre for more than six decades. In the beginning of his creative career, he translated many plays from English into Gujarati, namely, *Station Master* and *Vandara no Panjo*. *Sari Jatu Surat* is a dramatic transformation of *Ame Badha*. *Garib ni Jumpadi* is the first original play written by him. *Manu ni Masi* and *Rangilo Raja* are the most successful plays so far as the performances are concerned. Dhumketu has written *Eklavya* which is a very popular children's play. Yashodhar Mehta is another noteworthy writer. Along with *Mumbojumbo* and *Ranchhodlal and Other Plays*, he wrote five plays based on five different great personalities. The diction of these plays is very distinguished. He is very much familiar with theatre art and endowed with extraordinary language skills, in addition to profundity in artistic presentation. Shri Durgesh Shukla had also been serving the Gujarati theatre since 1934. That year he wrote *Urvashi* in a verse form. Thenafter, he wrote *Sundarvan, Pallavi Parni Gai and Roope Range Rani* for the Gujarati theatre. Pragji Dosa wrote plays for theatre groups such as *Chhorukachhoru, Charanraj, Ghar no Divo, Mangal Mandir, Samay na Vahen,* etc. which are worth mentioning. The dialogues are extempore, real and dynamic, but characterisation is shallow. Glaringly they are lacking in depth. Nandkumar Pathak has also written a three-act play named *Parki Jani*.

Apart from this, many playwrights have written so many other plays such as Jashvant Thakar's *Razia Begum*, Praboth Joshi's *Patta ni Jod,* Lilavati Munshi's *Kumardevi,* Hansa Mehta's *Himalaya Swarup,* Raman Vakil's *Urtantra*, Firoz Aantiya's six plays, Anant Aacharya's *Bhrahmachari,* Gunvantray Aacharya's *Allabeli*, Indulal Yagnik's *Varghodo*, Darshak's *1857, Jaliyawala Baug, Paritran*, Damu Shukla's *Kuwara j Sara,* Bhagvandas Bhukhanwala's *Raj nu Gaj, Jama-Udhar,* Rashmi Pancholi's *1942,* Gajendrashankar Pandya's Pavapati, Babulal Vaidya's *Dhingali Ghar* and *Ae Aavjo*, Pannalal Patel's *Jamai Raj, Vaitarni na Kanthe, Dholiya Sag-sisamna,* Govindbhai Amin's *Radium, Kalchakra,* Bhaskar Vahora's *Rankh na Ramakada*, Rambhaben Gandhi's *Raj ni Ramayan*, *Chakmak, Pranay na Rang, Koine Kahesho Nahi,* etc. These playwrights have contributed substantially in the field of Gujarati drama and theatre. Chunilal Madiya as well as Shivkumar Joshi are two dramatists with a difference. Shivkumar Joshi's plays such as *Sumangala, Sandhyadipika, Angarbhasma, Suvarnarekha, Saputara,* etc., have received great response in the theatre. Chunilal Madiya's *Hu ane Mari Vahu, Ramlo Robinhood* and *Sunyashesh* are very effective so far as performance is concerned. As Dr. Dhirubhai Thakar rightly points out that Madiya's plays are romantic in nature at the same time, they are full of variety and are in Sorathi dialect. He incorporated ancient, historical, political and social themes in his dramatic world.

Dr. Dhirubhai also notes that in the last five to seven years, the trends of absurd theatre are in full swing. In Gujarati theatre, Labhshankar Thakar and Subhash Shah introduced this type of play. *Waiting for Godot* was first translated by both of them entitled as *Ek Undar ane Jadunath.* Then many plays like *Jew Story, Two Executions, Cross Last Tape, Chairs, Hello Out There, A Man with a Flower in His Mouth* were translated and even performed. Madurai's *Jhervu*, Aadil Mansuri's *Pencil, Kabar, Minbatti*, Chhinu Modi's *Dayal na Pankhi* are written in the absurd style with original touch. These plays can create a great impact on the stage because of the dialogues in absurd drama style. Prompted by laughter, sometimes the serious message is missed. When the illusion breaks down, the vacuum and void come to the surface. Even the helplessness of the people comes to the surface.

In order to make the Gujarati theatre vibrant, the State and Central Governments sponsored a lot of competitions and schemes. Just like the Government efforts, certain voluntary theatres, charging no money for the performances and radio played a major role for the development of the Gujarati drama and theatre. Aa the number of plays written were very few in numbers, many novels were also dramatised. Darshak's *Zher to Pidha Jani Jani,* Chunilal V. Shah's *Roopvati,* Eeswar Petlikar's *Pankhi no Mado*, Pannalal Patel's *Madela Jeev*,

Kanaiyalal Maneklal Munshi's *Patan ni Prabhuta* commanded great respect in the field of Gujarati theatre. Both in Gujarati literature as well as theatre, one finds very few dramas. Compared to other arenas in literature, in Gujarat the field of drama is given less attention. Almost all plays are written in the same style. Gujarati drama and theatre can claim very few masterpieces. The height of the artistic qualities are lacking in these plays. Though the State and Central Governments try to motivate the people about Gujarati drama and theatre, there is a very little hope for getting quality plays. Gujarati has still to wait for the dramatist of the world's stature for years together. Extraordinary themes, excellent characterisations, spirited dialogues, melodious songs, aesthetic beauty, wonderful description, vivacity and the dialogue delivery work wonders. It is fervently hoped that a world classic will be produced in the near future.

Works Cited

Brahmbhatt, Prasad. *History of Medieval Gujarati Literature.* Ahmedabad: Parshwa Publications, 2002.

Brahmbhatt, Prasad. *History of Modern Gujarati Literature (Sudharak & Saksar Era).* Ahmedabad: Parshwa Publications, 2004.

Chaudhari, Raghuvir and Ratilal Borisagar. eds. *Gurjar Prahasan Sanchay.* Ahmedabad: Gurjar Grantharatna Karyalaya, 1998.

Mehta, Chandravadan and Hansaben M. Patel. *Children's Drama & Literature.* Ahmedabad: University Granth Nirman Board, 1972.

______. *Drama in Europe.* Ahmedabad: University Granth Nirman Board, 1973.

______. *American Drama.* Ahmedabad: University Granth Nirman Board, 1974.

______. *Japanese Theatre.* Ahmedabad: University Granth Nirman Board, 1975.

Nayak, Ratilal S, Somabhai V. Patel and Dr. Prasad Brahmbhatt. *History of Modern Gujarati.* Ahmedabad: Anada Book Depot, 2003.

Patel, Bahecharbhai. *The Medieval Gujarati Literature: A History.* Ahmedabad: Navbharat Sahitya Mandir, 1993.

Raval, Anantrai M. *Gujarati Sahitya: The Medieval Age, History of Gujarati Literature.* Ahmedabad: Gurjar Grantharatna Karyalaya, 1999.

Shah, Mahesh Champaklal. *Bharat's Natyashastra: Modern Relevance.* Ahmedabad: University Granth Nirman Board, 1997.

Thakar, Jashvant and Hasmukh Baradi. *Art of Acting.* Ahmedabad: University Granth Nirman Board, 1972.

Thaker, Bharatkumar. *Natak: shilp* ane *Sarjan.* Ahmedabad: Bharat Prakashan, 2007- 08.

Thaker, Dhirubhai. *An Outline of the Development of Modern Gujarati Literature- 5.* Ahmedabad: Gurjar Grantharatna Karyalaya, 2006.

Trivedi, Ramesh M. *Arvachin Gujarati Sahitya no Itihas.* Ahmedabad: Adarsh Prakashan & Shabdaloka Prakashan, 1993 -94.

______. M. *History of Medieval Gujarati Literature.* Ahmedabad: Adarsh Prakashan, 2000.

______. M and Natubhai Thakkar. *Gujarati Sahitya no Itihas ane Kavya na Tattvo.* Ahmedabad: Adarsh Prakashan, 2004.

17

A History of Indian English Drama

— Ram Sharma

India has a rich tradition of drama from the ancient times. India is a land of several types of dramas in several languages. Drama in India begins its journey with the Sanskrit plays. A.L. Basham, a prominent historian, expresses his views in this manner:

> The origin of Indian theatre is still obscure. It is certain, however that even in the Vedic period dramatic performances of some kind were given, and passing references in early resources point to the enaction at festivals of religious legends, perhaps only in dance and mime.[1]

Indian traditions are preserved in the *Natyasastra*,. the oldest of the texts of the theory of the drama. This play claims for the drama divine origin and a close connection with the sacred *Vedas* themselves. The origin of Indian English drama can be traced to the ancient rules and seasonal festivities of the Vedic Aryans. The dramatic performances of those times mainly included such events like depiction of events of daily life accompanied by music. Some members of the tribe acted as if they were wild animals and some others were the hunters. Those who acted as animals like goats, buffaloes, reindeers and monkeys were chased by those, playing the roles of hunters and a mock hunt was enacted. In such a crude and simple way was drama performed during the age of the Vedic Aryans. Later, different episodes from *The Ramayana (Ram Leela)*,

The Mahabharata and *The Bhagavad Gita* were chosen and dramatised in front of the people. This kind of performance is still very popular in India especially during the time of Dussehra, when the episode of the killing of Ravana is enacted in different parts of country.

There are refrences to drama in Patanjali's *Vyakarna Mahabhashya*, as well as Vatsyayan's *Kamasutra*, Kautilya's *Arthashastra* and Panini's *Ashtabhyam*. Thus, the origin of Sanskrit drama dates back to 1000 B.C. All literature in Sanskrit is classified into *Drishya* (that can be seen on exhibited) and the *Shravya* (that can be heard or recited). While poetry in all forms can be said to fall under the later, drama falls under the former. Drama in Sanskrit literature is covered under the broad umbrella of *rupaka*, which means depiction of life in its numerous aspects represented in forms by actors who takes various roles.

A *rupaka* has ten classifications of which *Nataka* (drama), the most important one, has come to mean all dramatic presentations. The Sanskrit drama grows around three primary constituents namely *Vastu* (plot), *Neta* (hero) and *Rasa* (sentiment). The plot could be either 'principal' (*adhikarika*) or 'accessory' (*prasangika*). The former concerns the primary characters of the theme and pervades the entire play. The latter serves further and supplements the main topic and relates to subordinate characters other than the chief ones. This is again divided into 'banner' (*pataka*) and 'incident' (*parkari*). The former is a small episode that presents, describes, improves or even hinders the primary plot to create added excitement. The latter has minor characters. The *Neta* or the hero, according to the definition prescribed by the *Natyashastra*, is always depicted as modest (*Vineeta*), sweet tempered (*Madhura*) sacrificing (*tyagi*), capable (*daksha*), civil in talks (*priyamvada*), belonging to a noble family (*taptaloka*), pure (*suchi*) articulate (*vagmi*), consistent (*sthira*), young (*yuva*) endowed with intellect (*buddhi*) enthusiasm (*utsaha*), good memory (*smrthi*) aesthetics (*kola*), pride (*maana*) and is brave (*Shura*), strong (*dridha*), energetic (*tejaswi*), learned (*pandita*) and pious (*dharmika*). The main category in which the hero of Sanskrit drama normally falls is the *Dheerodatta* that is he who is brave and sublime at the same time.

Bharata's *Natyashastra* is the most significant work on Indian poetics and drama. In it there is description in detail about composition, production and enjoyment of ancient drama, a wealth of information of types of drama, stage equipment, production and music. According to the legend, when the world passed from the golden age to the silver age and people became addicted to sensual pleasures and jealousy, anger, desire and greed filled their hearts. The world was then inhabited by gods, demons, *yakshas*, *rakshasas*, *nagas* and *gandharvas*. It was the gods among them who led by Lord Indra approached god Brahma and requested him thus:

> Please give us something which would not only teach us but be pleasing both to eyes and ears.[2]

Bharata ascribed a divine origin to drama and considered it as the fifth Veda. Its origin seems to be from religious dancing. According to Bharata, poetry (*kavya*) dance (*nritta*), and mime (*nritya*) in life is play (*lila*) produce emotion (*bhava*) but only drama (*natya*) produces flavour (*rasa*). The drama uses the eight basic emotions of love, joy (humour), anger, sadness, pride, fear, aversion and wonder attempting to resolve them in the ninth holistic feeling of peace. Thus, when the dramatic art was well comprehended, the *natyaveda* was performed on the occasion of the celebration of Lord Indra's victory over the *Asuras* and *danavas*. In the *Natyashastra* there is a verse in its sixth chapter which can be quoted as Bharat Muni's own summary of his dramatic theory:

> The combinition called natya is a mixture of rasa, bhavas, vrittis, pravrittis, siddhi, svaros, abhinayas, dharmis, instruments, song and theatre-house.[3]

The most celeberated dramatists of the ancient times are Ashwaghosh, Bhasa, Shudraka, Kalidas, Harsha, Bhavabhuti, Vishakha-datta, Bhattanarayana, Murari and Rajeshkhara, who enriched Indian theatre with their works like *Madhya-Mavyaayoda*, *Urubhangam*, *Karnabharan*, *Mrichkatikam*, *Abhigyana Shakuntalam*, *Malavikagnimitram*, *Uttar Ramacharitam*, *Mudrarakshasa*, *Bhagavadajjukam*, *Matta-vilasa,* etc. The supreme achievement of Indian Drama undoubtedly lies in Kalidasa who is often called the Shakespeare of India. The Sanskrit drama flourished in its glory till the twelfth century in India when the Mohammedan intrusion shattered the Sanskrit stage. But till the fifteenth century, plays of Sanskrit tradition were performed on stage in Tamilnadu, Kerala, Karnataka, Andhra, Utter Pradesh and Gujarat but thereafter, Indian dramatic activity almost ceased due to foreign invasions on India.

The beginnings of *Loknatya* (People's Theatre) are noticed in every state of India from the seventeenth century onwards. We see in Bengal *Yatrakirtaniya, Paol* and *Gaan* in Madhya Pradesh *Mach* in Kashmir *bhandya thar* and in Gujarat the forms were *Bhavai* and *Ramleela* in Northern India. There were *Nautanki, Bhand, Ramleela* and *Rasleela,* in Maharashtra *Tamasha,* in Rajasthan *Raas* and *Jhoomer* in Punjab *Bhangra* and *Song* while in Aasam it was *Ahiyanat* and *Ankinatya* in Bihar it was *Videshiya* and *Chhari* in West Bengal and Bihar.

The rise of the modern drama dates back to the eighteenth century when the British Empire strengthened its power in India. As Krishna Kriplani points out, the modern Indian drama "Owed its first flowering to the foreign grafting." With the impact of Western civilisation on Indian life, a new renaissance dawned on Indian arts including drama. Futhermore, English education gave an impetus and a momentum to the critical study of not only Western drama, but classical Indian drama. English and Italian dramatic troupes toured India and performed many English plays, mainly Shakerpeare's, in cities like Bombay and Madras. The Portuguese brought a form of dance drama to the West coast. A Russian music director, Rebedoff, is said to have produced the first modern drama in Calcutta towards the end of eighteenth century. Thus, the Western impact awakened:

> the dormant, critical impulse in the country to bring Indians face to face with new forms of life and literature, and to open the way for a fruitful cross-fertilisation of ideas and forms of expression[4]

In 1765 one Russian drama lover, Horasin Lebdef, and Bengali drama lover, Qulokhnath, had staged two English comedies *Disgaig* and *Love Is The Best Doctor*. But the real beginning was in 1831 when Prasanna Kumar Thakur established *Hindu Rangmanch* at Calcutta and staged Wilson's English Translation Of Bhavabhuti's Sanskrit drama *Uttar Ramacharitam*. Social drama of Girish Chanda Ghosh, historical dramas of D.L. Roy and artistic dramas of Rabindranath Tagore (*Muktadhara*, *Chandalika*) continued to reach upto the stage of realistic dramas during the period of the worst-ever famines of Bengal and the Second World War.

In 1852-1853, the famous Parsi Theatre was launched in Bombay which influenced the whole country in no time. Postagi Pharmji was the pioneer in establishing the Parsi Theatre company in India. Many new theatre experiences were brought up on stage during Parsi Theatre evolution in India. On the other hand, the amateur theatre also developed with the works of Bharatendu Harishchandra, acclaimed as the father of Hindi drama.

Indian English drama was inaugurated when Krishna Mohan Banerji penned *The Persecuted* in 1837. The real odyssey of Indian English Drama begins with Michael Madhusudan Dutt's *Is This Called Civilisation?* which appeared on the literary scene in 1871. Rabindranath Tagore and Sri Aurobindo, the two great sage-poets of India, are regarded the pioneer Indian dramatists in English. Tagore wrote mainly in Bengali but almost all his Bengali plays are available to us in English translation. His prominent plays are *Chitra, The Post Office*, *Sacrifice*, *Red Oleanders*, *Chandalika*, *Muktadhara*, *Natir Puja*, *The King of the Dark Chamber*, *The Cycle of Spring*, *Sanyasi* and *The Mother' s Prayer*. These plays are firmly rooted in the Indian culture in their themes, characters and treatment.

R.K. Ramaswamy appreciates his plays for depth and gravity of purpose and appreciates his dramatic art:

> — more than anything else, he has shown the way both in respect of ideas as well of methods, by which the soul of India could be realised and revealed in the realm od dramatic creation and representation.

Sri Aurobindo is the second prominent dramatist in Indian English Drama. He wrote five complete blank verse plays besides his six incomplete plays. His complete plays are *Perseus the Deliverer*, *Vasavadutta*, *Radoguna*, *The Viziers of Bassora* and *Eric*. Each of these plays is written in five acts. His incomplete plays are *The Witch of Ilni*, *Achab and Esarhaddon*, *The Maid and the Mill*, *The House of Brut*, *The Birth of Sin* and *Prince of Edur*.

The notable feature of Sri Aurobindo's plays is that they present different cultures and countries in different eras, with variety of characters, moods and sentiments. *Perseus the Deliverer* is based on the ancient Greek myth of Persues, *Vasavadutta* is a romantic tale of ancient India. *Rodoguna* is a Syrian romance, *The Viziers of Bassora* is a romantic comedy which takes one back to the days of the great Haroun al Rashid, while *Eric* is a romance of Scandinavia, a story of love and war between the children of Odin and Thor. In Aurobindo's dramas there is romance, heroic play, tragedy, comedy, farce— all different shades and varieties which we can expect from Indian English dramas.

As K.R.S. Iyengar observes:

> But all five plays are steeped in poetry and romance, recalling the spirit and flavour of the distinctive dramatic type exemplified in different ways by Bhasa, Kalidas and Bhavabhuti. Though, of course all have Aurobindonian undertones.[5]

Harindranath Chattopadhay also made significant contribution to Indian drama. He started his career as playwright with his play *Abu Hassan* (1918). He has written seven verse plays to his credit published under the title of *Poems and Plays* (1927) and all the seven plays are based on the lives of Indian saints. His *Five Plays* (1929) are all prosaic. *The Window and The Parrot* deals with the lives of the poor whereas *The Sentry's Lantern* is a symbolic display of the expectation of the arrival of a new age for the downtrodden people. *Sidhartha: Man of Peace* is an adventurous effort to dramatise Lord Buddha's life.

Another great dramatist is A.S.P. Ayyar who wrote six plays. *In the Clutch of The Devil* (1926) is his first play and the last one is *The Trial of Science for the Murder of Humanity*. P.A. Krishnaswamy has also his name in the history of Indian English drama who is famous for his verse play *The Flute of Krishna* which is very unusual.

Another dramatic voice on the Indian literary scene is Thyagaraja Paramsiva Kailasam. He wrote bilingually both in English and Kannada. Though Kailasam is considered the father of modern Kannada drama, he excelled with his full expression in his English plays such as *The Burden* (1933), *Fulfilment* (1933), *The Purpose* (1944), *Karna* (1964) and *Keechaka* (1949). G.S. Amur holds T.P. Kailasam in high esteem and lauds thus:

> A talented actor who appeared on the amateur as well as the professional stage, he brought to the writing of drama an intimate knowledge of the theatre. It is for this reason that his plays whether in Kannada or English, have a uniform technical excellence.[6]

Bharati Sarabhai is the modern woman playwright voice during the colonial era of Indian English drama. She has written two plays *The Well of the People* (1943) and *Two Women*. Of these two plays, the former is symbolic, poetic and is besides a notable contribution to the Gandhian social order, while the later play is realistic in its theme and content.

J.M. Lobo Prabhu is the last significant voice in pre-Independence Indian English drama. He has written over a dozen plays but only *Mother of New India: A Play of India*

Village in three Acts (1944) and *Death Abdicates* (1945) appear before Independence. His *Collected Plays* was published in 1956.

Up to post–independence era, drama in English could not become successful on Indian soil as a major current of creative expression. In other words drama could not be identified with the main stream or people, as it could not divert the attention of the people in a significant way. Although the pre–Independence Indian English drama is notable for its poetic excellence, thematic variety, technical art, symbolic significance and its commitment to human and moral values, post-Independence Indian English drama got some momentum when foreign countries started taking interest in Indian English literature in general and Indian English drama in particular. Many plays by Indian playwrights Asif Currimbhoy, Pratap Sharma, Gurucharan Das were successfully staged in England and USA and in this these playwrights got some recognition abroad. Encouragement to drama was received immediately after India got freedom in 1947 from several quarters but it was monopolised by the theatre in the Indian regional languages while Indian English drama continued to depend on other aspects. These plays have been written in prose but at the same time poetic plays also survived in the post colonial era.

M.K. Naik rightly opines:

> ...Tagore-Aurobindo-Kailsam tradition of poetic drama continues, but with difference in the hands of Manjeri Isvaran, G.V.Desani, Lakhan Dev and Pretish Nandy.[7]

Manjeri Isvaran's *Yama and Yami* (1948) is a dialogue in poetic prose, with a prologue and an epitogue, dealing with the incestuous love of Yami for her brother. G.V. Desani's *Hali* (1950), an entirely different kind of play, received high praise for its originality, symbolism and rich imagery.

Regarding the message of the play *Hali*, M.K.Naik remarks:

> *Hali* finds peace in the thought that man must transcend human love, go beyond life and death and even leaving behind his limited idea of godhead, develop in himself a god-like love and detachment.[8]

Lakhan Dev's *Tiger Claw* (1976) is a historical play in three Acts on the controversial murder of Afzal Khan by Shivaji. His two plays are *Vivekananda* (1972) and *Murder At The Prayer Meeting* (1976). The use of blank verse is flawless and the last play compels us to think of T.S. Eliot's *Murder In The Cathedral*. Other verse plays of the period include P.A. Krishnaswami's *The Flute of Krishna* (1950), M. Krishnamurti's *The Cloth Of Gold* (1951), S.D. Rawoot's *Immortal Song*, *Karm* and *The Killers* (1959), Satya Dev Jaggi's *The Point Of Light* (1967), Pritish Nandy's *Rites for a Plebian Salute* (1969), Hushmat Sozerekashme's *Vikramjeet* (1970), Sree Devi Singh's *The Purple Braided People* (1970), P.S. Vasudev's *The Sunflower* (1972) and S. Raman's *Karme* (1979).

The number of prose dramatists is larger in comparison to those who wrote in verse. The most prolific playwright of the Post-Independence period is Asif Currimbhoy, who has written and published more then thirty plays. Some important plays are *The Tourist Meeca* (1959), *The Restaurant* (1960), *The Doldrumness* (1960), *The Captives* (1963), *Goa* (1964), *Monsoon* (1965), *An Experiment With Truth* (1969), *Inquilab* (1970), *The Refugee* (1971), *Sonar Bangla* (1972), *Angkor* (1973) and *The Dissident M.L.A.* (1974). In spite of comprehensiveness, Currimbhoy's dramatic art has been criticised for the lack of a structured plot, embellished language and balanced characterisation. His dialogue shows the extreme poverty of invention and his language is not suitable to divert the internal drama of the clash of motives.

As the famous literary critic M.K.Naik observes:

> His symbols are often crude,conventional and mechanical but the greatest limitation of his technique is revealed especially in his later plays, in which Currimbhoy appears to confuse dramatic technique with theatrical trickery and stage gimmicks with dramatic experience.[9]

> Pratap Sharma wrote two prosaic plays *A Touch Of Brightness* (1968) and *The Professor Has A War Cry* (1970). His plays got success in foreign countries but they failed to be staged in our country. Sex, moreover remains the prominent theme of his plays but Pratap Sharma shows a keen sense of situation and his dialogue is often effective. Prof M.K.Naik lauds his dramatic craftsmanship for his keen sense of situation and effective dialogues.[10]

In the realm of Indian drama, Nissim Ezekiel's endeavour is acknowledged as a milestone for his exceptional poetic creed and rare dramatic sensibility. Nissim Ezekiel's *Three Plays* (1969) including *Nalini: A Comedy*, *Marriage Poem: A Tragi Comedy* and *The Sleep Walkers: An Indo-American farce* are considered to be a milestone in the dominion of Indian English drama. *Songs of Deprivation* (1969) is also a short play by Ezekiel. Gurucharan's *Larins Sahib* (1970) a historical play, deals with Henry Lawrence of Panjab. The play *Marriage Poem*, presents the conflict of a middle class husband caught in the conflict of commitments of married life and the desire of love. *The Sleep Walkers* is a diverting take off on national preconceptions and prejudices. In spite of strong sense of dramatic craftsmanship, Ezekiel could not change his poetic talent into appropriate dramatic talent. His plays are appreciated for symmetrical construction with abundance of irony. They reveal his sharp observation of the oddities of human life and behaviour. Ezekiel's poetics self swayed his dramatic creed but his plays make a 'pleasant reading'.

> In his satire of current fashion, in his exposure of prose and presence, Ezekiel comes very close to the spirit of some English social satirist in theatre.[11]

Contemporary Indian drama, deviating from classical and European models, is experimental and innovative in terms of thematic and technical qualities. It is not an offspring of any specific tradition and it has laid the foundation of a distinctive tradition in the history of world drama by reinvestigating history, legend, myth, religion and folklore with reference to contemporary socio-political issues. A cumulative theatrical tradition evolved by Mohan Rakesh, Badal Sirkar, Vijay Tendulkar and Girish Karnad, prepared the background of contemporary Indian English theatre.

Girish Karnad in the capacity of a writer, director and actor substantially contributed to enrich the tradition of Indian English theatre. His dramatic sensibility was moulded under the influence of touring Natak companies and especially *Yakshagana* which was in those days not accepted as a purified art form. His well known plays are *Yayati* (1961), *Tughlaq* (1962), *Hayavadana* (1970) and *Naga Mandala* (1972). He borrowed his plots from history, mythology and old legends but with intricate symbolism, he tried to establish their relevance in contemporary socio-political conditions. The play Yayati reinterprets an ancient myth from the *Mahabharata* in modern concept. The plot of the play *Hayvadana* is adopted from *Katha Saritasagar*, an ancient collection of stories in Sanskrit. *Tughlaq* is Karnad's best historical play where he mingles facts with fiction. Karnad projects the curious contradictions in the complex personality of Sultan Muhammad-bin-Tughlaq. In the play *Tale Danda*, he discovers the vital relationship between contemporary society and literature. His use of myth as a structure and metaphor in his play gives "new meaning to the post from the vantage point of view of present". In the play *Naga Mandala*, the conflict is between patriarchal and matriarchal views of society. It is about the life of Rani, a typical Indian woman in a male dominated society. She is married to Appanna, a wealthy village youth. The focus in the play is on sexual liberty of the sexes: male and female. In order to counter mail dominance, Karnad adopts a strange device in which King Cobra gets sexually involved with Rani and ultimately she becomes pregnant. Like his other female protagonists, she is encouraged to pass through chastity ordeal.

Regarding the position of Rani, Smita Nirula comments:

> Rani is never free to express herself, to be herself. She is either daughter, wife, lover or mother. She is always playing a role imposed upon her, except in her dreams in the lonely nights that engulf her. She is a woman used, abused. She can either live as a whore or a Devi. There is no element of person for her.[12]

Karnad's dramatic art lacks stability, still his success lies in technical experiment with an indigenous dramatic form. The collective efforts of Karnad and Kaavalam Narayana Pannikar are significant in their blending of the traditional forms of Indian theatre with the modern. Born in 1828, Vijay Tendulkar began his career as a journalist but from the very first play Grihasth in 1955 to *Safar* in 1992, his plays have given Indian theatre a rich and challenging repertoire. Leading the vanguard of the avant-garde Marathi Theatre, Vijay Tendulkar symbolises the new awareness and attempts of Indian dramatists of the century to depict the agonies, suffocations and cries of man, focusing on the middle class society. In all his plays, he harps upon the theme of isolation of the individual and his confrontation with the hostile surroundings. Influenced by Artaud, Tendulkar relates the problem of anguish to the theme of violence in most of his plays. He does not consider the occurrence of human violence as something loathsome or disgusting in as much as it is in note in human nature.

He says:

> Unlike the communists I don't think violence can be eliminated in a classless society, or for that matter, in any society. The spirit of aggression is something that human being is born with. Not that it is bad. Without violence man might have turned into a vegetable.[13]

While depicting violence on the stage, Tendulkar does not dress it up with any fancy trappings so as to make it palatable but rather keep it raw and natural. The plays *Chimanicha Ghor Hote Menache* (1960), *Kalojanchi Shalai* (1968), *Ek Holti Mugli* (1967) reflect Tendulkar's concern with authority and the idea of exploitation of the individual. In the plays *Silence! The Court Is In Session* (1968) and *Ghasiram Kotwal* (1972) the theme of oppression dominates. *Sakharam Binder* (1972) is a study in human violence amounting to a powerful dramatic statement. *Kamala* (1982) and *Kanyadaan* (1982) are written on the lines of naturalistic tradition. Kamala is a study of marital status as well as a study in the theme of exploitation. *Kanyadaan* is a complex play about the cultural and emotional upheavals of a family. Tendulkar was associated with New Theatrical Movement in Maharashtra. He presents a fictional reality in which the reality of life acquires a sharp focused character radiating rare dramatic power.

Badal Sircar too is a prestigious name in the realm of contemporary theatre. He represents New Theatrical Movement in India. He has created an appropriate 'people's theatre' a theatre supported and created by people. His dramatic career began with humorous play like *Solution X*. His earlier plays are *Evam Indrajit* (1962), *That Other History* (1964) and *There Is No End* (1971). All these plays are based on political, social, psychological and existential problems. *Evam Indrajit*, is a tale of a playwright who struggles in vain to write a play. In the play *There's No Need* Sircar develops the thesis that "We are all accused" and share the burden of guilt. Afterwards, he wrote *Pary Konodin*, *Jadi Aur Ek Baar*, *Palap* and *Pagla Ghoda*. His later plays *Procession*, *Bhoma* and *Stale News* are based on the concept of the Third Theatre. The play *Procession* is about the search for a 'real home' in new society based on equality. It suggests a 'real way' to new way in which man does not have to live exploiting man but should work according to his own needs. *Bhoma* is a dramatisation of the life of oppressed peasants in rural India. The analysis of these three plays suggests remarkable changes in Sircar's concept of a 'real home', a new society based on equality and free from the horrors of exploitation.

Tendulkar in 1967, established his theatre group called *Satabdi*. Sircar's first contact with Grotowski's 'Poor Theatre' influenced him greatly in formulating his Third Theatre. In Indian English drama the influence of Mohan Rakesh can not be ignored. He wrote in Hindi but for exceptional dramatic relevance, his plays have been translated into English and other regional languages. He published his first major play *Ashadh Ka Ek Din* in 1958, *Leharon Ke Rajhansa* appeared in 1963 and *Adhe Adhure* was first staged in 1969. The play *Pair Tale Ki Zamin* was completed by Kamleshwar after his death and was published in 1974.

As a playwright, his main concern was to portray the crisis of contemporary man caught in the web of uncongenial surroundings and the persistent threat to human relationship. Mohan Rakesh perceived drama as a complex art involving the uniform contribution of actors, scenic effects, light and music and effective stage direction. Mohan Rakesh made extensive experiments in theatre. He used words and languages not as dialogues or direct statements but as the tools of suggestion to convey the meaning beyond the verbal connotation. In *Ashadh Ka Ek Din*, he highlights the dangers of sycophancy that men of his age face for getting dignified official position. In *Leharon Ka Rajhans,* he reflects on the problem of relations between man and woman, ego clashes, divided self, illusions and nothingness. *Adhe Adhure* deals with the clash of ego between husband and wife, disintegration of family relationship, the prominence of individual interest against the commitments of the family. Besides, women dramatists also tried to enrich the soil of Indian drama by projecting the inner world of feminine psyche in the theatre.

Women's theatre coalesces with Street Theatre movement, using the same technique in performance and production. It can be attributed as a 'Theatre of Protest' because women writers expressed their resentment against the politics of exploitation on the basis of gender discrimination. They also revived the traditional myths of Sita and Savitri and tried to reinterpret the epics from women's point of view. The dramatic work of Usha Ganguli and Mahasweta Devi can be placed in this category. Mahasweta Devi emerged as a dramatist with a quest to explore something challenging and new. Her five plays are *Mother of 1084*, *Aajer Urvashi O' Johny*, *Byen* and *Water*. The play *Mother of 1084*, is a moving account of the anguish of an apolitical mother who had witnessed the horrors of Naxalite Movement. In *Aajir*, Mahasweta Devi deals with the issue of the rapid deterioration in values and their effects on society, particularly on illiterate people. *Urvashi O' Johnny* is a play written as regards 'emergency' through the love affair of Johnny with Urvashi, a talking doll. The play *Bayen* presents a moving account of harsh reality of a woman's life in rural India. The play *Water*, is the story of a professional water-diviner, Maghai Done who is an untouchable boy. Her plays represent a profound concern for human predicament and sincerely hope for the better future of mankind.

MAHESH DATTANI

Mahesh Dattani is arguably one of the best playwrights the country has ever produced. Born in Banglore on 7 August 1958, Dattani consciously preferred English as a medium of expression.He was almost obsessed with the desire to represent Indian soil and sensibility in the wake of globalisation. His famous plays are *Where There is a Will*, *Final Solutions*, *Dance like a Man*, and *Tara*. The development of Indian drama in English has indeed been a curious one because in order to establish a direct relationship with its audience, it has had to concede space to translations. Dramatists like Mahesh Dattani have benefited from the experience of the writers in regional language and they are working increasingly exhibiting their social concerns.

References

1. A.L. Basham. *The Wonder that Was India*. New Delhi: Rupa &co, 1987, pp. 434-435.
2. Bharat Gupta, *Dramatic Concepts:Greek and Indian-A Study of Poetics and Natya Shastra*. New Delhi: D.K. Printworld,1994. p.86.
3. A.B. Keith. *The Sanskrit Drama*. Delhi: Motilal Banarasidas, 1992. p.12.
4. Krirplani, Krishna. *Literature of Modern India*. New Delhi: National Book Trust ,1982. p.40.
5. Ramaswami, Shastri. *Rabindranath Tagore*: *The Poet and Dramatist*. Calcutta: Oxford University Press, 1948. p-47.
6. K.R.S. Iyengar. *Indian Writing in English*. New Delhi: Sterling, 1985. p.226.
7. G.S. Amur. 'Kailasam`s Quest for Greatness' in *Critical Essays on Indian Writing In English*. Madras: Macmillan, 1977. p.186.
8. M.K. Naik. *A History of Indian English Literature*. New Delhi: Sahitya Akademi, 1995. p.256.

9. Ibid., p.257.
10. Ibid., p.260.
11. Chetan Karnani. *Nissim Ezekiel*, New Delhi: Arnold Heinmann, 1974. p.126.
12. Narula, Samita. 'Evolving Mixed Feelings', *The Pioneer,* 11 sept, 1988.
13. Sachidanand Mohanty. 'Theatre: Reaching Out to People', The Hindu, New Delhi, February, 14, 199.p.5

18

New Challenges and English Theatre in India

—N. Shanta Naik

There is a traditional legend relating to the origin of Indian drama and theatre. The tale is found in chapter 1 of the *Natyashastra*. According to the tale, Brahma asked Indra to compare plays based on semi historical tales and have them acted by the gods. It is true that Sanskrit theatre was dominant in India all through the years. Pali, Prakrit, and other regional languages were just ignored. All types of traditional Indian local performances were infused with religious over tones. Indian theatre was very much influenced by the classical and folk dances of each region, for example, *Yakshagana* of Karnataka, *Bharatanatyam* of Tamilnadu, *Mohiniattam* of Kerla, *Odissi* of Odisha and Kuchipudi of Andhra Pradesh. Instead of classical dance and folkdance folk theatre like *Sannata*, *Srikrishna Parijatha*, *Gondalligarata*, *Yasagara,* etc., were popular in Karnataka.

When we start discussing English theatre and English drama in India, theatre in English has a long and more impressive history in Bombay dating book to the middle of eighteenth century. Indian English plays were performed by English actors for the entertainment of British soldiers and merchants and to the delight of local anglophiles. After independence in 1947, English language theatre patronised by Indian actors and directors actually grew in size and influence, mainly because English remained medium of communication.

Aliq Padmasee opines that the English-speaking population in cities is even growing and there is a greater demand for more plays in English. The sources of modern Indian English plays run the gamut from original ideas to adaptations of short stories, novels and films. Modern plays seem doomed to remain in the language in which they were created. Works of Utpal Dutt, Badal Sircar, Girish Karnad and Vijay Tendulkar testify. There is no existing English theatre worth talking about in India as it is in the regional languages.

In Bangalore *Little theatre* (BLT) and the recent group. '*playpen*' are associated with Mahesh Dattani. The first play written in English was by David Horst Rough. David who was a lover of India has written *The Ungrateful Man* for children. He adopted the pattern and technique of Sanskrit plays. He was familiar with Sanskrit and acquainted with Indian folk theatre as well as Sanskrit tales. *The Ungrateful Man* is completely based on well-known *Panchatantra stories*. He introduces *sutradhara* in his play as in Sanskrit plays. The experience with English plays is that the same audience come to see the English plays again and again which are performed on rare occasions. This 'Elite' class audience is not big enough of support for plays in English, as the cost of production far exceeds the income from the ticket sales. Without sounding commercial and mercenary it will do well to remember that drama is written to be performed and if audience is not forthcoming, naturally playwrights stop writing in English. There were many reasons for this state. English language was learnt by a few affluent sections and the upper caste people who were very close to the British. Their number was very minimal, while 99 per cent of other major communities were in the dark. Another interesting point is 50 per cent of the population was completely kept away form the main stream. Women did not get any opportunity of getting education and participate in any social gatherings.

The one modern English playwright who used myths and legends with imagination and creativity resulting in stage-worthy plays is Girish Karnad. Karnad who was influenced by western playwrights and Sanskrit plays, tried to make use of legends in folk narrative style successfully. His ability to building bridges between the elite and the folk theatre and has proved to be his strength and individuality. The two other very successful modern dramatists in English are Vijay Tendulkar and Badal Sircar. Vijay Tendulkar's play *Silence! The Court Is In Session* and Badal Sircar's *Evam Indrajit* have been extremely successful on the stage.

Gurucharan Das's *Larins Sahib* is a significant historical play. It provides a perspective on colonial consciousness in the context of the imperialistic global context.

It was 1846, seven years after the death of the formidable Maharaja Ranjit Singh, the Sikh Kingdom has suffered a crushing defeat at the hands of the East India Company. Henry Lawrence, already a legend on the Northwest frontier, is appointed the company's agent to the Government of the late Maharaja's boy son, Dilip Singh. Preferring Indian officers to British in an attempt to restore sikh self-respect, and endeavoring to root out corruption in the court Lawrence alienates his supervisors.

This provides a definite and unmistakable shift in perspective on colonial consciousness in the context of the imperialistic global perspective. Lawrence, the 'Larins Sahib' is seen to be different from what he is expected to be by the *Pukka* Sahibs. Henry Lawrence, the 'Sahib' of the play though he is the Lawrence of Punjab is the wrong Lawrence because he is "partially a native!" Gurucharan Das, used a technique to make metamorphoses of Lawrence to 'Larins'.

It is good to use philosophy of or employing characters and languages of aliens. The infected culture of India digested western culture and others making it a policy to adapt, in an age of modernisation.

The other playwright who has emerged in recent times is Asif Currimbhoy. He has written some plays of dissent. In his play *Goa,* the relationship between Portugal and India is represented. This provides another colonial context from similar to that of Larins Sahib. However, the play is not only about this aspect, perhaps not even mainly about it, as it can be argued with reference to the symbolic element as indicated in the speech of Senhora Miranda, When she says about her daughter, "She is Rose. And Rose is Goa; and Goa is Rose". The character of Portuguese Administrator and Goan Nationalist are significant in the context of change in colonial perspective when the Portuguese administrator says:

> This is Goa... my home no less than Lisbon where I was born. And we, the Portuguese came to India four centuries ago; we made Goa an enclave... ah, but my friend here, who calls himself a nationalist insists we made this into a colony instead of a small part of Portugal. (*Goa*)

The Goan nationalist responds:

> There is a change coming in evitable and my friend, you will be in the midst of it. (*Goa*)

Perhaps, Currimbhoy's plot highlights a conflict between a Portuguese official and a Goan nationalist. The dilemma of superiority and interiority is very much expressed in the play *Goa*. Title of the play itself is remarkable. All incidents revolve round the metaphor of Goa. One can witness the change in Currimbhoy's play, as he tried to distance himself from the Indian folk theatre as well as Indian arts.

Dina Mehata's *Brides are not for Burning* is play on burning issue of Indian male dominated 'Hindu society'. Double standards in an orthodox society maintain one rule for men and another for women. Indian marriage system is fouled by dowry system; the parents of bride are purchasing bridegroom. But the logic is she has to go to her in-laws' house where they torture her physically and mentally. A desperate bride commits suicide in order to save her parents from disrepute and financial oppression.

Dina Mehata's *Brides are not for Burning* exposes the hard realities of Hindu Society. Laxmi the protagonist represents thousands of Indian young women who become prey to dowry system. But Malini certainly rebels against customs:

> Don't you get smart ass with me' or what shit! Look at this ugly room' or when she says 'won't my sister's-in-law is impressed if I drive up with him in his Mercedes... No, they won't. They will think I I've taken to whoring.
>
> (*Brides are not for Burning*)

One may presume, the influence of English education, American, British, German feministic ideology might have influenced Malini. Certainly the new wave created a lot of changes in Indian society.

Talking about the English language on the stage in India Mahesh Dattni says:

> Should the play be read in class rooms I sincerely wish that English language teachers and staunch Wren and language teachers and staunch Wren and Martiners will not dismiss my syntax as bad English, or worse still, as incorrect. While knowledge of the rules of grammar is important, the richness and variety of the spoken word is study in itself.

With his amazingly new major concerns, Dattani energised Indian drama in English.

When we discuss Indian English theatre, we must know something about the pioneers of Indian theatre. Badal Sircar was an eminent playwright. When his play *Evam Indrajit* was first staged in Calcutta it was read as a period piece. It is contemporaneous as it deals with the people of modern society suffering from inability to grasp reality in totality. The play focuses on the problems of marriage, job security and bondage which are the very basis of bourgeois Indian society. Sircar's creation of Indrajit into four spectators like, Amal, Vimal, Kamal and Nirmal alias Indrajit, is quite interesting.Stage viewers get transformed into stage and become gazers. The purview of the gaze comprises spectator gallery as well ass stage for acting.

After Badal Sircar another important Indian English playwright known for his innovation is Girish Karnad. All his plays are transcriptions of myths. His experiment is myth creation and myth breaking was successful in the early period. He is the most notable personality among the Indian playwrights. Unlike his contemporaries Karnad is the only dramatist who has fully relied upon the rich fund of Indian culture available is the form of history, myth and folk tale. His first history-based play *Tughlaq* focused on corruption penetrating into religion and politics, taking the readers to fourteenth century medieval India. Socio-political events of the late eighties and early nineties prompted him to write *Tale Danda*.

Karnad As a conscious writer witnessed happenings in India and prepared a new equation in his play. Though he borrowed like William Shakespeare all his material from old myths, he succeeds in linking the same with modern social events.

One should not ignore the Bengali activist, writer Mahasweta Devi when we discuss Indian English Theatre. She stands unique among Indian writers in portraying the struggles of the subalterns, especially the untouchables struggling for their basic human rights. As she considers women as one group among the exploited, she explores women's subjugation as linked to the oppressions of caste and class in her writing. Mahasweta Devi's play *Mother of 1084* is set against the backup of the climatic phase of the suppression of the naxalite movement during the 1970's in the urban Bengal. The protagonist is a miserable mother who is illiterate pathetically ignorant of her own son Brati, the corpse number 1084, who had taken part in the naxalite movement and become a martyr.

The play begins with a phone call from the government morgue asking Sujata to identify corpse number 1084 and confirm whether it is her own favourite son, Brati. Her corrupt husband and other children are keen on hushing up the whole affair. The portrayal of Sujata's character illuminates the darker areas of life. Though Sujata is well aware of the corrupt ,degenerated values represented by her husband, she never ventures to disentangle from them and leads a compromising life.

Indian English drama has not fully developed like other literary forms. Except a few playwrights the neglected sphere of the society has not been projected. Now a dramatist from the lower caste has to emerge to write a fresh experience of his locality. The rich folk, myth, local theatre is nourished by the *shudras* and *atishudras*. English is an alien language to these people. The class which believed "Others make it yours" who were very near to the Colonial rulers and disallowed education to *shudras* kept them under dark for many centuries. The lower community people sustain rich Indian theatre.

At present the scenario has changed and attracted a class which all these days felt that theatre is for men of low status. Village is a centre for all kinds of activities like *Kolata, Dollukunita*, *Horse dance*, *Chau-dance*, *Mohiniattam*, *Yakshagana*. But highly sophisticated and urban centered English theatre is yet to develop in a radical way. There are many challenges it has to face. Let us hope that it will over come all these shortcomings and attract new elite class.

Works Cited

Dubey, Satyadev. 'Introduction', *Three Modern Indian Plays*. New Delhi: O.U.P., 1990.

Karnad, Girish. *Tale Danda*. New Delhi: Ravi Dayal Publishers, 1993.

Mathi, Nirai.S. *Mahaswetha Devi, The Rebel Play Writer of Mother of 1084.*

Richmond, P. Fardey and other (ed.) *Indian theatre*. Varanasi: Motilal Banarsidas Publishers, 1990.

Sircar, Badal. *The changing language of Theatre.* New Delhi: Indian council for Cultural Relation, 1982.

19

An Interview with Shri Hrusikesh Panda

— T.S. Chandra Mouli

T.S. Chandra Mouli: **Namaste, Sir! Thank you very much for according permission to record your impressions.**

Hrusikesh: It is an honour for me. You are offering me a wider platform to express my views as a writer. I am grateful to you.

C.M.: **Could you tell us about your childhood memories, please?**

Hrusikesh: That itself would make an autobiography. Since this interview follows an essay on my plays, I guess I can limit my response to this medium. My village in Orissa (like many others in the state) had a theatre-song-dance group. The landlord who was the local ruler patronised this. It was said that in our family for several generations before independence, the men went out to perform, particularly, in the through-the-night open stage theatres. The women managed the estate and the collection of land tax. When independence came, the abolition of the landlord system had been a foreseeable fact. My father who was an accomplished and recognised singer of *Odishi* at the age of 18 at All India Radio, Calcutta (this was the only station with a limited program in Odia language), did not get the support from his father for a career in music, and studied science. But he continued to write and stage plays in small towns, wherever he worked. In our village, the music sessions continued; but the theatre group disbanded with absence of patronage from the former landlord, my grandfather. One of my earliest memories was when I had gone to see a play with mother and siblings and fell asleep. When father came on stage, I was woken up from sleep, and I could not recognise him. That was around 1958, when I was three years old. The play was written and directed by my father. My father died in 1972, when I was not even 18. Around 2004, I discovered the manuscript of this play, went through this, tried to understand the creative process behind it, and wrote an afterword when this was published. The play was based on his immediate experience, but maintained an authorial distance. Then I recollected that evening when I was about three years old and identified the character played by father: a landlord trapped in situations of decadence. I could identify some characters he had drawn from real people from various strata from my village.

C.M.: **How about your academic career, sir?**

Hrusikesh: I was in two minds: study science or literature? Father said that I should study science in college; I can study literature on my own. In college I read a lot of literature, and even prepared notes for students of English literature for difficult texts like *The Sound and Fury* by William Faulkner! I was put to school in Class I, when I was three years old because I was too naughty. When father passed away, I had completed my Honours in Chemistry, and discontinued. Next year, I joined Utkal University to do M.Sc. in Chemistry. Born in a small town in Kalahandi district, I moved through seven schools and passed matriculation from Koraput high school. Later, I did a Ph.D. in English literature, also from Orissa. My guide was late Professor Biyotkesh Tripathy, who had taught creative writing in several American universities. The topic was: Creative writing with specific relationship between society and literature in fiction. The work made me conscious of the creative process.

C.M.: Has this study changed your style? Have you become more conscious about your style?

Hrusikesh: I have always been a spontaneous writer. I write only when moved [and often shaken] emotionally and intensely. At the time I started writing, I did not like the verbosity, or the *obiter dicta* of some major writers in Oriya. I wrote with precision with great regard for the intelligence of the readers. When I was beginning my Ph.D. work, I was also writing a novel *Sunaputara Loke* (The People of the Golden Hill) about the multiple displacements of people living in the hills and forests of Koraput, and the rise and fall of left-wing extremism. This novel spanned through 1945 to1985. I followed a chronological time-line because that was natural. This novel was also part of my Ph.D. work. My guide asked me to change the structure when I wrote this in English. I wrote this again, with the first chapter taken from the middle part of the novel, the second chapter about the past and the last part about rise and fall of extremism, something like *Sound and Fury*. I think that is why I remembered the book now. Meanwhile, the novel in Odia was published, won the by Bhubaneswar Book Fair Award and sold well. I have not published the English rewritten version of *The People of the Golden Hill*.

When my work began to be published by reputed publishers of Odisha, I had expected a very small readership, about fifty or hundred. I am still baffled by the fact that all the books have run into more than one edition, and the last book *Michha Khushi Sata Dukha* (False Happiness, Real Sadness) sold out in the Book Fair and the publisher had to bring the second edition in the midst of the Fair. I think that the Ph.D. in creative writing has not changed my style or concern; but it has helped me in answering questions about my writing.

C.M.: Do you mind sharing your professional experiences?

Hrusikesh: My father had wanted me to become a scientist. I did not become a scientist. I joined IAS. I was working as an

Executive Trainee at SAIL, had chosen this job over several bank officer jobs, did not like the posting in a city, and took the IAS examination. The first time I saw Delhi was when I came for my IAS interview. The interview was humiliating. One member thought that I was a panda or priest from the Puri temple, and asked me endless questions about them. Two other members asked about the forest dwelling communities of Koraput and why it was poor. I was all of 13 years old when I studied for one year in government high school there and passed matriculation. When the results were published in newspapers and radio (and possibly TV), I discovered a day late that I was the topper of the batch. Later, the results showed that I had only 42 per cent marks in interview and about 90% marks in written papers. This is symbolic of the discordant life of mine in the job. I have always worked for the poor and the disadvantaged. This concern has often led to conflict. When I was ADM of Koraput, there was a discussion about having land acquisition for one more hydro-electric project. I had visited the area where people were due to be displaced and found that they will be displaced for the *third time and they did not have valid land rights*. I stated this before the Secretary of the Government and he said: 'So what!'

These are foretold symbols of my professional experience. I have been often posted to *unimportant* posts, and I have not understood why they were called unimportant. For 18 months from December 2008, I was paid full salary without any work. My fault was that I wanted to raise the price of milk paid to farmers by 20 per cent when prices of other essential food items had gone up by 100 per cent. For several years, I had been trying to write a novel about economic history of Odisha from 1500. This was not about the megalomaniac ascendancy of monarchs nor about their escapades to capture a bride thousands of miles away. I was able to finish this novel because of my posting without work. I am grateful for the job. Or should I say joblessness?

Minor issues apart, my service has given me enormous opportunities to see places, meet people, and understand them. My mother and her brother persisted with me to take the IAS examination, even after I had got another job. The job has been a great exposure. At the end of the day, I have not misused my positions, which are often unimportant anyway, to further my cause in literature. On the other hand, my writing has been a cause of my persecution. An example is the story *A Report of the Starvation Commissioner* published later in English translation in *Indian Literature* of Sahitya Academy. This story was a result of intense suffering of experiences of indentured labor; and the publication of the story led to a second bout of suffering through privilege motion and threats of arrest. I was saved by public opinion and the court, but the agony led me to write these three long stories and published under the title *Michha Khusi...* mentioned above.

C.M.: **What are your views on drama as a genre? It is sometimes said that drama is the highest form of literature. Since you had been successful in short stories and novels, why did you choose the medium of drama? What makes a drama popular and academically impressive, please?**

Hrusikesh: There are writers/ theoreticians who claim that 'highest' form of literature is drama. Such debates are spurious. I wrote plays after I had published about ten volumes of short and long fiction. My first play was based on a story I had just written which was to be broadcast as a radio play in Hindi translation! I am grateful to the producer who gave me the courage to venture into this form. In 1994, I developed this into a stageable play. This gave me immense scope to experiment with my rudimentary knowledge of music. A play requires tight structure, a single set which is one more aspect of the structure, limited characters, positioning the characters through each dialogue so that s/he does not look redundant, have enough drama to hold audience attention; yet say something important. The impact of the play on the audience is visible immediately.

For all these reasons, writing a play is more challenging. However, I consider that a good film is the highest form of literature, because it has additional aspects like cinematography, editing, and special effects. I have derived the maximum creative satisfaction in the few films I made for the small screen: there I wrote the story, screenplay, dialogues and songs; composed the music, was the director, and sometimes gave the commentary.

***C.M.:* Have you received any awards for your films?**

Hrusikesh: No, I never worked in that direction.

***C.M.:* Could you throw light on drama in twentieth century, sir? Would you mind to comment on drama in postmodern period?**

Hrusikesh: The plays which were borrowed shamelessly and recreated in Odia language finished off the proscenium theatre. Even in 1958, when my father was writing and directing plays in small towns of Odisha, he was doing so as a matter of artistic duty and without any expectation of an award. I am happy that today plays have found their way back into local milieu and relevance.

***C.M.:* I did not get the point about awards.**

Hrusikesh: Those who wrote 'modern' and 'absurd' plays were considered serious writers. Those who wrote about the reality that they experienced were just mundane, ordinary and not worth the attention of critics.

***C.M.:* What characterises a postcolonial drama, please?**

Hrusikesh: Most of post-colonial drama in Odia language was not about the colonisers, but the exploitation by intermediary estate owners or landlords, who did not exist any more. Perhaps, there was inadequate understanding of the actual exploitative process of colonialism. Some of these plays were of the other order of 'absurd' plays, on which I have already commented. But then I am not a critic and not competent to answer this question.

***C.M.:* Do you agree with the view that your plays have postcolonial connotations? Please, elaborate.**

Hrusikesh: I have been concerned with the problems of the marginalised, the disadvantaged , the exploited, the displaced—but not as a theoretical set-up I built up for myself. It was more like my spontaneous and emotive concern. To that extent, I have been concerned with neo-colonialism from early 1990, when I saw this happening in Southeast Asia and South America, and later in India. In that sense *God-Demon* can have neocolonialist connotations.

***C.M.:* How relevant are your plays as symbols?**

Hrusikesh: That kind of interpretation will reduce the literary ambiguity of the plays. My readers and audience come from wide spectrum: students, workers, activists, other writers. The plays may mean different things to them. I may have intended a *rasa*, and the actor and the director may have expressed this. But the spectator may perceive a different *bhava*. One reason of the success of *God-Demon* among a large range of audience may have been that while the dialogues were often complex, the language and the drama captured the attention of the spectators who did not understand the express content of the dialogues. I am saying this now because you have asked this question; no doubt this is an afterthought.

***C.M.:* Have you consciously introduced political issues as allegories/symbols in your plays?**

Hrusikesh: No.

***C.M.:* What is your opinion about translation of Indian literature into English today?**

Hrusikesh: The most common kind is reductionist: the translator reduces the text to the level of his bi-lingual capability. The idioms of Indian language are reduced to some nearest English idiom which may appear hackneyed. Flora and fauna are not translated at all. The other kind is when the translator has sufficient command over both these languages.

For example, there is sufficient material available in the internet to find exact words for the flora and fauna; but needs a little more effort. I have rarely translated myself, but have tried to help the translators in these areas. The other aspect is, there should be more translation between Indian languages. After all, the necessity of such translation is far more significant because the number of readers is more and we owe this to our languages. I chose to write in Odia because I owed this to my mother tongue. The reason this is not happening is because while there is no dearth of studies and research support for theories of translation, there is no support for a person to learn a second language with competency sufficient to make the translation authentic as suggested above. My argument is that the institutions which support translation studies should support capacity building in language skills of a second Indian language. This program should support a two year capacity building with adequate financial incentive to attract potential translators with language skills and with aptitude for translation. I think that capacity building in language skills is far more important than studies in translation theories.

***C.M.:* Do you feel feminist movement had any impact on your writings? What are the major concerns of feminists?**

Hrusikesh: As I have said, I do not go by any theories. You either have empathy with the disadvantaged, including women, or you do not. This is something you feel. I write only when I am moved deeply, often disturbed, and sometimes when I am moved intensely; sometimes this feeling comes when I fail as a human being or as a person with public responsibilities. I have come across articles and a couple of students doing their Ph.D. on feminism in my writings. A professor recently took my interview as part of his post doctoral work; his topic is eco-feminism in my short stories and novels. My position, in brief, was: feminism did not start in twentieth century, it is complex, women are identified as *prakriti* or the manifest nature. As Arjuna tells Krishna in the *Gita*, a conqueror takes away the land of the conquered and with that the women. Village goddesses are worshipped under trees, but gods need temples. Feminism is a complex *feeling* for me, and is not about burning the bras.

***C.M.:* What is the present status of Oriya drama, sir? What about its future?**

Hrusikesh: There is no commercial proscenium theatre. So the artists who are engaged in theatre have some other avocation. I look at this as a positive development because even in remote and small places, plays are written and staged, festivals are held, and at least one international festival is held in Katak. Local theatre and music traditions are built into them, though they may be concerned with contemporary issues like degenerate political situation. I am happy because the writer and the artists have unlimited space to express themselves. And I have no doubt about the basic talent among them; some of them have moved on to films and have become famous. Mr. Sadhu Meher who is the only person from Odisha to win the best actor award in National Film Festival belonged to one such group. He was also kind enough to direct one of my plays in his home town last year. So you get the picture: even those who have rightly become famous are still rooted in this small theatre. The future will be pretty similar. Here, I must mention about the commercially successful open air theatre staged in the night, known as *jatra*. They have full time artists, playwrights, directors and producers. They are paid well, sometimes better than those in Odia films. I should know because once I was offered a decent amount to write a script for them; but of course I could not because I was unable to get into their wavelength and more than that I write only what I want to write. Their only earnings are from sale of tickets. Their commercial success comes from their cathartic presentation of both content and form. Since they have competed successfully against films, both Oriya and Hindi, they will continue to thrive. It is about time they are given some serious attention in the study of their dramaturgy.

***C.M.:* Some of your works in translation have done very well. Your short stories in Tamil translation by Mr. Tamilnadan won the Sahitya Academy award and also ran into several editions. The play *God-Demon* translated by Dr Lipipuspa Nayak was sold out within two years. Do you think that your literature is multicultural?**

Hrusikesh: In my writings in Odia I had the opportunity to use a large canvas because of my exposure. The register of idioms is also large because I have been exposed to them since my peripatetic childhood. Orissa is quite a gallimaufry of several sub-cultures. My job and my empathy for *ordinary* people have given me the scope to write in the background of various cultures. Mr. Tamilnadan once told me that the Tamil translation sold well because the stories had *universal* appeal. Since I write realistic fiction, there is a particular place, particular characters and specific local events. If these are understood by readers in other places and times, that is their literary sensibility, and I respect those readers. Of course I am happy that my written words are appreciated across places.

***C.M.*: Technology, movies and innovative Television plays appear to have had an adverse impact on drama all over the world.Is there a possibility to revive interest in drama? Your views, please!**

Hrusikesh: Yes. I have already said this earlier in the context of *jatra* and local theatre groups. One more point about *jatra* as a successful genre of play. They have the form and content of popular movies of India: corrupt politicians and officials, a rebel hero or heroine, rape and molestation, exploitation, verbose dialogues, and a loud structure. But one reason these plays have been successful is that there are live characters instead of movie pictures. This advantage will sustain. The proscenium theatre will survive because it is participative.

***C.M.:* What is your advice to teachers and students who desire to focus on Indian theatre?**

Hrusikesh: I am not qualified to give any advice. However, off and on, I have worked on Indian and Western poetics. A simple suggestion is: *Natyashastra* by Bharat (2nd century BC) should be a compulsory text [in translation, of course] in all special courses on theatre. It covers every aspect of dramaturgy, gives a multi- cultural perspective of Indian theatre and languages, and gives us the historical retrospective to understand our own plays. The other book I suggest is *Dhwanyaloka*, as an optional text on Indian poetics. I assure you that I have great respect for the theories of tragedy based on Greek plays.

C.M.: **Thank you very much sir, for sharing your scholarly views with us and providing new insights as regards Oriya drama and your writings. You are so kind.**

Hrusikesh: I am grateful, sir. I am honoured.

Index